HE

Please return or renew this item before the latest date shown below

HOUSEBOUND 1/19

Murray

The
Kaiser's Mission
to
Kabul

A SECRET EXPEDITION TO
AFGHANISTAN IN WORLD WAR I

JULES STEWART

Foreword by
**GENERAL THE LORD
RICHARDS OF HERSTMONCEUX**
GCB CBE DSOR

I.B.TAURIS
LONDON · NEW YORK

New paperback edition published in 2019 by
I.B.Tauris & Co. Ltd
London • New York
www.ibtauris.com

First published in hardback in 2014 by I.B.Tauris & Co. Ltd

ISBN: 978 1 78831 458 9
eISBN: 978 0 8577 3471 6
ePDF: 978 1 78673 939 1

A full CIP record for this book is available from the British Library
A full CIP record is available from the Library of Congress

Library of Congress Catalog Card Number: available

Printed and bound by CPI Group (UK) Ltd, Croydon, CR0 4YY

Contents

List of Illustrations   vii

Foreword by General the Lord Richards of Herstmonceux   ix

Acknowledgements   xv

Map of the Routes Taken by Niedermayer and Hentig   xviii

1   The Kaiser, the Amir and the Viceroy   1

2   We're Off to Join the Circus   27

3   Into the Fearful Wasteland   59

4   The Waiting Game   83

5   To Berlin the Hard Way   111

6   West to Berlin   131

7   East to Berlin   145

8   My Enemies' Enemy is Germany   159

Epilogue   195

Appendix 1   201

Appendix 2   205

Glossary   209

Notes   211

Bibliography   221

Index   225

List of Illustrations

1. Werner Otto von Hentig (courtesy of www.phototheca-afghanica.ch)

2. Oskar Ritter von Niedermayer as an officer, 1917 (courtesy of Gerd M. Schulz)

3. Habibullah Khan (courtesy of the Royal Geographical Society)

4. Nasrullah Khan (courtesy of the Royal Geographical Society)

5. Kaiser Wilhelm II (courtesy of the Library of Congress)

6. Mahendra Pratap (from *Asia Magazine*, Vol. XXV, Issue 1 (May, 1925), p. 383)

7. Enver Pasha (courtesy of the Library of Congress)

8. Niedermayer *c.* 1940 (courtesy of Gerd M. Schulz)

9. Wilhelm Wassmuss (author's collection)

10. Frederick John Napier Thesiger, Lord Chelmsford, Viceroy of India 1916–21 (courtesy of the National Portrait Gallery, London)

11. Charles Hardinge, Lord Hardinge of Penshurst, Viceroy of India 1910–16 (courtesy of the National Portrait Gallery, London)

12. Amanullah Khan (author's collection)

13. Mission caravans (courtesy of www.phototheca-afghanica.ch)

14. Mission photo (courtesy of www.phototheca-afghanica.ch)

15. Audience with Amir Habibullah Khan (courtesy of www.phototheca-afghanica.ch)

16. Niedermayer in Persian disguise (author's collection)

17. Expedition to Isfahan (courtesy of Gerd M. Schulz)

18. Bagh-e-Babur (courtesy of www.phototheca-afghanica.ch)

19. Bala Hissar (courtesy of Bill Woodburn)

20. Caravanserai (courtesy of www.imagesofasia.com)

21. Kabul bazaar (courtesy of www.phototheca-afghanica.ch)

22. Khawak Pass (courtesy of Hartmut von Hentig)

23. Turco-German caravan (courtesy of Hartmut von Hentig)

Foreword

By General the Lord Richards of Herstmonceux GCB CBE DSO

The year 2014 marks the commemoration of two signal events in the history of armed conflict. We observe the centenary of the First World War and the withdrawal of ISAF (International Security Assistance Force) combat troops from Afghanistan. The Great War was described in its day as 'the war to end all wars'. But it was not, of course, to be. Little more than two decades after the signing of the armistice in November 1918, the same European nations were once again pitched into an even more devastating conflagration. One in which several countries fought their former German ally. It is useful to reflect on this historical fact when pondering the future of Afghanistan and its history of shifting allegiances. We should not be too quick to espouse a sanctimonious 'I thought as much' if events in that country do not always go as smoothly as hoped.

As far as Afghanistan today is concerned, there may well be setbacks in the months and years ahead. But we can be confident that much has been achieved in laying the groundwork for greater political stability and economic prosperity. Afghanistan is today a totally different country to what it was under the Taliban regime. There are hopeful signs of a return to the path of reform that was in progress before the 1979 Soviet invasion. The majority of the Afghan people, insurgents and ordinary citizens alike, are weary of more than thirty years of bloodshed and civil strife. Most are prepared to make the concessions required from all sides to build a workable structure of government for the future.

The Kaiser's Mission to Kabul is a unique and, I found, a quite fascinating story. It links the two historical events cited above by placing Afghanistan, a country not often thought of as relevant to the European conflict, in the context of the Great War. This is the story of two young German officers, the Prussian Werner Otto von Hentig and the Bavarian Oskar Ritter von Niedermayer, whose extraordinary travels took them to the court of Amir Habibullah in Kabul. The book brings to light an almost forgotten episode of First World War history, moreover one that might have had a material impact on the outcome of that war. The trek to Afghanistan across the burning wasteland of the Persian desert, the encounters with swarms of deadly snakes and tarantulas and cut-throat bandits, reads like an Indiana Jones adventure tale.

These German officers, accompanied by a party of Turks, Indian revolutionaries and North-West Frontier tribesmen, made their way to Kabul in 1915 with the aim of persuading the Amir to rise up in arms against British India. That, at least, was the mission's official objective. It remains open to debate whether Kaiser Wilhelm II wanted the 'jewel in the Crown' of his cousin George V to fall into native hands, or if the German General Staff's real intention was to make trouble for Britain. Be that as it may, the British took the threat seriously. When the German plans were made known to Delhi via British spies in Kabul, Lord Kitchener, Secretary of State for War, estimated that if the Hentig–Niedermayer mission succeeded in provoking an Afghan attack on India, Britain would have to divert more than 135,000 men from other theatres of war to defend the subcontinent successfully.

After months of frustrating negotiations it became clear that despite promises of money, military hardware and territorial gains, Habibullah was not prepared to put at risk his profitable relationship with British India. The mission fell into disarray and in May 1916 Niedermayer and Hentig departed Kabul for their homeward journeys, travelling in opposite directions and undergoing even more harrowing times than on the previous year's march to Afghanistan. The two protagonists eventually made it back to Berlin, Niedermayer having been reduced to near starvation and forced into begging in his trek across Persia, while Hentig also suffered his fair share of tribulations on his crossing of the Pamir Mountains and China, to make his way to the US and from there by sea to Germany.

Once home, the two men resumed their military and diplomatic duties, and if they looked back with regret on the failure of the mission to Kabul, their legacy provides us with useful lessons for conducting our affairs with Afghanistan. Niedermayer, apart from taking credit for having modernised the Afghan armed forces, expressed a genuine fondness and respect towards Afghanistan and its people, a sentiment that was shared by Hentig. They made it a matter of principle never to offend the Afghans by purchasing any foreign-made goods during their months in Kabul. They taught the people new techniques for producing handmade cotton and other dress materials and, as Niedermayer states, 'The people listened eagerly when we told them about the state of affairs in the great world outside.' Hentig claims that the mission awoke 'an unknown national pride' in Afghanistan and made it possible for the minorities to play a role in the state. This, he said, was supported by engaging with youth eager to learn. Powerful words, especially when considering they were uttered a hundred years ago, when European powers regarded the Middle East and Asia as a source of mineral exploitation or an area for carving out buffer states between empires. The West would have done well to adopt similarly enlightened views on Afghanistan from the start of the 2001 invasion, integrating necessary military force with a more determined and better-orchestrated effort to help its people and rebuild their war-ravaged nation.

The Kaiser's Mission to Kabul is a story of high adventure set against a backdrop of diplomatic intrigue, with a cast of colourful characters like the insurgency leader Wilhelm Wassmuss, known as the 'German Lawrence', the romantic Indian seditionist Mahendra Pratap, and the archaeologist-cum-jihadist Max von Oppenheim. The book is a truly exciting read as well as a valuable tool for understanding the history and workings of Afghanistan, a country that will remain in the public eye long after the departure of the last contingent of ISAF combat troops.

To the people of Afghanistan

Acknowledgements

L ooking back on the months spent researching the story of the German mission to Afghanistan, while struggling to decipher a welter of centuries-old rivalries, antagonisms, covert activities and propaganda, a somewhat hackneyed but in this case very true adage comes to mind: 'This book could never have been written without the help of...' I realised at the outset that putting together a book on a relatively obscure sideshow of the First World War, moreover one that took place in a remote part of the world, was always going to pose a challenge. I had no idea of just how daunting a task I faced. But help was waiting in the wings. Firstly, anyone who sets out to write about Afghanistan's turbulent twentieth-century history owes a huge debt of gratitude to Ludwig Adamec's two seminal works on the subject, *Afghanistan 1900–1923* and *Afghanistan's Foreign Affairs to the Mid-Twentieth Century*. His flaw-less scholarship has helped guide me, hopefully in the right direction, on many occasions. It would be an imprudent writer indeed who set out on a literary journey across Central Asia without a thorough reading of Peter Hopkirk, the Great Game master. His *On Secret Service East of Constantinople* is of particular relevance to this episode in Afghanistan's history. Indeed, it was Hopkirk who pinpointed the real significance of the German mission to Afghanistan:

> Had they succeeded in unleashing the full fury of the amir's forces against the British in India, they might well have changed the course of the war.

Indeed, their names, like that of Lawrence, might have been remembered to this day. As it was, they had suffered great hardship and faced innumerable perils, only to see it all collapse in failure.[1]

One of my motivations for writing a book on the mission was to ensure that the names of these two splendid German officers and adventurers were not forgotten to History.

The story's two German protagonists, Werner Otto von Hentig and Oskar Ritter von Niedermayer, both left memoirs, but only one unofficial English translation exists of each of these manuscripts. I am profoundly indebted to Paul Bucherer-Dietschi, Director of the Foundation Bibliotheca Afghanica in Switzerland, for opening his archives and allowing me to view Werner Otto von Hentig's translated memoirs, among other documents. His Afghanistan-Institut near Basel (www.afghanistan-institut.ch and www.phototheca-afghanica.ch) is a treasure trove of documentation on Afghanistan. It is also Europe's main source of photos and research material on Hentig. I cannot thank him enough for taking time to cast his expert eye over my manuscript and provide many useful suggestions. Sincere thanks are due to Antony Wynn, the noted author and Middle East scholar, for spotting inaccuracies in the narrative.

I am also grateful to the Imperial War Museum in London, whose files hold the only English-language version of Niedermayer's narrative of the mission to Afghanistan. Gerd M. Schulz was an absolute godsend in generously providing me with his many wonderful photographs of Niedermayer and the mission. Helen Crisp once again gave selflessly of her time to read through my drafts and offer valuable suggestions for improvement. Anja Büchele (lumpenprinzess@yahoo.co.uk) was invaluable in helping to research key works on the Hentig–Niedermayer mission. She knew precisely what to look for, and by all accounts was intrigued by this little-known chapter in her country's history. Many thanks to Brigadier Bill Woodburn for dispelling the popular myths surrounding the destruction of Kabul's Bala Hissar fortress. My agent, Duncan McAra, has, as always, been a source of support and encouragement. Joanna Godfrey at I.B.Tauris has seen the manuscript seamlessly through the editorial process and is a delight to work with. There are others, including the helpful staff at the National Archives, the German Historical Institute, the Royal Society for Asian Affairs, the National Army Museum and the British Library, all of whom took a great deal of the pain out of searching their files. I hope my book has done justice to the efforts of all these people, with apologies, of course, to those whose names I may have omitted.

The names of countries and cities are given in the spelling commonly in use in the early twentieth century, that is, Mesopotamia for Iraq, Persia for Iran, Constantinople for Istanbul, and so on. For the title of Afghanistan's rulers, I have chosen amir instead of emir, although the latter is more widely used today. The reason is that amir was the accepted British usage a century ago. Anecdotally, I discovered that a British spy had been unmasked in Kabul when he delivered a letter, purportedly from a German agent in Persia, written in German but containing the British spelling of amir. He was hanged on the spot. The Afghan monarchs are throughout history variously referred to as king and amir. The title amir was used between 1834 and 1926, which includes the reign of Habibullah Khan, an astute and realistic ruler who hosted the visit of the 1915–16 German mission. Previous to that, from Ahmed Shah Durrani's ascent to the throne in 1747, the title was shah, or 'king' in Persian. The title reverted to king after 1926. Amanullah, who succeeded his father Habibullah in 1919, changed his title from amir to shah ahead of his European tour in order to give himself the same title as the monarchs he would be visiting.

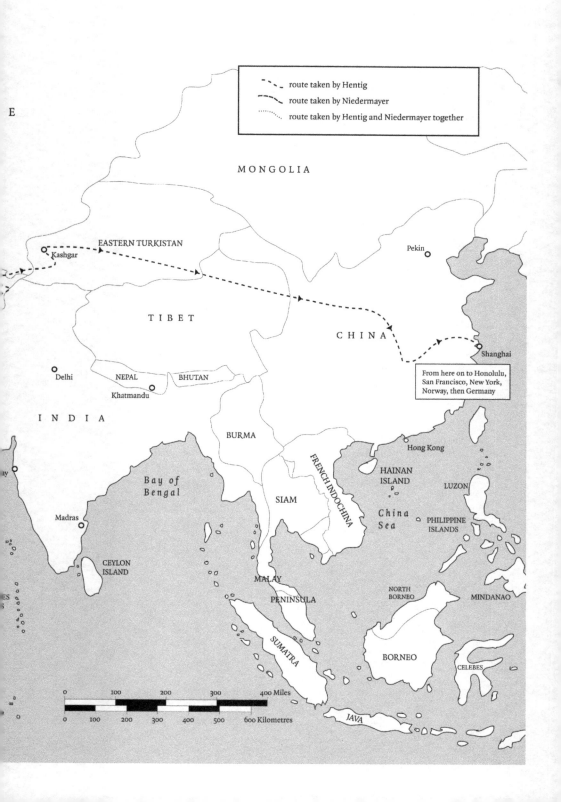

E

route taken by Hentig
route taken by Niedermayer
route taken by Hentig and Niedermayer together

MONGOLIA

EASTERN TURKISTAN

Kashgar

Pekin

TIBET

CHINA

Shanghai

Delhi

NEPAL   BHUTAN

Khatmandu

From here on to Honolulu,
San Francisco, New York,
Norway, then Germany

INDIA

BURMA

Hong Kong

Bay of
Bengal

FRENCH INDOCHINA

HAINAN
ISLAND

LUZON

SIAM

China
Sea

Madras

PHILIPPINE
ISLANDS

CEYLON
ISLAND

MALAY

NORTH
BORNEO

MINDANAO

PENINSULA

SUMATRA

BORNEO

CELEBES

0   100   200   300   400 Miles

0   100   200   300   400   500   600 Kilometres

JAVA

At that time the Central Powers were doing their best to foment such an agitation in India as would make it necessary for Great Britain to keep their troops in the country and perhaps send others from France.

ASHENDEN
SOMERSET MAUGHAM

1

The Kaiser, the Amir and the Viceroy

The morning of Sunday, 8 January 1928, brought welcome relief to Rome's shivering citizens after one of the city's most severe winters on record. Temperatures had plunged to 2°F over Christmas and, in the New Year, instead of enjoying a leisurely stroll to the shops and cafés, people found themselves trudging through blackened heaps of slush. That day, under a sparkling, cloudless sky that brought a hint of milder weather, a row of gleaming black Lancias stood lined up at the great domed Baths of Diocletian. The government motorcade attracted curious glances from office workers and housewives struggling to go about their appointed rounds. Across the road from the ancient public baths, at 9 a.m. a 12-coach train bearing King Amanullah of Afghanistan came chugging into Termini Station. Aboard the train, ripples of mirth were still to be heard in the royal carriage, where members of the royal party recounted in hushed voices the king's gaffe. This had taken place a few miles out of Chaman, Amanullah's birthplace, in what is today Pakistan's Baluchistan province. The Ruler of the Sublime God-Granted Government of Afghanistan and Its Dependencies had left his seat to answer the call of nature, and in the toilet he had mistakenly pulled the emergency cord, bringing the train to a screeching halt in the middle of the Khojak Tunnel.

Putting this incident behind him, the luxuriantly moustachioed, doll-like Amanullah and his audaciously unveiled wife Soraya kicked off the first week of their grand European tour as guests of honour at an air show hosted by

King Victor Emmanuel III and his prime minister, Benito Mussolini. The most dramatic event of that afternoon was a mid-air collision between two Fiat fighters over the Piazza d'Armi, killing one of the pilots. The next legs of the royal progress took Amanullah to France, Belgium and Germany, and finally to Britain on 13 March for a somewhat less dramatic inspection of Croydon airport, where the royal couple witnessed a special display by the Royal Air Force organised in their honour at Hendon aerodrome. This was followed by a spin around the English countryside, whose roads he pronounced superior to any in the world. The Afghan ruler was lastly treated to an underwater trip by submarine and a near-3,000-foot descent down a coal mine.

On his visit to Berlin in February, Amanullah met with President Paul von Hindenburg, who invited him to drive one of the city's new type A-II U-Bahn trains. To the amir's joy, his boyish enthusiasm for the state-of-the-art locomotive inspired the Germans to christen it the 'Amanullah-Wagen'. Amanullah employed part of his time selecting fittings for 80 rooms of a new palace he was having built in Kabul, designed by a German engineer. The simplicity of his choices astonished the local tradesmen. 'I am a modern prince,' he explained, 'and I have no intention of surrounding myself with the gewgaws of former rulers who, with all their ostentation, were not secure from assassination.'[1] It was a blunt and rather tasteless reference to his father, Amir Habibullah, who had been assassinated by an unknown assailant. Then a startling thing happened. On a tour of the AEG (General Electric Company) works, the amir dashed forward to embrace one of the onlookers, seized him by the hands, kissed him on both cheeks and drew him aside in animated conversation. In the ensuing confusion, police and bodyguards scrambled to intercept this astonishing breach of protocol. Amanullah brushed his security detail aside: he was delighted to encounter his old friend, Werner Otto von Hentig, looking perfectly fit at 42. After all he had been through on his crossing of the Persian desert, and later as he escaped through the Pamir Mountains and the Gobi Desert, Hentig, the long-distance swimmer, non-smoker and abstainer, would undoubtedly have attributed his hale and hearty state to a diet consisting mostly of milk and fruit, as well as to his morning ice-cold shower.

Amanullah turned to his entourage to introduce Hentig as 'my oldest and best acquaintance in Berlin'.[2] The king remembered Hentig as the diplomat and army officer whom he had met 13 years previously, as a 23-year-old prince in Kabul at the height of the First World War. At that time, the Prussian diplomat was leading a German-inspired mission that had journeyed in secret to Afghanistan with the objective of persuading Amanullah's late father, Amir Habibullah Khan, to raise his tribesmen in jihad and drive the British out of India. One might be tempted to think that as a neutral power in the Great War, Afghanistan played an insignificant part in a European conflict whose land battles in the East hardly stretched beyond the Ottoman Empire. But it was precisely Kabul's non-belligerent status that spared Britain having to divert tens of thousands of troops, desperately needed on the battlefields of France and Belgium, to deal with a German-orchestrated attack on British India through Afghanistan.

Not since the mid eighteenth century has Afghanistan, a nation of warriors, been a warring state. In 1747 Ahmad Shah Durrani sent his Pashtun tribes on a path of territorial conquest that was to carve out a vast empire, from eastern Persia to Kashmir, and from the Indian Ocean to the steppes of Central Asia. But with the king's death in 1773 his realm began to crumble under weaker rulers, men who were unable to hold their country's fractious tribes together and mount an effective defence against the ascendancy of their Sikh enemies. By 1818 Afghanistan was engulfed in civil war, resulting in a break-up into virtually independent fiefdoms. From that date until the deployment of US troops in 2001, more than 180 years later, with the sole exception of Amir Amanullah's preposterous month-long foray into British India in 1919, Afghanistan was the invaded rather than the invader, first by the British in 1838 and 1878, then by the Soviets a century later, and most recently by the US and its NATO allies. But no one really wanted to take on the burden of colonising this harsh land and its intractable inhabitants. They simply wanted to deny it to others.

Britain did not launch two costly invasions of Afghanistan in the nineteenth century to impose the Raj's dominion over its neighbour merely for the sake of territorial expansion. These campaigns were intended to parry a thrust by Russia in that same direction. Russian ascendancy in Afghanistan would have positioned the tsar's armies within easy reach of India through the passes that straddle what was at that time the Indo-Afghan border. There is no evidence, apart from some hawkish statements in Russian newspapers and journals, that Petrograd ever seriously considered stretching its army's supply lines across hundreds of miles of dangerous tribal lands to come up against a powerful British force waiting at the gates of India. Nonetheless, in 1838 Governor General Lord Auckland was persuaded by his hawkish advisers to mount an attack on Afghanistan. This decision was justified on the flimsiest of evidence, and no few outright lies. This misadventure resulted in the massacre of an entire 16,000-strong column on the disastrous retreat from Kabul.

It was a somewhat different picture when, 40 years after the First Anglo-Afghan War, Viceroy Lord Lytton sanctioned the second invasion of Afghanistan in 1878. By that time Russian divisions had rolled relentlessly across their empire's Muslim southern hinterlands, captured Tashkent, broken the power of the Khanate of Kokand, invaded Bokhara and established fortified posts far to the south of Uzbekistan's Jaxartes River (also known as the Syr Darya). They had also established the new province of Tashkent and captured the city of Samarkand, thus advancing the tsarist forces to within striking distance of Afghanistan's scarcely defended remote north-eastern border. The entire blitzkrieg operation had been carried out in less than five years. The spectre of Cossack patrols on the banks of the Oxus and the dispatch of a Russian diplomatic delegation to Kabul set alarm bells clanging in Whitehall as well as Calcutta. This was all the provocation Lytton and his generals needed to order another strike on Afghanistan, though one struggles to unearth any hard evidence to substantiate the claim that the Russians were playing at anything more than extreme brinkmanship, a game designed to keep Britain on the defensive diplomatically as well as militarily.

Germany had never been a significant player in the Great Game, the rivalry between the Russian and British empires that dominated Central Asian politics for most of the nineteenth and early twentieth centuries. Otto von Bismarck, the 'Iron Chancellor' who achieved German unification in 1871, was a staunch opponent of colonial expansion, determined as he was to turn his newly created nation into the dominant power in Europe. He suffered no moral uneasiness over Europe's ruthless scramble for overseas possessions; this was a matter of simple economics: colonialism, the chancellor believed, was not a lucrative business. Then, in 1883, nearing his seventieth birthday, Bismarck performed a radical volte-face. Germany embarked on a path of territorial acquisition, which in a few short years would see Europe's newest colonial player gobble up large swathes of Africa, from present-day Togo, Cameroon and Namibia on the continent's west coast, eastward to Tanzania, Burundi and Rwanda. The German Empire then leapfrogged the Middle East and Indian subcontinent, whose lands were mostly under the flags of France and Britain, to annex part of Papua New Guinea and a string of island possessions in the Western Pacific. Bismarck had little appetite for provoking the great colonial powers by challenging French and British dominance in Egypt, Mesopotamia, Syria or India. That would come later. His immediate dream was to carve out Germany's sphere of influence in Europe. But the death of Emperor Frederick III brought Bismarck's career to an abrupt end, for two years later he was defeated in a power struggle with Frederick's successor Wilhelm II. The hoary old father of his nation was given a dukedom and sent off to retirement, which he spent lambasting the new emperor and his ministers.

If Bismarck refrained from throwing down the gauntlet to Europe's historic colonial powers, the new emperor, Kaiser Wilhelm II, did not labour under such pusillanimous constraints. A grandson of Queen Victoria, a half Englishman who despised the British and their powerful empire, Wilhelm was a firm believer in the use of force in foreign politics, as well as the divine nature of kingship. True to his aristocratic Prussian upbringing, the German emperor and king of Prussia loved military display and strutting about in flamboyant field marshal's uniforms. Much has been made of the fact that Wilhelm had a withered left arm to explain these traits, as a compensation for the physical weakness that he took great lengths to conceal. As emperor, Wilhelm endeavoured to maintain and extend the royal prerogative and build Germany into a major naval, commercial and colonial power. In the late nineteenth century, shortly after Wilhelm ascended the throne, a shift in trade between the European powers and the Middle East took place. The spread of German finance and German commerce in the East increased at a rapid pace. The German firm Krupp was supplying the Turkish navy with torpedoes. Ludwig Loewe & Co. had equipped the Turkish army with weapons. In 1888 Deutsche Bank began issuing Turkish sovereign debt in the German market, for which there was a considerable appetite. The bank's presence facilitated trade and business between both countries and gave Germany a strong foothold in the Turkish economy. German textile manufacturers captured 20 per cent of a market that was previously dominated by British exporters. In 1895 German trade delegations to Palestine outnumbered their British competitors by more than five to one. British bidders were undercut in price by the Berlin engineering firm Orenstein & Koppel to construct a narrow-gauge railway to carry pilgrims from the Gulf of Suez to Mecca. Contracts for locomotives and rolling stock for other projects were awarded to companies from Munich, while contracts for bridge-building went to a Nuremberg engineering consortium.

Germany's expanding commercial supremacy in the Ottoman Empire came as an unwelcome development in Paris and Petrograd, with the memory of the Russo-Turkish and Franco-Prussian wars still fresh in the minds of many. Germany had been steadily gaining ground on her British and French rivals in terms of trade with Turkey. Between 1887 and 1910, the German proportion of Turkey's imports rose from 6 per cent to 21 per cent. In the same period, the intake of British goods fell from 60 per cent to 35 per cent, and of French goods from 18 per cent to 11 per cent. During these years, Germany's share of investment in Turkey rose to 45.4 per cent, more than the combined total for Britain and France. This alarming decline in commercial predominance notwithstanding, the British had nothing but good wishes for Germany's business endeavours in the Middle East. Far from regretting lost opportunities for British trade in the Ottoman dominions, The Times led the acclaim for Queen Victoria's grandson Wilhelm: 'If we were not to have these good things for ourselves, there are no hands we would rather see them in than in German hands.'[3]

Britain seemed equally unconcerned about the build-up of German military domination in Turkey. In 1886 Sultan Abdul Hamid II of Turkey had asked Germany for help in reorganising his army to resist the advance of the Russian Empire. Consequently, the kaiser dispatched General Colmar von der Goltz to Constantinople to train the Turkish Army in modern fighting techniques. Von der Goltz, whose puffy, bespectacled face and oiled, centre-parted hair could have been the model for a *Punch* lampoon, spent nearly a decade disciplining Turkish troops along Prussian lines. He returned to Berlin in 1895 with the exalted title of Baron Generalfeldmarschall Pasha and he was in many ways responsible for the pro-German sentiment that brought Turkey into the First World War on the side of the Central Powers.

Germany's pursuit of commercial and military expansion in Ottoman territories precipitated two key episodes of the pre-war years. Both should have sent a clear signal to the Western powers of the kaiser's determination to pursue his aggressive policy of *Drang nach Osten*, the 'drive to the East'. Wilhelm's visit to the Middle East and the advent of the Berlin–Baghdad railway set in motion events that led inexorably to the First World War. All that was required to ignite the fuse was the assassination of the Archduke Franz Ferdinand, heir to the Austro-Hungarian throne, in June 1914.

Jerusalem was a hubbub of pre-dawn activity on 25 October 1898. Great crowds had begun queuing around 4 a.m. to catch a glimpse of Kaiser Wilhelm II, who that morning was due to make his entry into the city, dressed in a field marshal's tropical uniform and wearing the Order of St John of Jerusalem. The German emperor's triumphal journey to Constantinople, Jerusalem and Baghdad had been obligingly arranged by the British travel company Thomas Cook & Son. Wilhelm and his wife Augusta Victoria of Schleswig-Holstein rode at the head of a procession of Ottoman and German officials, followed by a column of Turkish lancers who had accompanied Wilhelm on his sea voyage from Constantinople. The entire entourage numbered more than 2,000 officials, soldiers, retainers and cooks. It was a pleasant morning in Jerusalem after the oppressive, dust-laden sirocco that had swept over the city the previous day. A sea of white turbans lined the route to witness a spectacle the likes of which had not been seen in Jerusalem since the entry of Solomon. The significance of this Turco-German display

of grandeur in the Holy Land was not lost on the French and Russian diplomats, contemplating the pageant from the balconies of their legations.
The mile-long line of march to the city gates was festooned with German
and Turkish flags. The party passed under three great arches erected for the
occasion. At one of the arches a deputation of rabbis presented the emperor
with holy Torah scrolls made of polished wood from the Mount of Olives. The
kaiser then turned into a road leading to the Church of the Holy Sepulchre,
where he was welcomed by the Holy Catholic Patriarch. He later stopped in
at the Greek and Coptic churches to receive a blessing from their respective
patriarchs. Of all these ceremonial visits the one the emperor deemed to be
of supreme importance was his meeting with Jerusalem's Muslim mayor,
who conferred on Wilhelm the freedom of the city. The kaiser's credentials
in the Islamic world were firmly in the ascendant.

In Constantinople, the kaiser had grasped in friendship 'the dripping
hands of Abdul Hamid – stained with the blood of thousands of his Christian
subjects who had just been butchered in Armenia'.[4] This gesture of friendship
with the Ottoman ruler provoked sharp criticism in French, Russian and,
to a lesser extent, British political circles. But it was a necessary expedient,
for if Germany were to take her position as a power in the Middle East – and
ultimately the jewel in the British Crown that lay farther east – that path lay
diplomatically as well as physically through a cooperative Turkey.

Damascus was the final stop on Wilhelm's Middle East tour. The British
manufacturer and philanthropist Sir William Treloar, who accompanied
the imperial party, tells of the emperor's visit to the tomb of Saladin, followed by a great review of 10,000 Turkish troops and about 1,000 Bedouins
and Circassians who went through 'a sort of Buffalo Bill entertainment' on
horseback. In spite of all this pageantry and splendour, Treloar complains
that Thomas Cook & Son let him down in his accommodation arrangements,
as he was unable to get a bath at his hotel, whose proprietor 'does not like
water in the bedrooms'.[5]

On 8 November 1898 the kaiser laid his cards on the table before a throng
of thousands of bemused Arab onlookers: 'Let his majesty the Sultan [Abdul
Hamid], as well as the three hundred millions of Mohammedans who ven-
erate him as their Caliph, be assured that the German Emperor will always

remain their friend.'[6] The next day, translated into Turkish and Arabic and printed in gilt letters, the message was circulated among the population of Damascus. Wilhelm's appearance in Damascus and his speech to the multitudes stood as an undisguised challenge to Great Britain. It had been orchestrated by Max von Oppenheim, the chief Middle East expert in the Auswärtiges Amt, Germany's Foreign Ministry. Oppenheim was a noted archaeologist of Jewish origin who, as head of the Intelligence Bureau for the East, was to play a major role in promoting pan-Islamism and providing an impetus for Indian as well as Muslim nationalism. In Damascus, the kaiser at a stroke had publicly proclaimed Germany the dominant power in the Muslim world. Kaiser Wilhelm was thenceforth seen as one with Islam: quite literally, in fact, for the word quickly spread among the unlettered masses that the emperor had performed the hajj to Mecca and was on that holy spot converted to Islam. To his amusement as well as that of the German establishment, the kaiser became known as 'Hajji Wilhelm'. Some bizarre rumours went so far as to claim that following the emperor's example, the entire German nation had adopted the true faith. Berlin did nothing to dispute these fairy tales, which on the onset of war in 1914 neatly settled the question of why Muslims should throw in their lot with one army of infidels engaged in fighting another. The sultan's call for his people to rise up and slay their Christian oppressor may no longer have applied to the Germans, but it was definitely aimed at the British in India, who ruled over the world's largest Muslim population.

The kaiser's visit was to have included a journey up the Nile in an imperial flotilla, which had already been decked out and moored for the occasion. But he cut short his trip to dash back to Berlin on account of the Fashoda incident in Africa, a crisis that brought Britain and France to the verge of war when French troops attempted to seize control of the river and force the British out of Egypt. It ended in a diplomatic victory for Britain, as France failed in its attempt to exclude its rival from Sudan and Egypt.

Nevertheless, Wilhelm's Middle East tour had been a resounding success by any measure. His flamboyant public appearances before the masses had secured Germany's pre-eminence among European powers in the region. Even before setting off to Jerusalem and Damascus, the reward for the emperor's display of largesse towards the Muslim world had been quietly sealed behind closed doors in Constantinople. In secret talks with Abdul Hamid, Wilhelm promised large shipments of arms to equip the Ottoman army, as well as German officers to train its soldiers in their use. This all but guaranteed Turkey's allegiance to the German cause in the increasingly likely event of a European conflagration. As Great Britain and Turkey's deadly enemy Russia were soon to bring the Great Game officially to a close with the signing of the Anglo-Russian Convention of 1907, it looked almost certain that the next war would see these two great imperial powers fighting together as allies.

There was another issue on the agenda in the kaiser's talks with the sultan, a project that raised the hackles of Lord Curzon, who condemned it as a direct threat to the Indian Empire to which he was shortly to sail out to administer as viceroy. This was the proposed Berlin–Baghdad railway, which would reach out for the copper mines of the Taurus, the oil of Kirkuk, the tobacco, wool, cotton and grains of Mesopotamia and Kurdistan, and one of the richest markets in the world for German manufacturers.[7] Wilhelm needed Abdul Hamid's consent in order to run the line through Turkey to the Ottoman possession of Baghdad and south to the oil-rich Persian Gulf. It was now Germany's turn to play the Great Game with the Ottoman Empire and in Muslim lands beyond its frontiers.[8] Germany had been denied a great overseas empire, but the kaiser nurtured his dream of dominating the route from the banks of the Rhine to India by a series of railway links through Turkey, Syria and Mesopotamia. As originally planned, the section from Constantinople to Baghdad was to be 1,255 miles in extent. 'It was to be built by two German concessionaires, the Anatolische Eisenbahn Gesellschaft, organised in 1888, and the Baghdad Eisenbahn Gesellschaft (1903), both owned by a financial syndicate whose controlling member was Deutsche Bank.'[9]

Britain was involved in railway-building in Turkey more than 40 years before the kaiser's tour of the Middle East. The first line constructed in that country was a 75-mile link between Izmir and Aydın, running near the Anatolian coast, financed by British interests to facilitate the export of Turkish cotton to world markets. What Germany envisaged was something considerably more ambitious. Since 1888 it had been possible to travel from Berlin to Constantinople on that most romantic of railway journeys, by linking up with the Orient Express in Vienna. Less than a year after Wilhelm and his imperial entourage had arrived back in Berlin, sensational news emerged from that capital, announcing an agreement by Deutsche Bank and Ottoman Bank to finance jointly the continuation of the Anatolian railway. It was now obvious that Germany's ultimate objective was to convert all the rail networks of Asia Minor into a single great system, skirting the Russian frontier and giving Berlin an open sea route to India. This development was greeted with horror in Petrograd and bemusement in London. The sultan was happy with the project, especially if it were to include a branch line to Erzingjan in present-day Armenia, where the Turkish Army was headquartered. The genocide of the much persecuted Armenians in 1915, expedited by the rail transport of troops to that region, was the work of Abdul Hamid's successor, Mehmed V.

Britain already had cause to be worried about a railway pointing at the heart of India from another direction. In May 1888 the Russians had inaugurated with much fanfare a railway line from the Caspian Sea to Samarkand, which had just become part of Russian Turkestan. For the first time in history, the tsarist empire was perilously close to the gates of India. The railway was played up with the most inflammatory rhetoric ever heard from Russian military quarters:

> This [railway] is the beginning of the end and the end will probably be a future campaign by Russian troops in India. We stand close to Herat, near those famed gates to India, and the main obstacle, the Turkmen steppe [...] now resounds to the sounds of locomotive whistles and the waterless drifting sands are crossed by steel rails.[10]

This incendiary threat came from the all-powerful General Leonid Skobolev, the architect of Russia's ambition to destroy the Ottoman Empire and annex the Bosphorus.

By 1892, German investors had secured a concession for a line between Constantinople and the south-western city of Konya. The year after the kaiser's Middle East visit, the concession was extended from Konya to the Gulf. Then, in 1903, Britain began to awake from its pro-German complacency and Prime Minister Arthur Balfour instructed the Indian authorities to declare Kuwait a British protectorate. The Germans planned to make the sheikhdom the railway's terminus, but at a stroke it was converted into a bulwark in Britain's defensive strategy for India. Another Tory grandee to wade into the fray, with a warning echoed by the Committee for Imperial Defence, was Foreign Secretary Lord Lansdowne. 'We shall resist all attempts by other powers to obtain a foothold on [the Persian Gulf's] shores for naval or military purposes,' he thundered.[11] The Germans were singularly unimpressed by Lansdowne's bluster and, to drive home the point, that year they enabled the Ottoman government to float a loan whose proceeds were to be handed over to the Baghdad Railway Company, as the operator was now known. As war approached, however, there were some signs that investors had lost interest in the project.

It was left to the commander-in-chief, Lord Kitchener, to sum up the railway's dire strategic implications for the British Empire. In Kitchener's view, this project constituted nothing less than a highway to India. For that reason, Britain should find a way not to oppose, but to obtain a piece of the action as a partner, to ensure that the railway concession would not be held exclusively in the hands of a commercial as well as a potential military rival. The possibility of German domination of the line gave rise to some unsettling thoughts: Constantinople was to be brought within 48 hours of Berlin, and the Persian Gulf a mere four to five days' journey from the German capital.

Fortunately for Great Britain, Germany failed to have the Berlin–Baghdad railway up and running before the outbreak of the First World War, at which time only 867 miles of track had been laid down and not even all of these were in consecutive stretches. The engineering difficulties of running a railway line through the remote Taurus and Amanus mountains, coupled with a welter of diplomatic wrangles, meant that a year after the commencement of hostilities the railway was still some 300 miles short of completion. However, the plan itself stoked the fires of international tension and this contributed to a war between both countries becoming all but inevitable.

Influential statesmen and military leaders like Curzon and Kitchener, fearful that the railway would pave the way for a possible German offensive on India, would have done well to direct their anxieties elsewhere. In spite of Germany's massive investment in a fleet of warships in the run-up to 1914 – a development, it must be said, that caused almost no alarm to the First Lord of the Admiralty, Winston Churchill – the German surface sea force never posed a serious threat to Britain's all-powerful Royal Navy. After Britain's entry into the war in August 1914, Germany's designs on India were mapped out not by a sea but by a land route, a perilous passage that led from Constantinople to Tehran, eastwards across the wastes of the forbidding Persian desert and on to Kabul.

Afghanistan was to be drawn back onto the stage of international conflict after the short period of political obscurity that followed the end of the Second Anglo-Afghan War in 1880. A dangerous move in the Great Game came into play only five years later and it bore the hallmarks of Russia's perennial fondness for brinksmanship. In March 1885 the Russians attacked and routed the Afghan forces holding the oasis stronghold of Panjdeh in western Afghanistan. It was not just a light skirmish, for the Afghans lost 600 men in the fighting before being driven back to the Maruchak fort. Fortunately, it emerged that Russia's claims of Afghan provocation were not unfounded, for without this it would have almost certainly escalated into a war in which Britain was treaty-bound to intervene.

For nearly a century, Afghanistan had formed the centrepiece around which Britain and Russia played out their chess-board intrigue, feinting and provoking, employing every ruse in the book to keep their opponent on the back foot. Now, nearly a decade after the official close of this cold war between the two great European empires, with the signing of the Anglo-Russian Convention of 1907, the Government of India was confronted with a new enemy coveting the greatest prize in Asia: Germany. In August 1907, faced with the threat of a hostile Ottoman Empire and an expansionist Germany, the perennial Central Asian rivals Great Britain and Russia agreed to bury the hatchet, a diplomatic settlement achieved by the signing of the Anglo-Russian Entente in the Petrograd Winter Palace. There was only one possible invasion route that led to the gates of Delhi.[12] To the east lay the impenetrable jungles of Burma, whose inhabitants had been pacified in three wars between 1824 and 1886. On the seas, no European power was a match for the Royal Navy, which controlled access to the shores of India from Karachi to Calcutta. The suggestion that an enemy power might choose to deploy an army across the Himalaya to invade from the north would have caused an outbreak of hilarity in the mess of the General Staff Headquarters. Quite a different matter was the prospect of an invasion from the passes to the north-west, like the Khyber and Bolan, both of which were the natural way into India from the Afghan frontier. The Germans were aware of these vulnerable points of entry and it was precisely here that their strategy was aimed.

In framing the 1907 convention, the two great European powers had in effect acknowledged their respective weaknesses. Russia had overrun the khanates of Central Asia to the Oxus River, which became Afghanistan's northern frontier. The British had consolidated their sovereignty up to the Durand Line, thus demarcating the limit of India's North-West Frontier. But both empires suffered from vulnerabilities in their respective dominions.

> British India was militarily weak on all her frontier buffer states: Persia, Afghanistan and Tibet. Russia, too, was weak after having lost the war with Japan. Britain required an agreement which would ensure the safety of India. Russia needed a breathing space.[13]

The terms of this agreement made Afghanistan a British protectorate in all but name, and its ruler a feudatory of the British Crown. One of the treaty's five articles required Russia to abide by a hands-off policy in Afghanistan. Petrograd was obliged to conduct all political relations with Kabul through the British government and no Russian agents were to set foot on Afghan soil. Amir Mohammed Yakub Khan had relinquished control of his country's for-eign relations to Britain in 1879 with the signing of the Treaty of Gandamak, which put an end to the first phase of the Second Anglo-Afghan War. This accord was renewed in 1905 with Abdur Rahman's eldest son, Habibullah Khan, who had ascended the throne at age of 39, in one of Afghanistan's very few peaceful transitions of power. It was subsequently reaffirmed in the

1907 entente and would cause a great deal of bitter discord between Britain and Afghanistan in future years.

Britain and Russia also jointly addressed the problem of Persia, where a wave of revolutionary activity had swept across this Middle East kingdom in 1905. Much to the distress of both signatories, the progressive regime that replaced the old order in this country, whose vast newly discovered oil resources were to be tapped in a matter of months by the Anglo-Persian Oil Company, was plagued by political instability. Hence London and Petrograd ruthlessly took a scalpel to Persia and carved up the country into two separate zones of influence. Russia was given control of a northern strip of territory, Britain took the south-eastern sector, and a neutral east–west corridor was created between the two, not unlike Afghanistan's Wakhan Corridor, which was carved out to keep the British and Russian empires a safe distance apart.

British Foreign Secretary Sir Arthur Nicolson walked away from the negotiating table the undisputed winner over a Russia that found itself in the throes of economic bankruptcy. The most significant concession Petrograd got out of the deal was a free hand in commercial activities in Central Asian markets that were under Russian suzerainty. In spite of the diplomatic drubbing it had taken, the Russian government was relieved to have the heat taken off a confrontation that had been steadily notching up from cold to lukewarm, with the danger of erupting into all-out war.

'The nearer Russia and England have approached the Afghan frontier, the greater importance has Afghanistan acquired, embracing the main lines of operations from Russian possessions to India,' was how an influential Russian commentator of the day summed up the mounting tension.

> On this account, until the conclusion of the recent Agreement, a collision in Central Asia seemed inevitable, in which event Afghanistan would have played an important part, as being a powerful lever in the hands of one or other of the rival Powers.[14]

Amir Habibullah Khan came to the throne of Kabul in 1901 with the blessing of Lord Curzon, who later developed very different thoughts about the amir whom he had originally supported. In 1898, on the eve of his appointment as viceroy, the then Under-Secretary of State for Foreign Affairs suggested providing military support for Habibullah, the legitimate Afghan heir, fearing his right of accession as primogenitor was in danger of being challenged by a rival pretender. The usurper that Curzon had in mind was Habibullah's younger brother, the virulently anti-British Islamist Nasrullah. The amir had the foresight to hold Nasrullah's supporters in check by increasing army pay, an expedient he repeated whenever he felt threatened by disgruntled Islamist factions within the armed forces.

The reformist-minded Habibullah had at that time never set foot outside Afghanistan, yet he was bent on continuing the modernisation process ushered in by his father Abdur Rahman, who had introduced a number of mild European-style reforms into Afghan life. The reactionary Nasrullah, on the other hand, was the family's international traveller, having been sent to England on a diplomatic assignment by his ailing father in May 1895. The task fell to Nasrullah because Abdur Rahman dared not allow his heir to leave the country, knowing that treachery and insurrection lurked in certain quarters of the army and among the conservative mullahs. After docking at Plymouth, Nasrullah was received by Queen Victoria at Windsor, and he also attended the Derby and a review at Aldershot. His remit was to persuade the British government to accept the posting of a permanent Afghan ambassador to London, a petition that was politely but firmly turned down. Lord George Hamilton, Secretary of State for India, argued that Afghanistan was unfortunately not a safe place for British diplomats. More than one British legation in Kabul had in the past come to a violent end and the government had no appetite to risk another tragedy. Nasrullah sailed back to Afghanistan in despair, nursing a grudge against the British, which turned him into the most shadowy figure at court as well as an ardent supporter of Germany's attempt to overthrow British rule in India.

Nasrullah's older brother Habibullah was cut from a different cloth than his overpowering father Abdur Rahman. Physically, he was hardly an imposing figure, a bespectacled, avid fan of Jules Verne novels, of less than average height and with a waistline that betrayed his fondness for fine cuisine. In his favoured Western-style dress of waistcoat and tie, he could have been taken for a court chamberlain rather than the monarch himself. The Government of India was not allowed a European agent in Kabul, nor was it keen to send one to a place that offered no personal security. The memory was still fresh of the brutal murder in 1879 of the envoy Sir Louis Cavagnari by a mob of Afghan soldiers, rampaging through the city over unpaid wages. The British representative was a trusted Pashtun, a spy in all but name, called Malik Talib Mehdi Khan. This agent sent a report to the viceroy, describing the impact that Habibullah's exposure to British life and customs had on the amir:

> Since his return from India Habibullah has entirely taken to European methods of eating, dressing and so on. The *pagri*, *paijama* and *chogha*, a very graceful combination of attire, have all been discarded and have given place to hat, trousers and frock coat. Everyone who has any connection with the court has to provide himself with a morning and evening suit and a spare suit or two for odd hours, and if he is not dressed in the style prescribed for the hour he is either punished with a fine or censured. The mania is not confined to the men only, for the women have adopted European gowns in place of their Eastern garb.[15]

But it would have been wrong to underestimate Habibullah's strength of character. Lord Curzon, for one, soon found him to be a stubborn and formidable opponent during a diplomatic wrangle over the interpretation of the 1880 Treaty of Gandamak. Curzon set forth his demands for renegotiating the terms, under which it had been agreed that the Afghan ruler would receive an annual subsidy and undertakings to defend Afghan sovereignty against aggression by any foreign power, meaning Russia. The viceroy insisted on new concessions that would give Britain more extensive dominion over Afghan affairs. He found himself confronted with an untested, inexperienced ruler, yet one who to Curzon's frustration dug in his heels over what could only be interpreted as the viceroy's summons to a face-to-face meeting in Peshawar. Habibullah's position was that there were no grounds for renegotiating the treaty, so he would not be meeting Curzon in Peshawar or elsewhere. The amir cleverly countered Curzon's arguments by posing an awkward question: if the original treaty was personal and its undertakings had lapsed, did this not also apply to the agreement over the Durand Line and British control of Afghanistan's foreign policy, both of which had been negotiated with Abdur Rahman? After all, Habibullah reasoned, these treaties had been signed under the reign of Queen Victoria, who had died in 1901.

> When Habibullah refused any more concessions, Curzon in 1901 created a Pashtun province, the North-West Frontier Province [renamed Khyber Pakhtunkhwa in 2008] out of the Punjab at the cost of increasing cross-border tribal disturbances, and also began preparation for a third British invasion of Afghanistan among other measures.[16]

So incensed was the viceroy by Habibullah's rebuff that he raised the time-worn bogey in London of an impending Afghan–Russian alliance and called for a declaration of war, a demand that fortunately fell on deaf ears in Whitehall.

With customary arrogance, Curzon kept up the pressure on Habibullah who, after all, was a monarch, not merely a government official. But when the viceroy was on leave in London in late 1904, the acting viceroy, Lord Ampthill, sent Sir Louis Dane, the Indian Foreign Secretary, to Kabul with a draft treaty in his pocket. Habibullah countered Dane's treaty with one of his own, which simply confirmed the arrangements that had been agreed with Abdur Rahman a quarter of a century previously. London's overriding concern was to preserve stability on the North-West Frontier at a time when it was feared that Russia might use its influence to inflame the warlike spirits of the border tribes with the connivance of a disgruntled amir.

> Dane was instructed to sign the treaty, under which Habibullah received the arrears of subsidy due to him and no limitations were placed on his right to import arms. His prestige in Afghanistan was much enhanced by this emphatic diplomatic success.[17]

Until then, in an attempt to coerce Habibullah, the Government of India had prevented arms supplies ordered by the amir from passing in transit through India. Habibullah also persuaded the British to address him as 'Your Majesty' and acknowledge him as 'independent ruler of Afghanistan and its dependencies', though in matters of foreign affairs this was no more than a formality to pamper the king's vanity and standing among his people.

Habibullah was 34 years old before he embarked on his first and only trip abroad in 1907, six years after ascending the throne. That was at a time when Germany's expanding hegemony in the Middle East was beginning to raise the unwelcome prospect of the kaiser extending his commercial and military influence outside Turkey's borders, with only a poorly defended Persia standing between him, Afghanistan and, ultimately, India.

> When Germany, by one of the most audacious diplomatic strokes in the history of the war, forced Turkey to range herself with the Central Powers, visions arose in Berlin of the swift collapse of Britain's prestige in the East. The first palpable step in the *Drang nach Osten* had been taken, and taken with seven-leagued boots. The Ottoman armies, reorganised by German brains and led by German commanders, would soon be, it was thought, at the Persian Gulf; the next step would be to rouse Mohammedan Persia. With two out of the three independent Mohammedan powers on Germany's side, little effort would be required to bring the third, Afghanistan, into line. Then the end of Russian dominion over the Mohammedans in the Caucasus and Turkestan and the downfall of British power in India seemed to the Germans in sight.[18]

To keep Amir Habibullah on side, the British government invited him to visit India in 1906, where he would have an opportunity to witness at first hand the grandeur and might of the empire that controlled his kingdom's foreign affairs. On the afternoon of 2 January 1907, seven months before the Anglo-Russian Entente came into effect, creating a semi-effective defensive barrier of Persia, one of Habibullah's Rolls-Royces pulled up at Landi Kotal, at the top of the Khyber Pass, with a numerous escort of cavalry and infantry in tow. The amir was met by his mentor, Lieutenant Colonel Sir Henry McMahon, who was taken completely aback by one of Habibullah's first requests, which was to become a Freemason. The Afghan ruler who was in time to stand up to Germany's designs on India was, McMahon observed, 'a man of very strong and determined character, of very superior intellect and surprisingly well-informed on all general subjects'.[19] Habibullah was treated to a 31-gun salute, he was invested with the Grand Cross of the Order of Bath, he made an ascent in the military balloon, he shot a tiger, and in Bombay he had his first ever view of the sea, which he proclaimed 'quite a large tank'.[20]

Habibullah was by all accounts a more humane ruler than his father, the 'Iron Amir'. He refrained from having enemies thrown into boiling vats, torn apart, skinned alive, starved to death or grotesquely maimed. Since he came to the throne, the number of executions had numbered only around 20 a year, a trifle compared with the more than 10,000 people Abdur Rahman was reputed to have put to death in his 21-year reign. So what was behind the amir's desire to join the Freemasons – to play, in effect, into the hands of the Islamist advisers who had prophesied that nothing but evil could come from his association with foreign infidels? Habibullah's only stated rationale for joining was that he had come in contact with Freemasons, who had all struck him as good men. But he did ask for it to be done on the quiet, without the knowledge of his people. Given the amir's love of all things English, it seemed natural for him to want to add Freemasonry[21] to his Anglophile pursuits, along with golf and a fondness for treacle pudding. Habibullah was whisked off to the Calcutta Lodge, the only one in India that could fast-track his entry in all three degrees of initiation in a single meeting. Lord Kitchener was the District Grand Master of the Punjab at that moment. It was the commander-in-chief who persuaded the Grand Master, the Duke of Connaught, to grant the amir an all-embracing dispensation to leapfrog normal procedures and thus, at a meeting on the night of 2 February 1907, Habibullah became a Freemason. This act served British interests by drawing the amir into a closer relationship with the country that controlled his own nation's foreign affairs. McMahon says as much in his account of Habibullah's visit to India:

> I am convinced that his experience of Freemasonry with us played no small
> part in creating that trust and in preserving it unweakened through the

years to come. Among his [Habibullah's] last words to me on leaving India was the expression of a solemn vow to prove a faithful friend of England as long as England kept faith with him.[22]

To Habibullah's dismay, on his return to Kabul he found the city's bazaars teeming with rumours of his having become a Freemason. There had been an unfortunate leak from somebody in the entourage that had accompanied him to India. The country's fanatical mullahs, who knew nothing about Freemasonry apart from it being foreign and therefore tantamount to heresy, flew into a rage; calls to insurrection were issued at Friday prayers. Habibullah acted swiftly to confirm his credentials as an Afghan king and to dispel any notion that he had become an effete toady of his British masters. The amir called a durbar, or public gathering, of the leading disgruntled clerics to inform them that he had proudly become a Freemason for the benefit of his country. Furthermore, any mullah who expressed criticism of his action would pay for it with his head. To dispel any doubts about the seriousness of his warning Habibullah, who reserved to himself the right of passing death sentences, had a few of these recalcitrant mullahs summarily executed.

The kingdom Habibullah inherited, once the cultural capital of Islam, situated at the crossroads of a flourishing caravan trade route between Central Asia and the Indian subcontinent, had by the early twentieth century become an impoverished backwater. For centuries the trade between Turkestan and India had flowed over Afghanistan's high passes. Quite often these caravans numbered as many as 120,000 laden animals, including camels, mules and horses. The amir had returned from India, fired with modernising zeal.

> Habibullah began to rectify his father's one great omission – the failure to develop the country – and he initiated a number of projects, including the construction of factories, hydroelectric plants and road-building schemes. Some schools, based on foreign models, were also founded and made available to the upper class elite.[23]

He set up the first almshouses to care for his innumerable destitute subjects. Traffic police were introduced into Kabul to try, without much success, to put order into the city's bottlenecks of animal-drawn traffic. This did not apply to Habibullah's fleet of 58 motor vehicles, the only ones in the country. The amir strove to improve the postal system, at that time operated by dak runners[24] who carried spears to frighten off wolves in the mountain passes between Afghanistan and India. He had a golf course laid out near Jalalabad, on which by all accounts he played a good game. Woollen mills and modern tanneries sprung up in Kabul. Habibullah also had milestones erected on the roads, an innovation that had much impressed him in India. However, several problems arose with these markers. For one thing, less than 3 per cent of Afghans could read numbers. Secondly, the numbers were leaded to make them visible, and the lead was frequently gouged out by tribesmen to make bullets. The amir's drive to bring European culture into his country was eagerly taken up by Kabul's elite. For instance, many of the wealthy imported pianos from Bombay, which they learnt to play with one finger. One affluent entrepreneur was found to have sawn off the legs of a grand piano, so that he might play it sitting on the floor, Afghan fashion.

Under Habibullah, Afghanistan also saw the launch of its first illustrated newspaper, *Siraj-ul-Akhbar* ('*Lamp of the News*'), a bi-weekly lithographed sheet published by one of Afghanistan's greatest intellectuals, Mahmud Tarzi. The paper survived until the end of Habibullah's reign in 1919 and made Tarzi a spokesman for Islamic nationalism in Afghanistan. Often to the amir's chagrin, it published incisive analyses on a wide range of subjects, from the role of Islam and monarchy and the relationship of the two to fundamental questions of Afghan nationalism and modernisation in Afghanistan.[25]

One of the amir's most ambitious undertakings was the construction of a dam and hydroelectric plant in Kohistan, 50 miles north of Kabul. The plant's official purpose was to provide power for Kabul's cottage industries, such as the mint, a leather-goods factory, machine shops and woollen mills. An American engineer, A.C. Jewett, was brought in to do the job. This former General Electric engineer travelled to Kabul in 1911 to oversee the construction of the hydroelectric plant. Jewett remained in Afghanistan for eight years and his work set a precedent for the many American engineers who followed him in later decades to work on projects commissioned by Habibullah's successor, Amanullah, and later progressive rulers.[26] Jewett's account of his sojourn in Afghanistan reveals the rigours endured by a native of San Francisco who in the end found solace in the remote South Pacific, where he retired with a collection of teakwood tables, Peshawar draperies and an assortment of Afghan knives and guns. Habibullah had in mind another use for electrical power, the most revolutionary of early-twentieth-century technological advances. Most of the government offices he had visited in India were lit by electric light bulbs. So, too, would be his new palace, the Kasr-i-Dilkushah, outside the fortified Arg citadel in the centre of Kabul, for the enjoyment of the amir, his four wives, up to 100 concubines (including several European women) and 50 offspring. Habibullah had already furnished his various residences and offices with some European-style desks, typewriters, sewing machines and clocks.

The early years of Habibullah's reign were marked by relative peace on the home front, a state of affairs inherited from his father's merciless repression of the merest hint of rebellion or misbehaviour by his subjects. Apologists for authoritarian rule play up the claim that throughout Abdur Rahman's reign, which masqueraded under a thin reformist veneer, travellers in Afghanistan enjoyed complete safety of the roads, as was allegedly the case more than a century later under the Taliban, which also boasted its social-justice credentials. Thus Habibullah's domestic problems were not concerned with keeping the peace internally.

Before the First World War and the German diplomatic offensive on Afghanistan, the amir's difficulties were with the restless border tribes of the British side of the Durand Line. The most testing incident came in 1908, when a number of the frontier Pashtun tribes that had taken up arms against the British were severely punished in the army's retaliatory expeditions. When the news of the offending tribesmen's villages being destroyed and their crops put to the torch was brought to Afghanistan, hundreds of armed tribesmen passed through Kabul on their way to the frontier to help their brethren fight the infidels. This was when the amir's fanatical brother

Nasrullah showed his hand. Using his powerful offices of Commander-in-Chief of the Afghan Army and President of the State Council, Nasrullah ordered the release of 5,000 rifles and 500,000 rounds of ammunition from the Kabul arsenal to arm the rebels. When Habibullah learnt of this affront to his authority, he took swift action in a public address after the Friday-morning prayers to a multitude gathered on a bridge across the Kabul River. The harangue undoubtedly raised the hackles of the attendant mullahs, but it fell like music on the ears of British agents in the crowd. Habibullah called for a Qur'an and, opening the book, he challenged his listeners to show him a verse or chapter that called for jihad against one's friends. He threatened to tear out the tongue of anyone who dared preach jihad again, or chop off the feet of anyone caught marching off to the fighting. 'I, the Light of Faith,' he declared, 'I, the Torch of the Nation, have decreed and now repeat my decree, that no subject of mine shall lift a finger against the Feringhis ['foreigners'].'[27] The throng dispersed in desultory fashion from the bridge, while Habibullah got into his Rolls-Royce and drove back to his palace for tiffin. The amir's calculated risk in proclaiming his British friendship had worked, though he was later to pay dearly for standing up to the fanatics.

Habibullah might have persuaded some of his people to accept reforms on sensitive issues like education and initiate a feeble attempt to improve the lot of Afghan women by giving them access to schools. He could take credit for the foundation of Habiba High School, on the French lycée model, a military academy and a teacher-training college, all of which helped to open Afghanistan to the outside world. But the one area over which the amir had no influence was his country's geography. The travel writer Peter Levi, perhaps rather uncharitably, defines Afghanistan as

> nothing but a chewed bone left over on the plate between Imperial Russia and British India. It has never been a cultural unity in any period, and it is not so today. Nonetheless it is a political reality, unified in some way by its religion, Islam, and by its special physical geography [author's emphasis] and remarkable climate.[28]

In the early twentieth century, Afghanistan was bordered to the south and east by British India, an ally and protector of Afghan independence in all things but foreign affairs. To the north, the snow-capped Hindu Kush stood for centuries as a formidable deterrent to anyone reckless enough to contemplate an invasion over the rugged mountain passes. By now, however, roads had been built from Balkh, part of Afghan Turkestan since the time of Ahmad Shah Durrani, which made possible the passage of wheeled vehicles six months of the year. With the signing of the 1907 Anglo-Russian Convention the tsar was now, at least on paper, committed to friendly relations with British India. This relationship was upheld throughout the war years, during which Britain and Russia fought as allies.

The peril lay to the west at Herat, the historical passage to Afghanistan, through which had marched the armies of all the great conquerors, from Alexander the Great and Genghis Khan to Tamerlane and Babur. From Herat the road presents few obstacles for an invader from the Russian-controlled khanates or Persia. While the Russians were no longer feared as a threat to Afghan sovereignty, another European power had its eye on this timeworn route to Afghanistan and India. Southwards from Herat, the road runs to the fertile valley of Helmand, past Kandahar, to become the main route to western India. The British and Russians were uncomfortably aware of this weak spot in Afghanistan's defences, natural and political. So, too, was Kaiser Wilhelm, and it is here, in the early days of the Great War, that Germany prepared to launch its diplomatic attack on Afghanistan, with the objective of exploiting British India's neighbour to destabilise the Raj.

2

We're Off to Join the Circus

Topography was always the key factor in safeguarding Afghanistan's independence. The country's mountains, with many peaks of more than 20,000 feet, and the trackless deserts in which armies would need to depend for survival on drawn-out supply lines through hostile territory, were enough of a barrier to discourage invaders. 'Large invading forces could not easily support themselves in a country so barren of vegetation. Thousands of transport animals were required to supply the troops and keep open the routes of supply.'[1] Perhaps this helps to explain why, as German generals were courting the Ottoman's German-speaking Minister for War, Enver Pasha, the architect of the Ottoman–German alliance, the British still regarded the turbulent North-West Frontier as pivotal to India's defence. If German and Turkish forces were to attempt an invasion of India through Afghanistan, the vulnerable Pashtun land of the frontier was the only viable attack route.

Charles Hardinge was one of the most rapidly rising stars in the diplomatic service, and his close friendship with King Edward VII, as well as his dashing good looks and cultivated manner, ensured him a prominent place in London society. In 1910 he was made a peer and in that same year he was chosen to replace the capable though somewhat staid John Minto as Viceroy of India. Lord Hardinge presided over four main affairs during his viceroyalty: the Delhi Durbar held in 1911 to celebrate King George V's accession, the reunification of the two parts of Bengal that had been partitioned in

Curzon's time, the transfer of the capital of India from Calcutta to Delhi, and India's involvement in the crucial first two years of the Great War. Devising a wartime strategy that would ensure Afghanistan remained neutral and hence India safe from a German invasion proved the greatest challenge to Hardinge's diplomatic skills. On 7 August 1914, the viceroy broke the news to Habibullah that war had been declared in Europe between Russia, France and Britain on the one hand, as the Triple Entente, and Germany and Austria-Hungary on the other. Three months later Hardinge again had cause to deliver some distressing news to the amir: the Ottoman Empire had entered the war on Germany's side.

India's contribution to the war effort cannot be overemphasised. The 'jewel in the Crown' figured so prominently in the European conflict that Hardinge, as viceroy, signed a separate declaration of war by India against Germany and Austria-Hungary. Immediately on the outbreak of hostilities, and to the immense distress of the Commander-in-Chief in India, General Sir Beauchamp Duff, Hardinge offered the Home Government two divisions of infantry and one division of cavalry for overseas service. In all, within six months nine divisions were deployed from India, consisting of 80,000 British and 210,000 Indian officers and soldiers.[2] As the troops bound for the Western Front and the Middle East embarked from Bombay and Calcutta, Hardinge dispatched three Indian Army divisions to the North-West Frontier in anticipation of trouble from the rebellious Pashtun tribesmen. The viceroy's apprehensions were well founded. In less than a year from the start of the European war, the army had to fight off seven determined attacks by frontier lashkars, tribal fighting forces. Although the Indian troops were trained for combat in the rugged hills of the Pashtun borderland, Hardinge could take pride in the heroic account they gave of themselves in the trenches of Europe. A letter from a German soldier printed in the *Frankfurter Zeitung* bears witness to the Indians as formidable adversaries:

> At first we spoke with contempt of the Indians. Today we learned to look on them in a different light – the devil knows what the English had put into these fellows. With a fearful shouting, thousands of those brown forms rushed upon us. At a hundred metres we opened a destructive fire

which mowed down hundreds, but in spite of that the others advanced. In no time they were in our trenches and truly those brown enemies were not to be despised.[3]

India was left militarily in a precarious state. In the early months of the war, the country had been so depleted of fighting men that the total of British troops was reduced to 15,000, to garrison a territory larger than Europe. If ever there was a man in need of a friend, this was Lord Hardinge, who was faced with the monumental task of buttressing India's borders against attack. Fortunately for the viceroy, Amir Habibullah was that friend, or at least he professed to be. Within days of the outbreak of war, the amir had gathered the tribal chieftains at a *loya jirga*, or 'grand council', to proclaim Afghanistan's neutrality in the European conflict. The vast majority of the tribal leaders cared little which side emerged victorious in a war being waged between infidels – the more who fell, the greater the glory for the true faith. There were others who virulently opposed what they took to be Habibullah's pro-British stance. To them, the amir's declaration of neutrality signified his allowing India's colonial masters to carry on suppressing the many millions of Muslims bent under the yoke of British imperialism. The ringleaders were the amir's third son, Amanullah (later to succeed him as amir), Habibullah's younger brother and ambitious head of the armed forces, Nasrullah, and increasingly the newspaper editor Mahmud Tarzi, who represented the Young Afghan Movement, a revolutionary group modelled on Enver Pasha's Young Turks, which in the previous year had seized power in a coup. All three lobbied for Afghanistan to throw in its lot with Germany and the Central Powers. The political enemy Habibullah feared most was his brother, the fanatical and, according to quiet rumours, corrupt Nasrullah. The amir took great care to avoid inflaming an already smouldering enmity with his brother. This was evidenced when Nasrullah dipped into treasury funds to buy up Kabul's entire supply of cooking oil, inflating prices to make it inaccessible to all but the most affluent. When a deputation of angry citizens called on the amir to complain, instead of having his brother arrested, Habibullah sent a caravan of men and pack animals north to the Hazara country to buy oil for the Kabul market. This was not the first time Nasrullah had artificially manipulated prices, for he had previously used the same tactics to corner the kerosene market, with equally detrimental results for the impoverished people of Kabul.

Berlin entertained great hopes of fomenting discontent and anti-British hostility in India. On this matter Oppenheim, who among other callings was celebrated as Germany's outstanding Middle East archaeologist, had the ear of Chancellor Theobald von Bethmann-Hollweg. Within a fortnight of Germany's 1 August declaration of war against Russia, Oppenheim put forward his proposals in a memorandum to the chancellor: 'It will not be until the Turks enter Egypt and the fires of revolt flame up in India that England will be ripe for destruction.'[4] The title left no room for doubt as to Oppenheim's ultimate intentions: 'How to Revolutionise the Islamic Areas of our Enemies'. There were two factors that Oppenheim regarded as essential for the success of German propaganda in these Muslim-populated areas of Germany's enemies, namely Russia and, in particular, Great Britain. 'First, intensive and close cooperation between Germany and the Ottoman Empire [...] and second, a rigid and strict organisation of all such activities.'[5] That same month, the Chief of the German General Staff, Helmuth Johann Ludwig von Moltke, sent a memorandum to the Foreign Ministry, saying that, in his view, Berlin's treaty with the Ottoman Empire would make it possible for Germany to kindle revolutionary activity in India. Oppenheim was the architect of an Indian nationalist movement, the Berlin Committee, founded in 1914. There were 18 members, mostly educated Muslims, but also some Hindus and Sikhs. The most notorious of these was the polymath and ascetic Indian nationalist Har Dayal, who was immortalised in postwar fiction as Chandra Lal in Somerset Maugham's spy novel Ashenden. These revolutionaries, mainly students, were drawn from various countries, including Britain, from which some of them were forced to flee under suspicion of being involved in the 1909 assassination in London of William Hutt Curzon Wyllie, political aide-de-camp to the Secretary of State for India. Oppenheim saw to it that Germany gave a warm welcome to these Indian revolutionaries. He firmly believed that this sort of radical organisation could whip up revolutionary anti-British activity in Muslim lands, including Persia. As for Afghanistan, he considered this 'a considerable power, whose invasion of India could only meet with the greatest success'.[6] Oppenheim was himself in Germany at that time, having been expelled from Egypt by the British, who quite rightly suspected him of spying for Germany.

Oppenheim was again seen in the Middle East when in November 1914 the caliph issued a declaration of jihad which, it turned out, had been masterminded largely under Oppenheim's guidance and encouragement. The plan was for a qualified jihad against the enemies of Islam, who were named as Britain, France and Russia, conveniently omitting Germany. Despite being an infidel nation, Germany offered assurances of being a strong ally of Islam, with the staunchly pro-Muslim kaiser as its guiding light. Oppenheim believed that the prospect of an Islamic uprising would strike fear into the hearts of Germany's European enemies. There were up to 270 million Muslims in the world in 1914, but barely a tenth of them lived under Muslim rule. The rest were governed overwhelmingly by Britain, with smaller numbers under French and Russian suzerainty. Germany itself had 2 million Muslim subjects in East Africa.

Oppenheim held secret talks with several influential Arab chieftains to answer the caliph's summons to war, but his plans were frustrated by T.E. Lawrence ('Lawrence of Arabia'), who was rallying Arab support for an uprising against the Turks. Oppenheim and Lawrence were acquaintances of former days in the desert, when both were engaged in archaeological excavations in Carchemish, on the present-day border between Turkey and Syria. Lawrence took a violent dislike to the German, whom he contemptuously referred to as 'the little Jew-German-millionaire [...] He was such a horrible person. Invited me over to his place by his relay of post horses – six days' journey in thirty-six hours! Not for me, thanks!'[7]

If Oppenheim was the chief instigator of Indian nationalist plots to bring down the Raj, the man responsible for putting them into execution was Franz von Papen, who in 1914 was serving as military attaché to the German Ambassador in Washington. A dashing aristocrat, von Papen, who in the next war served briefly as vice-chancellor under Adolf Hitler, was accused by the United States of engaging in outright terrorist activities, such as a conspiracy to blow up American railway lines and a canal connecting Lake Ontario to Lake Erie.

A few weeks after Germany declared war, von Papen, through his agent Ernst Sekuna, was in touch with Indian seditionists who had set up an office in New York's Upper West Side. The Germans told the Indians they would finance a consignment of arms and munitions to be sent from California to Mexico, and onwards to India. It was a worthwhile and affordable undertaking, although von Papen held to a more realistic assessment than General von Moltke of the damage Germany could inflict on British India:

> We did not go so far as to suppose that there was any hope of India achieving her independence through our assistance, but if there was any chance of fomenting local disorders we felt it might limit the number of Indian troops who could be sent to France and other theatres of war.[8]

That was about the most he believed Germany could achieve. He confided in his memoirs that, in his opinion, the shortage of sufficiently qualified agents and a lack of realistic thinking made the overthrow of British rule in India a pipe dream. 'Instead, they hoped that by creating a number of local disturbances they would compel Britain to retain in India troops which would otherwise be sent to the [Western] Front.'[9] Von Papen paid the firm Krupp $200,000 to assemble a shipload of weapons to be sent to Mexico under a bogus bill of lading. The German government was thus using the territory of a neutral country to sponsor a gun-running plot, which in the end went almost comically wrong. What became known as the *Annie Larsen* Affair was a complex operation, involving the transportation of weapons, first from New York to Texas, and then from the port of Galveston to San Diego by sea on the schooner *Annie Larsen*, which was to carry the arms to Burma for overland transport to India. The ship made for Socorro Island off the coast of Baja California, where she was meant to be joined by a specially chartered oil tanker, the SS *Maverick*, which in turn would hide the contraband in its empty tanks and make for Karachi as its first port of call. It was at that point that the scheme started to fall apart. The *Maverick* arrived late at Socorro and the *Annie Larsen* began to run out of fresh water. Without a condenser on board the schooner was forced to head for the Mexican mainland to replenish her water supply. When the *Maverick* reached the rendezvous point her captain was told of the *Annie Larsen*'s sailing, and he spent nearly a month waiting for the ship's return to Socorro. Meanwhile, a US warship came to search the *Maverick*'s hold and, finding nothing, her skipper was told to sail on. The *Annie Larsen* returned a few days later to find the tanker gone. The Germans tried desperately to arrange another meeting point, but by that time the *Maverick* was on its way to Java, where it was seized and impounded by the Dutch authorities. 'In the meantime, the British Secret Service had got wind of the affair – how, I shall never know – and caught up with the *Maverick*.'[10] On 29 June 1915, acting on a tip-off from British agents, the *Annie Larsen* was raided off the coast of Washington state and its cargo of weapons was seized. Several persons implicated in the plot blew the whistle on Germany's involvement and six months later von Papen was expelled from the US.

The first direct German intrigues in India came to the surface shortly after the Ottoman entry into the war in October 1914. British intelligence services had detected a number of attempts to organise an uprising by Indian nationalists, mainly in the Muslim-dominated areas of Bengal. These conspiracies were swiftly nipped in the bud by the army, resulting in the round-up of a handful of German agents a few days before the revolt was meant to take place. The viceroy heaved a sigh of relief on learning that the German-orchestrated plot had been aborted, although for a while the ability to keep the lid on the plotters' seditious activities was in doubt. 'I shall breathe more freely when Christmas [1914] is over, for that was the moment selected by the conspirators for the execution of their nefarious scheme,' he told Sir George Roos-Keppel, Chief Commissioner of the North-West Frontier Province.[11] In 1915, the following year, the Indian revolutionaries attempted a second insurrection at the same time of year, which became known as the Christmas Day Plot. The Germans were meant to participate in this operation by staging a raid on Madras and the Andaman Islands penal colony. This, too, was thwarted by British intelligence, with the help of double agents. As Germany's plan to destabilise India became more apparent and determined, Hardinge spent some uneasy hours pondering the trustworthiness of the amir's purported neutrality, not to mention his ability to deal with anti-British elements in Kabul. 'At the outbreak of war with Turkey,' the viceroy reflected in his memoirs, 'the attitude of the amir had been a source of some anxiety to me and the Government, since a hostile Afghanistan might have been a real danger to India.'[12]

The opening salvoes of the First World War played into the hands of Islamist elements in Afghanistan and on the rebellious North-West Frontier, as well as among the Indian revolutionaries who were bent on overthrowing the Raj, all of whom sought to discredit the image of Britain as an omnipotent imperial power. It was widely propagated in mosques and in the bazaars, in the first months of hostilities and especially after the Ottoman declaration of war against the Allies, that the smart money should be on the Central Powers. Britain's enemies in Afghanistan, from the conservative clergy to army cadres who fell under the spell of the mullahs' preaching, took heart in Germany's rapid advance through Belgium and northern France, the fall of Serbia and Montenegro and the expulsion of the Russians from Poland. The most powerful propaganda weapon was the British disaster at Gallipoli in April 1915 and the Allies' failure to open a supply route to Russia through the Dardanelles. The news of British battleships having met disaster at the hands of Turkish shore batteries and the heavy casualties inflicted on British troops during the beach landings on the Gallipoli Peninsula further inflamed the pro-Turco-German factions in Kabul. Their supreme moment of joy came when the government in London decided to bring the expedition to an end, at the cost of half a million Allied casualties, mainly British. Following close on the heels of the Gallipoli calamity, a British expedition rolling across the desert to the holy city of Baghdad was stopped in its tracks by the Turks, and to make things look even worse, a British division was forced to capitulate at the siege of Kut-al-Amara. 'Ottoman intervention, as far as the Germans were concerned, was now working out tolerably well.'[13]

*

The Emperor Babur's 500-year-old burial garden, Bagh-e-Babur, stands on a 27-acre site near the Kabul River. Today, as in the past, it is common to see families out for a leisurely afternoon stroll in the formal enclosure, sitting down to a picnic under the fruit trees or simply paying a visit to the grave of the great Central Asian prince who had the garden laid out after conquering Kabul in 1504. In the days before the Afghan capital was in many areas reduced to rubble during the civil war that brought the Taliban to power in 1996, a sprawling mud-brick palace stood in a corner of the Bagh-e-Babur. It was built by Amir Abdur Rahman in the late nineteenth century and soon became an Afghan royal residence, known also as the *haremserai*, or Queen's Palace.

In early autumn 1915, the Bagh-e-Babur was a bustle of carpenters, plasterers and assorted labourers pushing wheelbarrows and carrying ladders to and fro. The Queen's Palace was being smartened up in preparation for the arrival of some distinguished visitors. The bazaars buzzed with speculation over the identity of these mysterious dignitaries. It was assumed they were British, for Habibullah had not softened his opposition to Nasrullah's jihadist demands. The amir took every opportunity to reiterate his neutrality in the European war, 'neutrality' for the pro-German clique being a euphemism for support for the British cause. It was no secret that Habibullah was pushing for an increase in the annual subsidy he received from British India, which at the start of the war amounted to 1.8 million rupees, or £10,500 in today's money, a huge sum at that time. People reasoned that the forthcoming visit had to be the amir reciprocating his British friends' hospitality on his tour of India. Lieutenant Colonel Sir George Roos-Keppel, the scholarly soldier serving as Chief Commissioner of the North-West Frontier Province, had just received a report at his Peshawar office from one of his Afghan spies in Kabul. Roos-Keppel forwarded a copy of the memorandum to Lord Hardinge. The viceroy had for some time been aware of the unwelcome news in the report, the confirmation of which caused him considerable dismay, but not a bit of resignation.

> When orders were received for the Bagh-i-Babur to be made ready for the reception of guests it was generally taken for granted in Kabul that a British

mission was on the point of arrival, and the utmost surprise was felt when the German party arrived from the West.[14]

The tale of how two German envoys happened to make their appearance in Kabul in September 1915 had its origin more than half a year previously in the mud-filled trenches of Europe's battlefronts. Werner Otto von Hentig was a dashing 29-year-old diplomat with a number of consular postings under his belt, in Peking, Constantinople and Tehran. He was therefore acquainted with the whys and wherefores of the East and its political intrigues. Hentig was called up when war broke out and had been fighting on the Eastern Front for seven months. He was wounded in the battle of the Masurian Lakes in north-eastern Poland, during a German offensive that succeeded in outflanking the Russians and driving them into retreat. One morning in early spring of 1915, Hentig was handed a telegram with orders to present himself without delay to the General Staff in Berlin.

Hentig was given no clue to the reason for his urgent transfer, but he felt no regrets at quitting the trenches. He prepared his horse for the journey west, through the still-icy wind and cold of the plains, passing on his way gathering points of the wounded, where men lay on the ground in dirty, blood-soaked uniforms. He rode his exhausted mount day and night westwards across Poland's snow-laden Augustów county, observing the devastating the effect of recent heavy artillery barrages on the forests. Sporadic exchanges of fire echoed in the woods, between German troops and Cossacks who had become detached from the main body of the retreating Russian First Army Corps. In his haste, Hentig had left his pistol behind, so he took special care to avoid contact with the desperate Cossacks or, for that matter, with his German comrades who in the dead of night might easily have taken him for an enemy officer. Once through the forest, the darkness was broken by beams of light from German lorries and Hentig knew he was in safe territory, a short ride from the East Prussian Headquarters at Loetzen.

Three days after leaving the trenches, a washed and rested Hentig, in clean uniform, found himself in General Staff Headquarters in Berlin, facing a table of senior army officers. His orders were brief and to the point: the kaiser had personally commanded Hentig to lead expedition to Kabul, there to employ all diplomatic means necessary to persuade the amir to take up arms against British India.

Six months before Hentig's recall from the Eastern Front, at an advanced position at Nancy in north-eastern France, Lieutenant Oskar Ritter von Niedermayer of the 10th Bavarian Field Artillery Regiment was under heavy bombardment from Allied troops. Unlike Hentig the diplomat, Niedermayer was a professional soldier, almost a year older than the man with whom he was to share a heroic epic. He was a Bavarian of forceful personality, very wiry and with a fierce look of determination in his hard, penetrating brown eyes. Niedermayer's army career began at the age of 20, when he enlisted in his Bavarian regiment's officer training academy. He excelled at geography and the Persian language, two subjects that rendered him eminently suitable to undertake the greatest adventure of his life. 'Niedermayer was a man to whom military discipline was almost instinctive. He was just that kind of man who made the German Army almost invincible.'[15] These qualities would stand him in good stead on his epic expedition to Afghanistan, and on the even more arduous journey home. Niedermayer's commanding officers recognised the young officer's talents early on, and in 1912 they granted him leave to undertake a privately funded journey to Persia and India. The voyage enabled Niedermayer to acquire a close knowledge of two countries that were to loom large in Germany's wartime Eastern strategy. During his journey Niedermayer also established his credentials as a rugged explorer, by becoming the first European to survive a crossing of the Dasht-i-Kavir salt desert in south-eastern Persia, a place totally unsuited to supporting life, where temperatures in excess of 150°F have been recorded.

Niedermayer spent nearly half a year in Persia on a research furlough from his unit, much of which he passed in the company of the Austrian art historian and Orientalist Ernst Diez. One day in early 1913, while passing near Turshiz, the present-day Kashmar, Niedermayer was attacked by a gang of thieves and robbed of all his money and surveying equipment. On his return to Tehran he stormed into the German legation to lodge a complaint with the legation secretary, a young diplomat named Werner Otto von Hentig. This was the start of an ambiguous relationship between the two Germans, an alliance that would be severely put to the test in the hellish crossing of the Persian desert, and later strained almost to the limit in the oppressive world of Afghan palace intrigue.

One year later, in 1914, First Lieutenant (later Captain and finally General) Oskar von Niedermayer and his men were taking heavy fire from French troops at 200 yards, in a forest near Metz in north-eastern France. Niedermayer realised his position would soon be overrun by enemy infantry, so he gave the order to retreat. The column made a dash from the forest to find cover in the village of Champenoux, a few miles to the south, where Niedermayer set about furtively sketching the French positions. Later in the day Niedermayer, accompanied by his adjutant, Hans Jakob, was leading the men farther south, towards the town of Pontois, when a staff car pulled up alongside in the rutted dirt road. From the passenger seat the 5th Royal Bavarian Infantry Division commander, General Gustav von Schoch, beckoned to Niedermayer and handed him a telegram. The message was from the Bavarian War Ministry asking Niedermayer if he was prepared to join an expedition abroad, giving no further details. 'Do whatever you think would be of greatest service to your country,' Schoch said. 'You've got two hours to think it over.'[16]

Travel was as deeply embedded in Niedermayer's blood, as was soldiering, and he concurred with Hentig in that any opportunity to quit the vermin-infested trenches while still being of service to the Fatherland was a welcome development indeed. Niedermayer had a suspicion of where he was to be sent and he agreed, albeit with certain misgivings, to take part in the venture, provided he could take along his trusted adjutant. For Jakob, it would prove to be a fateful undertaking. The two men boarded a train at the Gare de Metz-Ville (once a grand palace that had served as Kaiser Wilhelm II's residence when the city was under German rule) bound for Munich, where on arrival they were handed orders to proceed directly to General Staff Headquarters in Berlin.

There I learnt that the affair in question was a combined German-Turkish expedition to Afghanistan, for the purpose of stirring up trouble for the British in India. The details were to be provided by the Ministry for Foreign Affairs. My orders were to appear before a committee of high-ranking officers, who made it [the mission] sound a most attractive proposition.[17]

A party of 25 Germans had already been dispatched to Constantinople, where they spent their time indulging in the sumptuous splendour of the Pera Palas Hotel (built to host the passengers of the Orient Express) and treating the Turkish staff with extreme insolence and rudeness. There was only one person of repute in this drunken, rowdy entourage, and he was the only one ever to have set foot in Persia, the difficult terrain they would have to cross on their journey to Afghanistan. This was Wilhelm Wassmuss, the shadowy, elusive adventurer who was later dubbed by the British the 'German Lawrence', an allusion to the romantic revolutionary Lawrence of Arabia. Wassmuss's battlefield enemies had no hesitation in voicing their admiration for this dashing German agent.

> Of those who worked against Allied interests in Persia, the palm must undoubtedly be awarded to the notorious Wassmuss, who was a thorn in our sides practically throughout the war. The history of this gentleman's adventures [...] will be worthy of a place among the most remarkable romances of this or any other age. He completely closed the Bushire-Shiraz road during a great part of the war. He succeeded in seizing the British Consul and the British colony in Shiraz early in the war and keeping them prisoners among the tribesmen for several months. [...] Legitimate methods of capture failed entirely.[18]

The rest of the group had been haphazardly drawn from the ranks of the Colonial Service. These men had spent most of their time in Africa, where abusing the local populace was considered a colonial officer's prerogative. A few of them owed their appointment to political patronage, perversely from the Naval Ministry. With his recent firsthand experience in Persia and India, Niedermayer was the obvious candidate to lead the mission. The Turkish Minister of War and leader of the Young Turks Movement, Enver Pasha, had personally pushed Niedermayer's candidacy. He had been made aware of the young German's expert knowledge of the region, and of his resilience in hostile conditions. Wassmuss was also keen to bring him on board, to guide the mission if not actually to serve as its leader. Niedermayer demurred: he thought himself too junior in rank to take on such a heavy political responsibility, or so he claimed. In truth, Niedermayer's travels in the year before the war had left him sceptical of any real challenge to British rule by Indian revolutionaries. On the other hand, he recognised the mission's potential for inflicting military damage on Britain, which was one of his reasons for agreeing to take part in the venture. Not least of all, there was that irresistible lure of adventure.

Like Niedermayer the soldier, Hentig the diplomat harboured certain doubts about his personal role in the expedition. 'Never even in times of peace had a German come out of Afghanistan,' Hentig reflected in his memoirs.

> Strong patrols by British and Russian troops along the Afghan frontier on the Indian as well as the Turkestan and Persian side had intercepted all traffic with that little-known country. To reach the closed land in time of war, when the Russians had increased the Cossack units in Persia to an unheard of extent, or through Baluchistan, where the British had pushed thousands of their Indian troops, was a task I could not take on without earnest thought.[19]

'Surely there would be someone more suitable to undertake this task,' Hentig thought. In the same breath, he realised that those colleagues whose names came to mind were charged with other critical wartime duties, or lying under the mud of Europe's killing fields.

Enver Pasha, the German-trained Minister of War who in January 1913 had seized power in a coup, had persuaded the sultan to proclaim a jihad against Britain two months after Turkey joined the war on Germany's side. Turkey, the centre of the Ottoman Empire, at that time wielded the greatest spiritual influence in the Muslim world. 'The German foreign office predicted that the sultan's actions would awaken the might of Islam and promote a large scale revolution in India.'[20]

Reports were circulating in Berlin that the sultan had sent an emissary, Khalifa Abdul Majid, on a journey to Kabul, carrying with him the symbolic sword of jihad as a summons for the Afghans to join the holy war against the infidels. German officialdom rejoiced at what they took to be Turkey's first step in an all-out offensive against British India. The British government took a different view: faced with strong pressure from his Muslim brethren, this was the first real test of Habibullah's professed neutrality. After a few anxious days, Delhi and London were reassured by the amir's canny handling of his Turkish visitor. He informed Majid that while he was in total sympathy with the sultan's call to arms, as ruler of Afghanistan he found himself trapped between two great powers, Britain and Russia. He assured the envoy of his loyal support and that, as a good Muslim, there was no question that he would obey the sultan's command. Then the amir played his trump card: Habibullah said he awaited the Turkish armies that even now must be marching towards his kingdom. Once this mighty force was on Afghan soil he would be ready, Allah willing, to lead the hosts of Islam by their side. The amir knew full well that the 'hosts of Islam' existed solely in the realm of demagoguery at the Friday mosque sermon, at least for the moment. Habibullah sent Majid home to Constantinople in the confidence that he had acquitted himself with the supreme voice of the Muslim world, and more importantly with his British next-door neighbours, who represented the supreme voice in his country's foreign affairs, as well as being the chief donor to his treasury.

As far as Germany's military strategists were concerned, the British Empire's most vulnerable point was India, and the catalyst for its eventual downfall would be a rising of the country's vast Muslim population. A memo from the German General Staff, issued as early as 24 August 1914, concurred with Enver Pasha's forecast, claiming that the Indian revolution would begin with 'an invasion by the amir of Afghanistan'.[21] Germany's military leaders and the Foreign Ministry were ecstatic over reports from two almost legendary

Asian authorities. One was the archaeologist Oppenheim, who had been posted to Turkey as an anti-British agent, where he did his utmost to rouse the politicians, the military and radical clerics to jihadist fury. The other was the Swedish explorer Sven Hedin, who supplied the Germans with his superb maps of Central Asia and who in the Second World War maintained a controversial relationship with Germany's Nazi leadership, including Adolf Hitler. Both claimed that British rule in the East was under threat and that Afghanistan was the key to unlocking the gates of India.

The personal link-up between Niedermayer and Hentig did not come about until the groups under their respective leadership were well advanced in their travels, after setting out separately from Constantinople. The seeds of personal conflict that later became a factor in the mission's failure were evident from the outset. Niedermayer considered the entire venture to be a strictly military undertaking: the objective was to convince or coerce Habibullah into waging war on the British in India, with the support of Turkish troops and the bellicose Pashtun tribes of India's North-West Frontier. The diplomatic function was subordinate to Germany's military aims, hence Hentig played a secondary role in the expedition. Hentig, on the contrary, saw the mission's role as that of a diplomatic offensive aimed at cementing relations with the amir, who should be induced to sign a treaty committing his country to the German cause. In this way, Hentig maintained, Afghanistan would be drawn into the Central Powers camp, throwing Britain's India defence plans into disarray.

If one were to evaluate objectively both men's approaches, it was Hentig who stood the best chances of success. The German General Staff had no intention of diverting several divisions from the European theatre of war to a remote corner of Asia. Much less did Berlin wish to embark on a suicidal operation to march troops across the Persian desert into Afghanistan or confront the logistical nightmare of descending on India through the mountains of Central Asia. There was also the ever-present risk of Turkey refusing to commit its forces to the campaign, a fear borne out by later events.

This antagonism between the two German leaders gave rise to confusion over command and control of the expedition.

> Once they arrived in Afghanistan, the diplomatic-political aspects of the Mission were clearly predominant, with Hentig in charge. He alone had official credentials – named as *Kaiserlicher Vertreter* ['Imperial Representative'] in the Chancellor's letter to the amir – and he alone was responsible for the Mission's finances. At times Niedermayer and Hentig seem to have reported independently. In any case, orderly reporting channels were disrupted from the outset.'[22]

The Hentig–Niedermayer mission, as it can justly be called, found itself plagued by a host of problems once inside Afghanistan, but even well before that the greatest challenge of all was to reach their destination. Speed was of the essence, as Hentig notes in his account of the journey. At an earlier date, he claims, a mission to Afghanistan would have posed a serious threat to India's defences,

> devoid as [India] was in the beginning of the war of Indian or even English leadership. This was not done, because it [a mission to Kabul] had never been foreseen, because no one had thought of it. Now a communication by land with Afghanistan and through this country to northern India seemed indispensable.[23]

Wassmuss led his party of 25 to Constantinople early in September 1914, with Niedermayer following later that month. As noted earlier, the Wassmuss contingent fell into a state of disarray from the moment it checked into the hotel, where some of the Germans adopted a ridiculous cloak-and-dagger pose by signing in as secret agents. Enver Pasha was not amused by their antics. He complained that the men were of the lowest calibre, loud, lazy and almost constantly drunk. They were openly contemptuous of Turkey and all things Turkish, and on several occasions they had to be physically ejected from cafés for giving offence to public propriety. From the moment the Turkish War Minister met the party in Constantinople his enthusiasm for the mission went on the decline. With the exception of Wassmuss, the only Persian-speaker in the group, the rest struck him as bickering lightweights. This view was substantiated by the fact that the only maps of Afghanistan they carried 'were copied from Alexander Keith Johnston's general atlas of the world'.[24] Johnston was a nineteenth-century British geographer whose maps were kept at the Foreign Ministry in Berlin.

Niedermayer was dispatched from Berlin in the hope that he might pull this motley group together, albeit always under Wassmuss's leadership. Niedermayer and his faithful adjutant Jakob travelled via Vienna through still neutral Romania, which did not enter the war as a Russian ally until August 1916. There they picked up two more German members of the expedition, Hermann Consten and Wilhelm Paschen, both of them explorers with Asian experience and some language skills under their belts. The party soon ran into trouble with Romanian customs officials, however, causing an incident that could have been scripted into Monty Python. In order to disguise a shipment of arms they were transporting to Afghanistan, Berlin had the truck convoy registered as a travelling circus. The Romanians halted the convoy for inspection when they became suspicious of the 'tent poles', as they were listed on the way-bill, that protruded from under a tarpaulin. These were discovered to be wireless aerials for telegraphy sets and, moreover, a further probe of some unusually large cases revealed an arms cache of machine guns and around a million rounds of ammunition, which the Romanian police concluded could scarcely be considered 'fireworks', as listed in the documentation. Once the Germans' escapade was revealed, the Romanian press had a field day with the affair. Photographs of the confiscated 'circus equipment' were circulated to papers round the world. After much haggling and an exchange of telegrams with Berlin, not to overlook a discreet sweetener to the customs officers, a chastened Niedermayer and his party were able to carry on to Constantinople, a city they found to be in a state of high political tension, with a declaration of war expected momentarily.

The adventure-seeking Wassmuss had by now had his fill of inactivity. He set off from Constantinople on his own, heading in Lawrence of Arabia-fashion for the British-held positions in southern Persia, where he aimed to raise the tribes in revolt against the foreign occupiers. Despite his misgivings, Niedermayer was now placed in charge of the mission by default. He dismissed a few of what he described as 'the noisier and ruder members' of the group.[25] At the same time, he took on two trustworthy aides: one was his own brother, Fritz Niedermayer, who joined the expedition as chief medical officer, and the other was Lieutenant Walter Griesinger, another adventurer who would later spearhead a separate group in an attempt to incite Persia to war against Britain.

On 5 December 1914, less than six weeks after Turkey joined the German cause, Niedermayer and his party of Germans, which was now swollen by an escort of four Turkish officers and 27 troops, departed Constantinople to follow in Wassmuss's tracks. They sailed across the Bosphorus to the seaport of Haidar Pasha in Asia proper, where a caravan of lorries had been assembled for the drive south. The plan was to spread destruction among the enemy, and with this in mind the initial target chosen was a British-held oil refinery at Abadan in Persia. Niedermayer's proposal was to block the Euphrates River below Abadan with a Turkish gunboat and a German steamship and to set fire to the oil tanks and the refinery. The Turkish authorities were in agreement with the plan and Niedermayer began to lead his men through the Mesopotamian desert towards Basra in order to supervise the arrangements. To his dismay, however, the group was halted en route by a telegram that arrived from Berlin, countermanding their plan to attack and destroy the refinery. The General Staff expected the facility to fall into German hands when their armies marched victorious across the Middle East and they wanted it in serviceable condition to fuel the war effort.

> Niedermayer was to await the arrival of a mission with special equipment that was being sent for this purpose. But he refused to have anything to do with the new proposal, which he implies (in his memoirs) was responsible for preserving Abadan for the British.[26]

After boarding a train for what was to be a comfortable journey down to the Berlin–Baghdad railway terminus, Niedermayer's party received a foretaste of harrowing times ahead when they reached the foothills of the Taurus Mountains. The group was forced to continue by ox-cart to the ancient city of Aleppo on the main caravan route across Syria to Baghdad, slowing them to a bone-rattling crawl that turned the 550-mile journey from Constantinople into an eight-day ordeal. Waiting for him at Baghdad's Casino Hotel was an advanced party whose members included several German soldiers: Wilhelm Paschen, Günter Voigt and Kurt Wagner, among others.

There is an old Arab proverb that goes like this: 'When Allah created hell he thought he could improve on it, so he added flies and called it Mesopotamia.' Iraq, as it is today known, gained independence from Ottoman rule after the First World War and in 1921 it was created a kingdom under Faisal I, who had been recommended for the job by the British traveller and spy Gertrude Bell. Another female British adventurer, the intrepid Freya Stark, visited Baghdad in the early years of the twentieth century. Her description of the city would appear to substantiate the Arab proverb's portrayal of an unsavoury place.

> True happiness, we consider, is incompatible with an inefficient drainage system. It is one of these points on which we differ most fundamentally from the East, where happiness and sanitation are not held to any particular connection. In spite of many efforts, Baghdad still remains triumphantly Eastern in this respect.[27]

It was to this squalid desert flea pit of 145,000 souls that Niedermayer now headed. If nothing else, again citing Stark's experience, he could look forward to a warm reception from the native population.

> It was the fashionable thing to be anti-British in Baghdad at that time. To be anti-British made you successful either as a lawyer, a politician or a journalist. You were a patriot as well, which is as near as one can get in politics to having one's cake and eating it.[28]

The travel writer Robert Byron also visited Baghdad around the same time as Stark, and took a no less scathing impression of the city. 'The air is composed of mud refined into a gas. The people are mud-coloured. They wear mud-coloured clothes, and their national hat is nothing more than a formalised mud-pie.'[29]

Niedermayer sent the main body of his party to Mosul, north of Baghdad, and on 21 February 1915 he and Jakob, now reunited with Wassmuss, set off for Baghdad in a long caravan of horsemen and wagons. The south-easterly route took them across a hard, red-earth desert road strewn with tyre-bursting flint, which flanked the course of the Euphrates until it reached a greener landscape at the Syrian desert town of Deir ez-Zor. From there they drove on behind six lorries laden with baggage and supplies towards the marshlands, much of it below sea level, for the final slog to Baghdad, in all a 450-mile trek from Aleppo. Niedermayer's mission had reached the dusty city, a hybrid of the worst of East and West, having successfully eluded detection by British patrols.

Enver Pasha had envisaged the mission as a Turkish-led venture to carry the sword of Pan-Islamism across the lands of the East. The Ottoman Empire would reap the glory for inciting India and its vast Muslim population to revolt and overthrow British domination.

> Enver Pasha declared shortly after Wassmuss left the expedition that all its personnel were to be subject to the overall command of a Turkish officer, Rauf Bey. The Germans were to put on Turkish uniform immediately or surrender their stores and return to Constantinople.[30]

The Germans saw things differently. Turkey's wholesale massacre of its Armenian minority provoked an outcry in the German Church – Catholic as well as Protestant – and this led to a backlash from Constantinople that ended with the summary expulsion of German diplomats who had protested at the atrocities. Therefore, when Niedermayer arrived in Baghdad, where the Turco-German mission was to join forces, he encountered Rauf Bey, the leader of the Turkish contingent, in an ugly mood. Rauf Bey addressed Niedermayer in flawless English, informing him that if he carried on to Afghanistan he would do so on his own, as the 1,000-strong contingent of Ottoman troops quartered in Baghdad would be shifted to Basra to wage war against the British. In other words, the Turks had withdrawn their military support from the mission.

> Even so early in the war did the incompatibility of German and Turkish intentions appear: the former regarded England as the main enemy; the latter Russia, and indeed for the English they hardly entertained a dislike. The Germans wished to use Turkish authority to unite Islam and they looked to an effect in India. The Turks felt only a desultory enthusiasm for Islam compared to their ever-growing enthusiasm for the Pan-Turk movement, and they looked for an effect in the north-middle and central-east.[31]

Niedermayer decided to push on to Afghanistan, ignoring Enver Pasha's objections.

There was another facet to this confrontation between two of the Central Powers' allies. Germany had agreed to assume the cost of the expedition, and Wassmuss and Niedermayer were determined not to become the tools of Turkey's imperialist policies. Niedermayer, the ultra-patriotic Bavarian military man, who harboured no doubts about German superiority over what he took to be inferior fighting forces, was unwilling to serve under Turkish military leadership. There never was much love lost between the German officers and their Turkish counterparts during those first weeks of the mission. 'Turkish pigs', 'odious nation', 'pack of dirty Turks': these were but a few of the epithets articulated in Baghdad by Lieutenant Griesinger, the artillery officer Niedermayer later dispatched to south Persia to incite the tribes to attack the British.[32] Quite simply, what happened was that 'command and control disagreements collapsed the Wassmuss-Niedermayer Mission when they refused to work under Turkish command'.[33] Rauf Bey informed Niedermayer that the Germans stood little chance of being allowed to cross the border into Afghanistan. Habibullah had so far maintained absolute silence with regard to the mission. The Turks, for their part, were convinced the British held the amir securely in their pocket. Niedermayer was equally certain that Enver Pasha harboured deeper motives for giving the order for Rauf Bey to abort Turkey's military support for the mission. The Turks, Niedermayer suspected, were suspicious of German designs on Persia, a land in which Berlin's relationship with the Muslim population, with the figure of Kaiser Hajji Wilhelm at the forefront, was a bit too cosy for comfort.

On instructions from Baron Hans Freiherr von Wangenheim, Germany's ambassador to the Ottoman Empire, Niedermayer was now assigned the role of the mission's sole military commander and strategist, and this was done with Wassmuss's blessing.

> It was impossible to consider an advance as a single body into Persia. It appeared to me that if we split up into groups the expedition would be more mobile. It would also be more capable of overcoming physical, as well as political and military difficulties in the mountainous frontier district of Persia and afterwards in the highlands of the interior.[34]

Niedermayer faced the decision of how and when the party of around 30, deprived of their strong Turkish military escort, should hazard the crossing of Persian territory. He chose a north-easterly route via Kermanshah to the once-glorious Isfahan, Persia's third largest city, which lies 200 miles south of Tehran. The party set out for the Persian border on 23 January 1915 and few regrets were heard in the ranks at quitting Baghdad. Niedermayer alone knew that hazardous and testing times lay in their path. Past experience had exposed him to the perils now awaiting in the barren wasteland towards which the mission headed, from snake-bite and sunstroke to dysentery and maddening thirst, not to overlook the ever-present menace of marauding bandits. For the others it would be a baptism by fire. Niedermayer's plan was to create a line of communications across central Persia to Afghanistan, so exploiting the corridor between the Russian and British zones.[35]

On 14 April 1915, Otto von Hentig stood on the rear platform of the Vienna Express and watched the lights of Berlin fade into the darkness of night.

After spending a short time in Constantinople finalising the details of his expedition, he moved swiftly on to Persia and by late June, he was on his way from Tehran to link up with Niedermayer in Isfahan. By this time Niedermayer had embarked on his eastward trek, splitting his party into three to improve their chances of passing undetected into Persian territory. The indomitable loner Wassmuss was now active in the market town of Shushtar, distributing pamphlets prepared in Berlin to incite the tribesmen to join the war against the British. He was arrested but managed to escape, and after leading his pursuers on what was more than a 100-mile chase through the desert he arrived at Bebehan on his way to the Gulf. Here he was betrayed by a local chieftain who planned to sell him to the British. But by the time a platoon of soldiers arrived to take their prisoner, the quick-witted Wassmuss was already on his horse, wending his way to Bushire on the Gulf, where in May 1915 he set about organising the southern tribes of Tangistan to revolt against the British.[36]

In his memoirs Hentig recalls that before leaving Germany his first task was to put together the mission's team. 'I took only two Europeans with me from Berlin. The expedition would need a medical man, so I called upon my old friend of Persian days Major [Dr Karl] Becker.'[37] Becker had served in the Garde-Jäger-Bataillon, which until 1918 had formed part of the Gardekorps of the Royal Prussian Army. He was stationed at the German government hospital in Tehran in the two years prior to the war and was familiar with all the diseases and ailments the party would be exposed to on the desert crossing to Afghanistan. He was also reputed to be a fine horseman and crack shot, two aptitudes that were more than likely to prove useful on the journey.

> Another German I chose was a young chap from Magdeburg, Walter Röhr [a merchant and a fluent speaker of Persian and Turkish], who had been living in northern Persia since he was seventeen. When the war broke out he rushed back to Germany, hiding in a small sailboat. This enabled him to slip undetected past the English blockade at the port of Basra, and then continue his journey to Magdeburg overland via Baghdad and Constantinople. Röhr was experienced in handling caravans, native drivers and guides.[38]

It turned out to be a heterogeneous group, for apart from his two German companions the expedition was joined by two Afridi tribesmen from the North-West Frontier and two high-profile Indian nationalists. The Afridis, Abdur Rahman and Subhan Khan, travelled at their own expense from the still-neutral United States. Before the war Indian revolutionaries had established cells in New York and San Francisco, from where they hatched their plots to oust the British from India. Another six Afridi warrior tribesmen accompanied the mission as a military escort. These men, former soldiers in the Indian Army, had been taken from a German prisoner-of-war camp. The Afridis, like all good Pashtuns, for whom warfare was a way of life, when fighting under a foreign banner remained largely indifferent to the cause they were called upon to defend. Hentig later picked up another Indian Muslim prisoner of war, Sayed Ahmed, who came highly recommended for his culinary skills.

The two Indian revolutionaries who had been forced upon Hentig by the German Foreign Ministry were shadowy figures to whom a secret British report referred as 'unnamed Indian gentlemen'.[39] They soon became quite well known to British intelligence as the dour, bespectacled Mahendra Pratap and his Islamic scholar colleague Maulavi Barakatullah. They were both involved in the Ghadr ('Rebellion') Party, a group of radical Indian expatriates operating mainly out of San Francisco. It was set up in 1913 under the leadership of Har Dayal, who was drawn to the cause of violent revolution by the failed assassination attempt on Viceroy Lord Hardinge the previous year, which he claimed as the work of the Ghadr Party. Like many of his fellow militants, Har Dayal was a highly cultured Indian, educated at St John's College, Oxford, as a State Scholar in 1905. He threw up this scholarship two years later to devote his talents to revolutionary work and arrived in California soon thereafter to help set up the Ghadr Party. At the start of the war the US authorities arrested Har Dayal as an undesirable alien and asked for his deportation for carrying out seditious activities on neutral territory. But no sooner had he been granted bail than he absconded to Switzerland with Barakatullah. The Indian Government entertained no doubt that Har Dayal was acting with the connivance of Germany, for at a public meeting in California in 1913 he openly proclaimed that Germany was preparing to go to war with Britain, and that it was time for Indian patriots to get ready for the coming revolution.

Through the Ghadr Party's network, seditionists in India were supplied with propaganda and arms. The plot to incite Indian Army troops to mutiny was in part one of Germany's earliest efforts to topple the Raj. Hence the so-called Hindu–German Conspiracy, which came about under the aegis of the Ghadr Party. The US was chosen as the organisation's main base, given its remoteness from India, Washington's strict isolationism, and also the existence of a large body of Indian students and immigrant workers who were seen as ripe for recruitment to the insurgent cause. Moreover, the US's anti-colonialist traditions ensured that many public figures, including influential Irish-Americans, sympathised with Indian nationalism. The German Foreign Ministry secretly gave its support to what amounted to a terrorist organisation, for their tactics were bombs, not dialogue. The Ghadrites had nothing but contempt for the Congress Party's espousal of non-violent resistance.

Barakatullah was holed up in Tokyo in 1914, keeping himself at arm's length from the Indian Criminal Investigation Department (CID), which was doing its best to infiltrate the Ghadr movements and round up the leading seditionists. Delhi banned Barakatullah's inflammatory newspaper from entering India and brought pressure on Japan to deport the Indian agitator, who was finally told to leave in May 1914. He booked passage on a freighter bound for San Francisco, where he spent his time hatching plots and addressing rallies, urging his compatriots to return home and take part in the coming revolution.

Pratap was by far the more intriguing of the two conspirators, being at once a high-born Indian prince and a quirky visionary who founded a hotch-potch universal creed called the Society of the Servants of the Powerless, which dubiously claimed Lenin as one of its converts. The Germans took this 28-year-old fanatic very seriously, however, to the extent that he was received by Kaiser Wilhelm in Berlin and, to Hentig's great irritation, was appointed titular head of the mission, though in reality Pratap never exercised any authority over Hentig and Niedermayer. Pratap was put up at Berlin's

Continental Hotel where, had his messianic spiritualism endowed him with the powers of foresight, he might have pondered the realities of advocating the violent overthrow of British rule in India. One of his fellow guests at the hotel was the Irish nationalist Sir Roger Casement, who sought German support for a rebellion in Ireland and was hanged in London for treason in 1916. When Pratap arrived at the Bellevue Palace in the Tiergarten for his send-off private audience with Wilhelm, he found the kaiser

> standing alone in a field-grey uniform [...] His face was ruddy and his blue eyes flashed. I was introduced to him in English, and immediately he entered into English conversation with me. He spoke English like a foreigner, but it seemed to me that he did this purposely, as if to stress the fact that it was the language of the enemy.[40]

Wilhelm conferred on Pratap the Order of the Red Eagle and told him to convey his personal greetings to Habibullah in Kabul. 'A German officer [Hentig] was to accompany me, as well as some Indian Mussulmans,' Pratap later wrote, leaving little doubt as to whom he considered to be in charge of the expedition, a status imbued with reality in his mind only.[41]

Alarmed by the mishaps and confrontations that had beset Niedermayer's efforts to reach Afghanistan, the Army High Command in Berlin spared no effort to smooth the way for Hentig's diplomatic mission. Whatever problems the Hentig–Niedermayer expedition faced, a lack of money was not one of them. Germany lavished $63,500 in funding on the operation, a fabulous sum a century ago. Of this, $12,000 was held in an account in Germany and the rest deposited in gold with Deutsche Bank in Constantinople. It stands as a tribute to Teutonic probity that the unspent portion was actually returned to the German government after two years of wandering across Central Asia.

Becker, Röhr and three of the Afridis were the first to depart Berlin, followed by Hentig, Pratap and Barakatullah. The rest of the Afridis went last, travelling via Vienna to Constantinople, where they all assembled at the luxurious Pera Palas Hotel. In his three weeks in Constantinople, Hentig spent part of his time paying protocol visits to Ottoman dignitaries, including the caliph, who received him 'clad in black frock coat, with a red fez on his head and a huge diamond on his ring finger'.[42] As he was leaving the grand chamber, the caliph's parting words were, 'Be on your guard with the English and don't let them catch you.'[43] Hentig then bowed out of the room to make the final preparations for the onward journey, an operation nearly as burdensome as putting Napoleon's Grande Armée on the march. This involved withdrawing a large sum in gold coins from the mission's Deutsche Bank account, which had to be securely packed for the journey by rail and camel caravan. There was a huge stockpile of gifts for the amir, which it was hoped would serve as an inducement to abandon his neutrality.[44] Hentig filled numerous cases with gold watches and an array of German novelties which included 12 alarm clocks, gold fountain pens, gold-plated rifles with telescopic sights, an assortment of Mauser pistols, binoculars, cameras and compasses. Hentig realised his early apprehensions were justified as he watched this tremendous cache of gadgets and artefacts being packed for transport: 'As our strength lay in mobility, problems of luggage taxed our ingenuity.'[45] Months later, before they reached the Afghan border, some of these presents, including a one-ton cinema projector, had to be unloaded from the backs of the exhausted pack animals and abandoned in the desert. Also discarded was a case containing German letters of diplomatic recognition in magnificent morocco bindings which were to be delivered to 26 Indian princes.

After celebrating Bismarck's centenary on 1 April 1915, one fine sunny morning in early May the party left Constantinople and was ferried with all its baggage to the Asian side of the Bosphorus. By this time, the mission had swollen to around 20 members, with the addition of Kazim Bey, a Turkish officer designated by Enver Pasha to accompany the party, and another several servants.

With Niedermayer well on his way across Persia, British spies were beginning to pick up pieces of intelligence from Turkey and Persia concerning suspicious movements by foreign nationals moving eastwards towards Afghanistan. The British relied on a Muslim agent by the name of Hafiz Saifullah Khan, who was stationed at Kabul and was allowed access to court officials and state functions. In his report of 31 March 1915, shortly before Hentig and his party set out from Berlin, Khan informed the viceroy that a small party of Indians had crossed into Afghan territory, almost coinciding with 'the arrival at Herat of four respectable men from Turkey who wish to see His Majesty [Habibullah]'.[46] The identity and purpose of these Turks was not known, but they were most certainly the advance guard of a softening up exercise whose aim was to undermine Habibullah's neutralist policy. The hand of Nasrullah, Habibullah's hard-line Islamist brother and army chief, is alluded to in Khan's dispatch, when the British agent finds out that the order had been given to the armoury to clean and make ready 95,000 German-made rifles and 600 Maxim guns. 'The work, it is said, is being conducted in absolute secrecy.'[47] Furthermore, Habibullah's shura, or 'advisory council', had quietly been approached by Turkish sources as well as the Pashtun tribes of the frontier, pleading for Afghanistan to make common cause with Germany against the British. Acting on this information as well as reports from field officers in the Middle East, the viceroy wrote to the amir, informing him about a number of German agents in Persia who were intending to enter his country. Habibullah and Hardinge both knew that trouble was coming to Afghanistan. Hardinge told Habibullah that under international law, he had every right to arrest any uninvited and armed foreign nationals entering his country without permission. The viceroy spoke of Germans, Indians, Persians and other foreigners numbering in their hundreds, marching towards the Afghan border, although it is not known how or where Hardinge obtained this extraordinary bit of intelligence. Habibullah reassured an anxious viceroy in a letter that Afghanistan stuck by its commitment to neutrality, adding that such foreigners would not be allowed to roam freely about the country. 'I write to say [...] that Your Excellency need have no anxiety about the movements of these parties, for firstly they will not enter Afghan territory.'[48] Habibullah added that if the Germans did manage to cross the border they would be disarmed at once. The viceroy was given false assurances on both counts.

Niedermayer conceived a plan to send his party into Persia in three small groups, a tactic he as well as Hentig had employed in the past to disperse the enemy's attention from a large body of intruders. Over a five-day period in late March 1915, as the early spring sun blazed with a foretaste of greater hardships in the imminent desert crossing, the Bavarian zoologist Zugmayer and the Teutonic xenophobe Griesinger, along with Fritz Seiler, started off on their trek to Kerman. Niedermayer offers no explanation for his decision to jettison these two expedition members, but he must have realised that they could easily become the source of friction with the Afghans. His concerns were well founded: the 425-mile journey from Baghdad to Isfahan took them two months and, as Griesinger records, their jolliest moment was spent with a detachment of Swedish gendarmes who were serving in Persia as a rural police force and maintained a significant involvement in pro-German politics. They arrived in Kerman in July 1915, 'where Zugmayer promptly announced himself to be the German Consul, even though he had no accreditation as such from either the German Legation in Tehran or from the Persian Government'.[49] They were enthusiastically welcomed by the local populace, as well as the nationalist ranks, who caught the scent of the gold the Germans carried with them. 'Splendid dinner with liqueur, port wine, beer, champagne, wine, coffee cognac and whisky. In the evening, very merry. Zugmayer very drunk.'[50] In a word, not the most appropriate sorts to accompany a diplomatic mission to an Islamic kingdom. In the event the boorish Griesinger, in contrast to the diplomatic finesse and charisma displayed by Wassmuss among the south Persian tribes, failed miserably in his attempt to incite the tribes of Kerman to rise up against the British.

With his customary military composure, Niedermayer was unruffled about the crossing into Persian territory. Ahmad Shah Qajar had declared his country's neutrality in November 1914, acting under pressure from Britain and Russia, which wanted Persia as a territorial cushion against Turkey's proclamation of jihad. This was welcome news to Niedermayer: he planned a desert crossing through unoccupied land with a party of around 30. They needed to take care to avoid Russian patrols in the northern district and the British who patrolled the Gulf region, which was inhabited by tribes long under British influence. Niedermayer was aware of the dangers of leaving Ottoman territory. German and Austrian consular officials in Baghdad could use their good offices to ensure the mission safe conduct to the frontier, but once inside Persia they were on their own. Once again Niedermayer split his expedition into smaller parties, with instructions to meet at Khanikin, a Mesopotamian border town due west of Kermanshah in Persia. From there they crossed the frontier as a single strong party, and once on Persian soil Niedermayer travelled north-east to Tehran, while the rest of the group proceeded to the final rendezvous point at Isfahan.

Hentig was at this time not far behind, riding the Baghdad Railway across the broad grassy plains of Central Anatolia. They had passed a gap in the Taurus Mountains through which Alexander had marched on his conquest of Mesopotamia. Then after two days they found themselves at Konya, the ancient capital of the Ottoman Empire, where stands the tomb of Rumi, founder of the Mevlevi order of dervishes. From this spot it was an inter-rupted series of rail and horse-cart stages, changing over wherever the line was blocked by steep mountain passes, to reach the well-stocked markets and bustling cafés of Aleppo, in which city Hentig called a two-day halt. Embarking on the next leg involved a new mode of transport – three flat barges which Hentig and Kazim Bey had commissioned for the river journey down the Euphrates. These vessels carried 260 animals and their drivers, while Hentig and Pratap travelled in houseboats which completed the flotilla that slowly floated south towards Baghdad. On their approach to Falluja, a few miles from Baghdad, they were attacked by what Hentig described as 'a Biblical horde of locusts, followed by a swarm of millions of flies',[51] thus confirming the Arab proverb about the pestilential city. On 1 June 1915, 45 days after leaving Berlin, Hentig and his group departed the bungalows that had been provided by the German legation in Baghdad to begin plying the ancient trade routes that led to Persia.

Haste was of the essence: British agents had detected German activity in spite of Hentig's efforts to mask their presence by having his party split into separate quarters in Baghdad.

In Aleppo and Baghdad we knew our movements had been reported by enemy spies, but so long as the column remained within the boundaries of the Ottoman Empire there was relatively no danger. Now we were nearing the borderlands, I suspected that we were being followed.[52]

The first real trouble arose within the mission itself when Mahendra Pratap threw a tantrum on hearing that Italy had entered the war on the side of the Allies. His faith in the German cause suddenly collapsed and he begged to be left with the Turkish commander Kazim Bey. Pratap had been badly bitten by mosquitoes on the river journey and was suffering violent attacks of malaria. A bout of dysentery added to his misery. Hentig would have dearly liked to grant his wish and rid himself of this pompous Indian, but General Staff orders were to escort Pratap to Afghanistan to be used as a bargaining tool with the amir. Hentig therefore arranged for his troublesome companion to be transported in a wagon, while he himself rode north to Tehran to finalise details of the journey to Kabul with Prince Heinrich Reuss, the German envoy to the Persian shah. Reuss himself, after an aborted attempt to seize control of the government in November 1915, with the Russians at the gates of Tehran, realised that Persia was a lost cause and returned to Berlin.

On the afternoon of 28 June 1915, Pratap and the others caught sight of Isfahan, whose gleaming blue minarets stood out against the sky only a two-hour carriage ride away. This last leg took a bit longer than expected, however, as their cart lost two wheels on the rocky ground, spilling its occupants into the road. It was not until nightfall that the sorry little cavalcade trundled into the narrow streets and pulled up at the German consulate. Hentig had already arrived from Tehran and prepared to greet the party with a warm supper. Another German traveller joined them at table, Oskar von Niedermayer, and over coffee and brandy it was decided that the two groups, one under Foreign Ministry auspices and the other under General Staff command, would join forces and march together to Afghanistan.

3

Into the Fearful Wasteland

H entig and Niedermayer pondered their route on the maps stored at the Isfahan legation, which during the war was the centre of German diplomatic influence in Persia. They concluded it would be suicidal to attempt a breakthrough of the Russian lines in the north. To trek southwards made no logistical sense since Herat, their chosen point of entry into Afghanistan, lay almost due east. Nor was the southern route a sensible option, for this would take them straight into the arms of the British armoured convoys patrolling that sector. The only way forward had to be through the forbidding sands of the Dasht-i-Kavir, the Great Salt Desert, which only a handful of the sturdiest nomads and the most desperate of bandits would attempt to enter in summer. The two Germans carefully marked out the few spots along the route where they were likely to find food and water. Hentig was undeterred: 'The Kavir had the reputation of being impassable in summer. It was a drastic decision, considering our weaker and less hardy companions. Since the task had to be accomplished, we firmly believed it could be done.'[1] Food and water were purchased from local merchants for the desert crossing, along with 36 camels, 12 packhorses and 24 mules.

The first week of July 1915 marked the start of their trek into the scorched wilderness. Niedermayer departed with Wilhelm Paschen, the soldier from South-West Africa, along with a number of Persians and six Austro-Hungarian escapees from a Russian prisoner-of-war camp. The first untroubled 75 miles took them to the village of Na'in on the edge of the desert. Awaiting them at this outpost was the old Persian hand, Röhr, who had put together an additional supply of pack animals. Hentig got his first taste of the perils the desert harboured the evening they set out on horseback into the uncharted realms of central Persia. Leaving Na'in behind the main group, he soon lost his way in the dark and wandered aimlessly for hours. It was not long before he felt the first symptoms of dehydration, an almost certain death sentence in that arid land. Then, around midnight, Hentig's ears pricked up to what he took to be the pack animals' bells, but in his disorientated state he found himself unable to track the direction of the sound. The faint tinkle of bells was heard again at dawn, but it was soon lost in the windswept desert, and in despair Hentig crawled into a shaded spot to await his fate. Fortune was with him that day, for shortly two nomads came across the prostrate German and his mount and led them to the village of Anarak, where his much relieved comrades came out to greet him.

Hentig learnt from Röhr and the others that their march to Anarak had likewise been anything but agreeable. The main body had strayed off the trail in the night and missed the watering holes marked on their map. Not expecting to be deprived of water on the march, they had extravagantly drained almost the entire supply in their goatskins and what little remained had leaked out into the sand from the porous hides. When the sun rose the next morning, some of the men became almost unmanageable and had to be restrained by the Persian escort, who fortunately in the light of day soon picked up the trail to Anarak. Pratap's penchant for hyperbole was on this occasion not without cause: 'After fearful anxiety and suffering we stumbled, utterly exhausted, into the oasis of Anarak.'² It was a classic, almost an action-movie sequence of last-minute salvation. Catching the scent of water, the animals bolted up the green hillside to plunge their snouts into the watering hole. The men gorged themselves on pomegranates, figs and almonds from the orchard, and promptly collapsed behind the walls of a caravanserai (a walled rest stop) to sleep. Fountains gushed up in the streets, men in light cotton robes were gathered around the whitewashed mosque, abundance was everywhere in the town of 2,000 inhabitants, and on the following day it took all the will the Germans could muster to rouse the men and the animals to strike out once more into the desert.

Reports filtering in from native scouts prompted the Germans to take the caravan in a more north-easterly and seemingly safe direction, for the news that reached their camp was that the Russian positions were concentrated mostly at the Afghan border region, still hundreds of miles distant. Further south, the usable wells were three to four days' march from one another, and most of them were guarded by spies who had already sent word to the British of the mission's progress since leaving Isfahan in two groups, on 1 and 6 July 1915.

Whichever direction they chose, their greatest fear was not so much a confrontation with hostile tribes, brigands or even the Russian and British patrols: what would tax their fortitude to the breaking point was the raging furnace and furious dust storms awaiting them in one of the most desolate places on earth. 'The Iranian sun made us realise our helpless situation in the midst of a vast, flat desert, where no sheltered spot was available.'[3] Niedermayer reflected on their plight upon reaching the oasis of Shah Pars. There the mules and camels quenched their thirst on the brackish water, but to the men and horses it was undrinkable and tasted of poison. 'Before long, a strong, hot wind rose [...] bringing with it the finest grains of sand, which penetrated into the respiratory organs, eyes, clothing, even into articles enclosed in firmly fastened packs.'[4] Hentig expressed similar horror at their ordeal:

> The sudden light [of dawn] was the hardest to bear. All dreaded the first sign of light on the eastern horizon. The Kavir seemed to eat into our lives. Salt penetrated our skin, collecting on hands and faces. The bite of the salt upon our bodies was almost unbearable.[5]

The relentless sun and salt were almost beyond endurance, but still other dreads lay in wait in the desert wastes. Much of the crossing was made under the stars, when the temperature dipped to a level that offered the travellers some comfort – certainly more than the average 104°F in the shade which they were forced to suffer by early morning. On one stage beyond Anarak the men drew their weapons at the sound of ominous rustling noises ahead of the caravan. They had been warned of the possibility of a surprise attack

by Russian patrols. On this occasion the noise turned out to be the shuf-
fling of an immense number of venomous snakes, which had crept out of
their holes at night, poised to strike. Niedermayer and a few of the others
dismounted and pulled on leather gaiters to walk ahead of the caravan,
armed with sticks and whips to drive the snakes from their route. Exhausted
but unscathed by these loathsome reptiles, at 2 a.m. they pulled up at the
deserted caravanserai of Meshedcheri, which stood half buried in the sand.
Despite its tumbledown state of abandonment, they found drinkable well
water and even some patches of pasture for the animals.

An even ghastlier encounter with desert vermin awaited them on the
next day's march. The caravan suddenly found its way blocked by a cluster
of tarantulas, which Niedermayer blithely dismissed as a not unusual occur-
rence in the vicinity of snakes. In fact, he took a rather dispassionate view
of this new and grisly visitation. 'In spite of their horrible appearance and
their evil reputation amongst the Persians, they are not poisonous, although
their bites may certainly cause injury.'[6] The path was cleared by beating the
ground with sticks and the column moved gingerly on its way.

On 23 July, the caravan lumbered into the town of Tabas, the largest of
Persia's desert oases, after having coped for three weeks with terrible sufferings in the Kavir. Their best hope of reaching the Afghan border, still
200 miles north-east, though across less inhospitable terrain, would be
through the use of deception. This meant travelling light and at speed. The
main portion of their baggage was sent back in the care of Becker, the idea
being to divert the Russians' attention, and then for the baggage column
to rejoin them by forced marches through the remaining sector of desert. A
mule train was sent ahead, carrying the bare necessities of food and ammunition. A third section, a camel caravan, was loaded with water and food
under instruction to follow the horsemen as far to the rear as practicable.

Becker's retreat led to his being knocked out of action for the duration
of the war. His party was spotted and surrounded by a Russian patrol and
he spent several days fighting them off until he ran out of ammunition.
Before abandoning his position with some of his Afridi volunteers, Becker
buried the gold his camels were carrying to attempt a break through Russian
lines. Most of his men were shot or captured and Becker took a bullet in the

chest as he ran for safety. The local tribesmen helped him to make good
his escape and whisked him to safety in their village, where he was nursed
for a fortnight until he was able to travel. But when Becker returned to the
spot where he had buried the gold, he found the Russians waiting for him.
Taken prisoner, he continued to work as a physician in a Russian camp and
was eventually repatriated to Germany, where he was killed in the next war
during the Soviet siege of Berlin.

From Boshruyeh, a small, barren settlement 50 miles north-east of the
pleasant comforts of Tabas, the mission was now heading into the most
hazardous part of their Persian crossing, a point roughly in line with Russian-
held Meshed to the north and the British garrison of Birjand to the south.
The telegraph line between the two enemy outposts was well guarded,
with spies lurking in every oasis settlement along the trail. This line was
known as the East Persian Cordon, 'which had been set up to protect the
Indian and Afghan frontiers against German incursions'.[7] It was an effective
Anglo-Russian defence network and before long the mission's presence was
detected. On the seventh day out of Tabas, the Germans' forward scouts
galloped into camp, bringing reports of a 150-strong column of Russians,
carrying two guns and two machine guns, who were rapidly advancing
southward from Meshed. This was to be expected. Niedermayer's bold but
risky plan was calmly to await the Russian approach and then, when the
enemy's men and horses were most spent, to strike out rapidly into the
desert on a meandering path.

Niedermayer's plan worked: having successfully outrun the Russians, the
caravan continued on its northward course, aiming for the frontier oasis of
Yazdan and the hope of safety on the Afghan side of the border. The British
were aware that a German mission was on its way towards Afghanistan,
though at this stage they had scant intelligence on the identity of these
mysterious travellers. Reports were routinely telegraphed to Roos-Keppel
in Peshawar, and it was clear from his memos, dispatched to Lord Hardinge
at his summer residence in the cool hills of Simla, that a German mission
was expected, although the tactical feints through the desert were showing
some success. In early August Roos-Keppel wrote: 'Afghanistan appears
quite quiet and I cannot hear of the arrival of any Germans or Austrians yet.'[8]

Niedermayer and Hentig marched on from Boshruyeh. In this secluded spot Niedermayer made sure the men had proper training in the use of fire-arms, a skill that it was assumed they would sooner or later need to put into practice. Then Hentig came up with the idea of sending a runner with a letter for the German minister in Tehran, bearing news that the column planned to push northwards. Hentig selected for the job the man he deemed the least cunning of his escort, in the hope that he would fail to evade capture by the Russians and that the letter would be intercepted. He was not disappointed. On 7 August the column set out along a faint camel-caravan trail on what was to turn into a week of quick zigzagging marches from one water-hole to the next, often on the move from late afternoon to the following morning for 15 hours at a stretch. The planned break through the Russian lines seemed a more promising risk than attempting to cross the British stronghold to the south, which in any event would lead them away from their destination.

That said, with two heavily armed columns of Russian cavalry bearing down on them, there was for the moment no option but to turn the caravan southwards. The mission was not remotely in a fit condition to confront a force of this size. Many of the men were suffering from an assortment of ailments: some were nursing broken bones sustained after passing out and dropping, exhausted, from their mounts in a heat that soared to an unbear-able 143 °F in the shade. Niedermayer could count on only four able-bodied men to bear arms. In their debilitated state, there would be no escaping the dreaded Russians, who were notorious for showing no mercy to their enemies.

Niedermayer and Hentig observed the faint dust cloud on the horizon through their binoculars. They waited until nightfall, moving under the cover of darkness in the hope that the desert wind that came up at night might wipe their tracks with a thick covering of sand. At dawn, the Russians were spotted advancing hard on their heels. The party, exhausted to a man, would have to make a desperate stand, for there was no hope of pushing the column deeper into the desert. Those few who were able to hold a rifle took shelter in a ditch to face the oncoming enemy, wait until they had them in range and prepare to sell their lives dearly. When the column came into sight with the naked eye, the men's sense of dread instantly turned to one of alleviation, no doubt mixed with fury at the duff information they had been fed by the scouts. The attacking column of 'Russian troops' turned out to be Germans, part of their own group who had been chasing after the main body to bring in fodder for the mules.

With renewed determination, Hentig and Niedermayer started off on their final push to the Afghan border. 'We were now certain of one fact: although smaller bodies of the enemy might still be encountered in the desert country lying between us and the Afghan frontier, yet the main forces of the East Persia Cordon were now in our rear.'⁹ As they rode east, the air cooled delightfully and they were greeted with the almost forgotten sight of green-clad hills rising to Yazdan, the last Persian oasis nestled in a salient on the border. 'Beyond lay Afghanistan [...] We cast a last farewell glance in the direction of Persia, where we had left so many of our party, and then, in spite of our fatigue, we began the descent in good spirits.'¹⁰

The Turkish officer Kazim Bey rode off to a nearby village in search of provisions for the half-starved men. Hours later he returned empty-handed, and to make things worse Yazdan turned out to be a dried up water-hole. As they debated how to obtain supplies for the crossing into Afghanistan, a few of the mission's stragglers stumbled into camp, bearing heart-rending tales of having passed bloated, sun-blackened corpses of men and animals who had suffered one of the most horrible fates to befall a desert traveller. There was no hope of turning back to give the men a proper burial, so their thoughts turned to the days ahead and how the mission might be received in the forbidden land of Afghanistan. Niedermayer and Hentig knew nothing of this country, which throughout history had treated foreign intruders as enemies. Of the merchants who had been granted permission to proceed as far as Herat, when this suited the Afghans, it was not uncommon for them to be led blindfolded. Those who crossed the frontier without a permit from the Afghan authorities, as had a recent party of Russians, were routinely murdered and their heads thrown back at night across the frontier in sacks.

On the evening of 19 August 1915, a column of some 50 bone-weary Europeans, Turks, Indians and Pashtuns marched slowly past a lone watchtower perched atop a rocky pinnacle, its western wall facing the high plateau of the Persian desert, and to the east the hills of Afghanistan. For the German mission, it had been arduous months of hardship and narrow brushes with death since the start of their journey from Berlin.

The Indian nationalist Barakatullah, a well-known figure in Afghanistan and elsewhere in the Muslim world, was dispatched with Kazim Bey and a few Afridi officers to deliver the news of the mission's arrival to Mahmud Serwar Khan, the governor of Herat. Afghans have long memories, particularly when it comes to remembering foreigners who have come to subjugate their land. It was less than 80 years previously that a Persian army, supported by Russian officers, had laid siege to Herat for many months and were only driven off by Lord Palmerston's gunboat diplomacy, when the foreign secretary landed a contingent of marines on Persian soil. Barakatullah needed to persuade the governor that the men gathered at the frontier were not Persians, and certainly not the despised Russians. These were Germans whose amir, moreover, had become a follower of the true faith. These men came as liberators, not conquerors, sent by the kaiser to free his Muslim brothers of India from the infidel's oppression.

The Governor of Herat was not the only one to learn of the mission's arrival in Afghanistan. On the day that Barakatullah's advance party was riding from the border to Herat, Roos-Keppel in Peshawar was handed a telegram from one of the British agents stationed in Afghanistan. As feared, the report informed him of a group of around 70 (the number was somewhat exaggerated) foreigners who had entered Afghanistan from Persia. They were encamped at Pahra, a village a few miles south-west of Herat, awaiting the governor's permission to proceed to the city and from there to continue on to Kabul. An even more disturbing piece of intelligence was that the Afghans were preparing to roll out the red carpet for the mission, having been impressed by some extravagant promises that the German members of the group would, like their kaiser, convert to Islam after bringing the war against the English to a successful conclusion. 'They said that they were preaching jihad, by the orders of the Sultan of Turkey, the Shah of Persia and the *ulema*, or highest Islamic scholars, of the Sunnis and Shi'as.'[II]

Presently a detachment of Afghan worthies rode out to greet the expedition and welcome them to the city as guests of the Afghan government. A large caravan with cooking utensils and servants appeared first on the road, followed some distance behind by a distinguished patriarch of about 65 with a long grey beard and dressed in a British general's uniform. This was Mahmud Serwar Khan, the governor of Herat, riding at the head of a retinue of 30 cavalrymen and court officials. The visitors could scarcely believe their eyes when they entered the vast walled city. They were met by the spectacle of fields of orchards, flowering gardens, the tinkle of fountains and magnificent gleaming mosques. It was all freshness and greenery, a sight unlike anything they had imagined in their 40-day crossing of Persia's devastating wasteland. Some of the mullahs at the city gates encouraged the people to kiss the Germans' hands as Hentig and Niedermayer passed through the arches, smartly turned out in their army uniforms.

That was on 24 August: in keeping with Afghan custom, they were obliged to rest for several days in an information purdah, until such time as the governor determined it appropriate to summon them to his presence. That was not until 28 August, but meanwhile Mahmud Serwar Khan lavished an almost regal attention on his guests. Rich, luxurious meals were served twice a day, apart from breakfast and afternoon tea. A troop of artisans – saddlers, blacksmiths, fullers, tailors and cobblers – were sent to the palace where they were lodged to re-equip the guests and provide Hentig, Niedermayer and Röhr with new uniforms. Habibullah's undertakings to Hardinge had been totally disregarded. The Germans, albeit under close surveillance, were given unhindered access to the city and its magnificent historical sites.

As they rested in the shaded courtyard of their palatial quarters, Niedermayer and Hentig took stock of the expedition's results in terms of human cost. They had departed Isfahan with 140 men, plus 236 baggage animals and mounts. They appeared so formidable a force to native agents working for the government of India that by the time news of the mission's progress reached Hardinge in Simla, the viceroy was being fed reports of several columns of hundreds of European, Turkish and Indian invaders on the march, some armed with machine guns. The truth was that the weary column that entered Herat on 24 August had been reduced to 37 men and 79 animals, roughly a third of the mission's original strength. But Niedermayer was not deterred: 'The result gained was worth the sacrifice. The main part of the caravan had reached Afghanistan. A difficult task had been accomplished and our Mission carried out.'[12]

Basking in the warm sunshine, surrounded by bowls of raisins and dates, was an almost forgotten pleasure, but this was not why the Germans had risked their lives on the journey to Afghanistan. They were growing impatient with their luxurious inactivity. Four days later their breakfast was interrupted by the fanfare of trumpets, announcing the arrival of the governor. This was but a protocol visit to enquire after his guests' well-being. Thus, after an exchange of pleasantries, Niedermayer and Hentig were invited to present themselves at Mahmud Serwar Khan's palace the following day for a more detailed discussion of the purpose of the mission and their plans for the onward journey to Kabul. Hentig assumed the role of protagonist at a second meeting, lavishing on their sprightly, joke-cracking host his assurances of Germany's friendship and, what was of greater appeal, an undertaking to recognise Afghanistan's full independence in the conduct of its foreign affairs once the Central Powers achieved their ultimate victory over Britain and Russia. Hentig then floated the idea of Afghanistan joining its Muslim brothers of Turkey in declaring war on the Allies. In return, Hentig held out a dazzling pledge to cede to Afghanistan vast tracks of territory stretching from Samarkand to Bombay. Mahmud Sewar Khan listened with enthusiasm to his German guest, to whom he explained that these proposals would best be put to Amir Habibullah, who was, after all, the only person empowered to dictate Afghan policy. He dismissed the Germans with the promise that they could expect to depart Herat on the 400-mile trek to Kabul within a fortnight.

On 7 September 1915, the column marched out of the Kabul Gate on the start of their journey over the Hazarajat Mountains of central Afghanistan, which were already flecked with patches of autumn snow. Paschen was the only German member of the expedition who failed to recover his strength during their sojourn in Herat. He was escorted back to Isfahan to spend two months convalescing before returning to Herat, where he remained while the others carried on towards the capital. Compared with the horrors of the Persian desert, it was an uneventful, brisk 24-day march to Kabul, a crossing that camel caravans usually took upwards of a month to complete. 'On several days, when stages were short, we covered two in a single day. It was hard riding. But we had nothing to bother about arrangements.'[13] It would be an exaggeration to say that the passage was accomplished in luxurious style, but it must have seemed so for the mission's members, whose memories were still haunted by the weeks of thirst and blazing heat in the Dasht-i-Kavir, not to omit the encounters with poisonous snakes, scorpions and tarantulas. The governor of Herat had sent one of his retainers, with a large retinue of cooks, servants and a military escort, to look after the men's every need. He saw to it that the mission was properly housed each night and that they were served good food all along the way.

There is an easier, albeit more circuitous, eastward route across Afghanistan, one that traverses less mountainous terrain and takes the traveller through a warmer climate. This is the southerly road to Kabul via Kandahar. Habibullah wisely sent instructions to Mahmud Serwar Khan to dispatch the German mission through the central Hazara country, most of whose people, descendants of the thirteenth-century invasion by Genghis Khan, adhere to the Shi'i sect of Islam. It was feared that the fanatical Sunni Muslim Pashtuns of the south could all too easily be stirred to jihad, had the Germans chosen to take their anti-British campaign to the people. The last thing Habibullah wanted at this stage was to destabilise his southern dominions, which ran contiguous with British India. In fact, the moment Habibullah learnt of the mission's arrival at Herat he lost no time in reassuring Hardinge of his enduring neutrality: the amir was desperate to avoid upsetting the apple cart at this auspicious moment, when a jittery viceroy was about to grant Habibullah an increase in his annual subsidy.

The journey from Herat had been uneventful, one might even say restful, and the fresh mountain air so invigorating that men and beasts soon found themselves restored to health and in a much fitter state, even in the high passes, where they encountered frozen water under their feet and icicles hanging from the rocks. One pleasurable task they needed to perform, for the first time since departing Constantinople, was to build a fire to shelter against the cold night air. On 1 October 1915 the caravan cleared a ridge to come within sight of the Kabul valley, where in the distance they could make out the Bagh-e-Babur and its palace, where the mission was to take up residence. They had been a year on the march and were now in sight of their destination. The riders sent out to escort the Germans into the city the next morning brought refreshments in the form of ten different varieties of raisins, almonds and other nuts, along with pastries, pistachio biscuits, apples, figs and pomegranates. The following day the Germans changed into clean uniforms to begin the descent to the capital. They were met at the gates by a large detachment of troops, infantry, cavalry and gunners, led by a young Turkish officer in uniform and red tasselled fez. This was Khairi Bey, who the following year commanded the defence of Medina against besieging Arabs and was currently employed by Habibullah as a military instructor with the Afghan Army. He was sent to escort the mission to their palatial residence in the Bagh-e-Babur. As the party moved onwards, the amir's troops lined the roadside and presented arms with European precision. All seemed to bode well on their arrival in Kabul.

Their living quarters were luxurious beyond what they had enjoyed in Herat. Literally hundreds of the amir's servants and attendants were sent to look after the honoured foreigners. No sooner had they set foot in the palace than they found a warm bath and a sumptuous banquet waiting for them. It looked like no effort had been spared to make them feel like royal guests, all of which led them to expect an effusive welcome by the amir. But even before the day was out, a pall of doubt descended on the Germans, who discovered that their splendid palace was in fact a prison. The amir had guards with fixed bayonets posted at every entrance to prevent contact with anyone from outside the compound. This applied especially to pro-Turkish members of the royal family, mainly Habibullah's brother, Nasrullah, and the amir's son, Amanullah. The mission was confined to quarters and a despondent Niedermayer expressed the general mood when he lamented, 'One thing was clear to us – our work here would be no easy task.'[14]

They spent a full week languishing as high-living detainees until a letter finally arrived from Habibullah, bearing words of 'welcome'. The men were told by way of explanation that the amir had been absent from Kabul and was now making preparations to receive the expedition's leaders in an audience, which would take place in a few days' time. Meanwhile, all was far from well behind the high palace walls. Hentig had been struck down with a severe bout of malaria; however, their request for an urgent visit by the Turkish court physician fell on deaf ears. Misfortune then turned to tragedy when on 9 October Niedermayer was woken by one of the frequent earth tremors that rock Kabul and went downstairs to the garden to check on their horses. At that moment a man rode up breathlessly proclaiming that Jakob, Niedermayer's faithful adjutant, was dead. He had been too weak to complete the crossing from Herat and was left behind at Badasia, a week's journey from Kabul, in the care of native servants, but despite all efforts to restore him to health he had succumbed to fever. Niedermayer recalls that he staggered forward and caught hold of the nearest tree, unable to utter a word to his distressed colleagues. He was devastated by the loss of his adjutant, coming on the heels of the realisation that the mission, for now, had been left effectively powerless. Medicines ordered to treat Jakob's fever had been delayed a fatal week in reaching Badasia. His body was brought to Kabul and buried on a hill above the Bagh-e-Babur palace. Niedermayer felt outrage at his personal loss and at the mission's impotence. 'It was useless to attempt forcible measures. We decided to adopt the only means that might bring success: we went on a hunger strike.'[15] The idea of depriving themselves of food was too extreme a measure for everybody but the Germans, who none-theless stashed a store of fruit and pastry in their rooms. They then rather sanctimoniously refused to join their companions, who sat down to meals with no misgivings after the privations suffered in order to reach Kabul. This all amounted to a political conundrum for Habibullah, who received with consternation word of the 'hunger strike'. On the one hand, the amir was worried about the political implications of the Germans' action. It would not bode well for a potential ally, who might one day emerge victorious in the war, to find that their emissaries had been mistreated by the Kabul government. That said, Habibullah dared not offend his British neighbours for the sake of a handful of Germans. Turning to his protector, the amir had informed Hardinge that the Germans had been interned and that he would soon be able to report on what they wanted from him and his government.

After a further three-day wait, the Turkish physician turned up at the Bagh-e-Babur and confirmed in confidence what the Germans already suspected to be the case. Habibullah, he informed them, was firmly secured under British influence. Lord Hardinge maintained weekly contact with the amir, imploring him – a tacit warning would be more accurate – in every letter not to waver from his commitment to neutrality. Dr Munir Bey administered quinine to Hentig and treated the other ailing members of the expedition, and then he gave them a confidential briefing on political affairs in Kabul. It brought solace to the all but captive Germans to hear that the amir's younger brother, Nasrullah, stood firmly in support of the cause of the Central Powers, as did a majority of the common people. As court physician, Munir Bey kept close contact with the amir's family and the highest-ranking dignitaries of Kabul, thus his word was taken as reliable. The doctor left the compound, taking with him a gift of rare brandy of First Afghan War vintage, which Niedermayer had found stashed in a cupboard. That same evening, the Germans celebrated what they considered to be their first diplomatic victory, confirmation that at least part of the court was with them. They uncorked a second bottle of the 75-year-old brandy, and they all fell hopelessly drunk around the fire.

By now Hafiz Saifullah Khan, Hardinge's official agent in Kabul, had provided him with a detailed account of political developments since the Germans' arrival. These weekly reports gave the viceroy grave cause for concern, as it looked like the amir's guests were settling in for a long stay. 'The fact that warm curtains are being provided for their rooms as well as other requirements for the cold season indicates that they will pass the winter in Kabul.'[16] What could Habibullah be playing at? Hardinge mused. The Afghans had never tolerated the prolonged presence of infidels in their country, not unless they came with offerings that were of interest to the amir. Had the Germans and Turks made the journey to Kabul with proposals of military aid? Should he allow himself to be persuaded to cast his lot with the enemy, to appease the Turks, or in the hope of recovering lost territory, such as the long-coveted winter capital of Peshawar, or even a sea outlet through Baluchistan? Habibullah was prepared to hear both sides, weighing up the pros and cons of what each had to offer.

The viceroy had good cause for apprehension. A short while after the Germans' arrival the amir convened a shura of elders and village headmen to discuss what was to be done about the mission. The assembled greybeards came up with two suggestions and left it to the amir to decide on what action to take. Either one, if put into effect, would have been enough to put the Indian army on high alert. One truly Machiavellian proposal was to strike a secret alliance with the Turkish members of the mission, conditional on their supplying a war arsenal, while deferring the call to jihad until a suitable moment for raising the frontier tribes to action. So as not to arouse suspicions in Delhi, a durbar should be held in the presence of the British agent in Kabul, at which the German mission would be publicly repudiated and their members driven out of the durbar in disgrace. The other, more forthright, suggestion was that under Turkey's proclamation of jihad, it should be declared that Afghanistan was obliged to respond by ending the country's neutrality and mobilise its forces for war. Habibullah kept his counsel and upon dismissing the durbar, he sent a party of court officials under cover of darkness from Paghman, his summer residence in the hills north of Kabul, to the Bagh-e-Babur to discuss arrangements for the first royal audience with the Germans.

The welter of reports coming out of Kabul appeared to confirm the version of the Turkish court physician, to the effect that the people, under the influence of Nasrullah and his anti-British faction, had embraced the German cause. This view was reinforced by a British engineer by the name of Lynch, employed by the amir to manufacture soap, candles and smokeless powder. He had fled Kabul, hastening to Delhi in disgust at the prevailing pro-German mood. Once in the Indian capital he complained to the British authorities that the Germans 'are treated like rajahs and we [the British] are treated like dogs'.[17] Everyone in Afghanistan with the exception of the amir, in Lynch's opinion, was bitterly hostile to the British. 'Though, mind you, I don't think they'll dare do anything as long as H.M. [the amir] is alive.'[18] This was an extremely unwelcome development, for if Habibullah's non-intervention policy was being subverted under his very nose, how could he possibly hope to contain the warlike tribes of the North-West Frontier who were waiting for a signal from the mullahs? Hardinge still had faith in the amir's sincerity, yet at the same time 'the situation on the Frontier was very disturbed and inspired grave anxiety'.[19] In the first year of the Great War, roughly up to the time the Germans set out on their march from Herat to Kabul, the frontier had been the scene of repeated attacks by Afghan tribesmen on the Indian side of the Durand Line. Since 1849, the year in which the Raj annexed the Punjab and the North-West Frontier region after defeating the Sikhs in two wars, the Pashtun tribes had kept up an almost relentless wave of raids on British civilian and military targets. The standard government reprisal was the 'butcher and bolt' tactic whereby British columns were dispatched to demolish an offending tribe's villages, destroy their farmland, and then beat a hasty retreat. It was not a strategy designed to win hearts and minds, but neither side displayed much interest in engaging in constructive dialogue, so the tit-for-tat battles continued throughout the century of British rule on the frontier.

It looked like the tide might at any moment turn against British control of the North-West Frontier. Nasrullah and the palace revolutionaries were taking every opportunity to whip up anti-British hostility among the mullahs (who needed little encouragement) as well as the general populace. Hardinge knew, through the government's chief officer in Peshawar, George Roos-Keppel, that the frontier tribesmen were a law unto themselves: Habibullah exercised almost no influence over the tribes, certainly a good deal less than did the fundamentalist clerics of Kabul. Roos-Keppel's frontier expertise was unmatched by any soldier-administrator of his day. He had published a grammar of the Pashtu language, translated arcane Pashtu historical works and co-founded Islamia College, now the undergraduate school of Peshawar University. But first and foremost he was a soldier of the Raj. Roos-Keppel was of Anglo-Dutch descent and answered to Gilbert and Sullivan's 'very model of a modern major-general', with his silk turban and ermine-collared greatcoat, a pair of hooded eyes gazing sternly above a formidable moustache, he was for all the world a man possessed of a Churchillian self-confidence. Through personal contacts in the tribal areas, he was aware that news filtering in from the European front would have a powerful impact on their actions: any sign of weakness would be taken as a signal to attack the British. For the Pashtun tribes, any Allied reverses in the war against Germany were taken as an invitation to revolt en masse. This was communicated to Hardinge:

I am afraid that the fall of Warsaw and the continued unbroken successes
of the Germans in Russia are having a bad effect on public opinion. Also
I am afraid that amongst other communities a belief is growing in the
invincibility of Germany and that nothing will alter this until we start a
steady forward move in the West.[20]

It was necessary at all costs to keep the amir on side and this required a
persuasive voice at the highest level. Hardinge came up with the idea of
asking King George V to write personally to Habibullah, as a fellow monarch, reminding the amir of his agreement to observe a neutral policy in the
European war. On 24 September 1915, George V sent a letter on Buckingham
Palace headed notepaper expressing his gratification at the amir's continued
friendship with Britain:

Your Majesty has maintained the attitude of strict neutrality which
you guaranteed at the beginning of this war, not only because it is in
accordance with Your Majesty's engagements to me, but also because
by it you are serving the best interests of Afghanistan and of the Islamic
religion.[21]

It is curious indeed how George asserts that ignoring the caliph's summons to jihad was in the best interests of the Islamic religion, when in
fact it constituted a blatant offence against the teachings of the Qur'an.
The king then went on to appeal to Habibullah's sense of historical duty,
by reminding him that in troubled times his late father Abdur Rahman
had kept an abiding friendship with the British monarch's own mother,
Queen Victoria.

It is unlikely that the delivery of a letter, even so regal a missive as this
one, had ever been surrounded by such a display of pomp. The amir dispatched the chief of the Dakka garrison to the Khyber Pass to receive the
letter, which had been sent via Delhi, under the escort of a company of
mounted tribal irregulars. An honour guard of the Khyber Rifles was sent
to greet the Afghan deputation at Landi Khana, a town a few miles inside
British territory, where a large marquee with refreshments had been erected

for the occasion. Habibullah rose to his feet when he was handed the document in Kabul by the Dakka commandant, who in exchange was given a brace of British-made Lee-Metford rifles as a gift for his orderlies. Whether or not Habibullah was won over by King George's effusions of friendship, the one incentive the amir could not ignore was Hardinge's attached note, advising the amir that the government of India had authorised a 2-lakh-rupee (200,000) increase in his annual subsidy. In 1915, this was equivalent to £25,000. 'It is hoped that this earnest token of goodwill will not only strengthen the ties of friendship between the two governments,' Hardinge wrote, 'but will add to the power and prosperity of the Afghan Government.'[22] Habibullah was anything but a fool and knew he had the British government's back to the wall. He was determined to exploit his position to the fullest. The amir thanked Hardinge for the increased subsidy but, alas, both he and his ministers considered the amount insufficient in view of the value of Afghan neutrality and the expense of keeping his country out of the war. Habibullah asked for a payment of 44 lakh rupees (4.4 million rupees, or £550,000 in the currency of the day), part in gold and part in rupees, out of the balance of his allowance, which amounted to some 49 lakh rupees a year (£612,500). Hardinge considered this an outrageous demand, but in a letter to the Foreign Secretary he acknowledged that Habibullah might in fact require additional funds, to keep the mullahs quiet and his army properly equipped. The viceroy considered the possibility that the amir could also be testing British India's good faith and its financial solvency, so it was agreed promptly to honour the amir's request.

Then came the waiting game, a traditional Afghan ploy to demonstrate which party has the upper hand. The days and weeks passed and still there was no reply to King George's letter. Hardinge was left to fret over what might be transpiring behind closed doors between Habibullah and the German envoys. 'The delay causes us some anxiety, and would seem to indicate that antagonistic influences are at work,' the viceroy noted in a dispatch.[23] The late dispatch of the amir's reply is one of those diplomatic incidents tinged with irony. King George's letter was typed instead of handwritten, something Habibullah regarded as a flaw in etiquette. In order for the amir to reply in the same manner as the British monarch, Habibullah needed to procure a typewriter, a task that took several weeks. In the end, the amir was given a Persian typewriter on which his scribe replied in Persian, which was the language of the Afghan court. Habibullah dismissed the British worries about his commitment to neutrality, as was expected, but the real value of this exchange of letters was its use as leverage in dealing with the Germans in their forthcoming meetings.

Early autumn of 1915, with India's forces stretched close to the breaking point, was not an auspicious time to be deploying fresh brigades to counter the threat of a German-inspired tribal uprising, which in turn would most likely be a precursor of a full-scale Afghan invasion. Hardinge grasped the gravity of the crisis: when Lord Kitchener, Secretary of State for War, asked for more British regular battalions from India to be sent to Europe, Hardinge and his commander-in-chief, Beauchamp Duff, flatly turned down the request. Kitchener estimated that Britain would have to send more than 135,000 troops from other fronts in order to defend the subcontinent successfully. India had at the time only eight British battalions and these had all been deployed to the frontier. There was not only the threat of the Germans in Kabul opening the gates to an offensive by Turkish troops. A question mark hung over Persia, which had yet to declare, while Wassmuss and his fellow German rabble-rousers were doing everything in their power to spread trouble across the country. The home government sided with Hardinge and dispatched four British battalions from Mesopotamia as reinforcements for the depleted army in India.

On the morning of 26 October 1915, a fleet of Rolls-Royces pulled up outside the Bagh-e-Babur, summoning Niedermayer, Hentig, Mahendra Pratap, Moulana Barakatullah and Kazim Bey to the amir's mountain retreat, a palace set in dense woodland and surrounded by bungalows and pavilions for his court entourage. The two Germans donned their freshly pressed army dress uniforms for the drive north from the capital. Hentig somewhat tactlessly donned the spiked helmet of the Colonial Service for the journey on Afghanistan's only tarmac road. The helmet was so admired by his hosts that he later presented it as a gift to the Crown Prince. This marked the start of the Hentig–Niedermayer offensive aimed at drawing Afghanistan into the Great War.

Their arrival at the summer palace was heralded by a trumpet fanfare, imparting to the amir's guests a sensation of self-importance that was before long to prove ill-founded. They were ushered into a large brown reception tent in the palace courtyard, where after a few moments spent admiring the splendid tapestries and carpets, the court chamberlain made his entry. 'His Majesty the Amir, the Shining Light of the Nation and the Religion, is prepared to allow you into the sight of His Countenance,' he thundered.[24] They rose as one and were escorted outside to the royal palace, where Habibullah stood in a small room with windows set high in the walls, whether to keep the sitting area cool or deter a would-be assassin was a matter for speculation.

In accordance with Afghan convention, the visitors were obliged to follow a strict protocol when presented to the amir. Mahendra Pratap led the party into the sumptuously carpeted reception chamber. As the Germans had been granted permission to enter Afghanistan on the understanding that this was a diplomatic mission, so as not to cause the British government undue alarm, the Indian was followed by Hentig, with Niedermayer a few paces behind. Kazim Bey came next, and lastly Barakatullah. They took their places at a table laden with a rich assortment of dried fruits and sweetmeats, Habibullah seated at the centre, flanked by his younger brother Nasrullah, his sons Amanullah and Inayatullah, and two *sardars*, or high-ranking noblemen. Niedermayer recalls his first impression of the amir as a man of short stature, with a close-cut black beard and small keen eyes behind gold-rimmed spectacles. He cut a sporting appearance in a tweed jacket of English tailoring and he carried a stick and gloves. 'He had some difficulty expressing himself, owing to a speech defect and slight deafness, and he often spoke quickly and rather loudly. He understood some English and Turkish, but Persian was the Court language.'[25]

Habibullah observed his guests with some bemusement and it soon became apparent that he was not lacking in a sense of humour. Hentig ceremoniously presented the amir with three letters, one from Emperor Wilhelm II, another from Chancellor Theobald von Bethmann-Hollweg, and the third from the sultan of Turkey. Habibullah gave the letters a cursory glance, and then remarked laughingly to Hentig that the German diplomat looked a bit young to be leading so high-powered a diplomatic mission. But Kaiser Wilhelm's typed letter, like that of his cousin King George, piqued the amir's vanity. Hentig skilfully parried his host's complaint by explaining that the kaiser had typed the letter from the battlefield, without the benefit of a calligrapher at hand. Habibullah then opened the formal talks, saying he regarded himself a man before whom his visitors wished to lay out their goods. 'I will think over for what purpose I can use them, and I will then make my choice.'[26] To this Hentig boldly retorted, 'We did not come to present merchandise or conduct commercial business. We have come to reveal what you will not read in the enemy press.'[27]

The amir engaged each member of the mission in conversation, until he noticed one pair of eyes resting too long on his mutilated hand. 'My fingers were torn off by the explosion of a gun barrel,' he explained. 'But not a German one,' Hentig said. 'No, an English one.'[28] The chit-chat went on until noon, when the amir and his entourage left for midday prayers. Then came lunch, a banquet that was attended by a clutch of government officials, signalling, the Germans hoped, the start of serious negotiations. On Habibullah's right sat Mahendra Pratap, for whom a special meal had been prepared by a Hindu cook brought up from Kabul. Barakatullah acted as translator for the group, while the Germans and Kazim Bey managed to get by with the little Persian they had mastered.

To their dismay, the amir stubbornly evaded discussing of anything of import. So Hentig put it to him in straightforward fashion that if Habibullah sought full independence from Britain, it was in his interest to join the Central Powers and declare war on Britain. Kazim Bey reminded the amir that this was the course his own country had taken and, furthermore, the last thing Turkey wished to see was a religious split among Muslims. Barakatullah added his weight to the debate by imploring Habibullah to close ranks with India's downtrodden Muslims. Pratap and Barakatullah deployed every argument they could muster, even attempting to seduce the amir with a repeat of their promises of new territory to be annexed to his kingdom once Germany had declared victory. All this, they emphasised, could only be achieved if Habibullah allowed Turkish and German forces to launch a strike at India through Afghanistan.

The meeting was conducted in a friendly atmosphere, though it could not be said the Germans held out much hope for an early, much less an easy, success in their negotiations. Habibullah was brimming with courtesy and charm, to the extent that he personally served his guests from the delicacies spread before them – all of which, Hentig noted, were first sampled by the amir's official taster. Habibullah was aware of the perils that went with occupying the throne of Kabul and he even kept his drinking water in 'a locked silver samovar and his glass had a special opening'.[29]

The amir expounded his dilemma to his guests in plain language: he was caught in a vice between Britain's and Russia's two great empires. Afghanistan was lacking in financial and military clout to defend itself against these foreign powers. It was British India, he was quick to remind the Germans, that provided the lion's share of Afghanistan's finances. As the afternoon wore on, it was becoming obvious that the cunning Afghan ruler was holding out for a solid commitment of money and troops, something that the Germans were not empowered to deliver. Niedermayer noted:

> He was much under British influence, and was certainly not of the type
> of black chieftain who could be induced by a gift of a few glass beads to
> undertake a fanatical war against our enemies, as many people at home
> have pictured him.[30]

On the other hand Nasrullah, he reasoned, although considered the amir's intellectual inferior, 'might possibly prove a very valuable tool in our hands'.[31]

The talks in this first meeting, as well as in those that followed, almost always carried on into the late hours, interrupted only by evening prayers. The Germans eventually saw they were getting nowhere. It was a frustrating state of affairs for Hentig and Niedermayer, to say the least, when recalling the sufferings they had endured to reach Kabul. 'The impression gained from our first audience was not particularly encouraging. We had confirmation of the fact that Habibullah was possessed of qualities which would have been most creditable in a German.'[32] The mood in the Rolls-Royces that whisked the envoys back to Kabul on 26 October was as dark as the night sky.

4

The Waiting Game

S everal days later the mission was again summoned to Paghman, a meeting that turned out to be as fruitless as their first encounter with the amir. The Germans were beginning to wonder if Habibullah's game was simply to wear them down to a point at which they would either table a firm offer of material aid, or return home and allow him to communicate the good news to his paymaster Hardinge. These days were likewise a trying time for Habibullah, with tension mounting on his Indian border, where certain frontier tribes were preparing themselves to launch a great coordinated attack on British territory. They had already invited some of their coreligionists from the formidable clans of Waziristan to share in the looting. Trouble was also brewing to the west in Herat, where it was reported that several of the Germans and Turks who had remained behind were spending their days swaggering about the city in large numbers, causing a good deal of friction with the local populace. It was also disclosed that they were 'working some sort of machine, supposed to be a wireless telephone or telegraph, making surveys of the district, drawing maps and furtively obtaining general information regarding the country'.[1] To the amir's dismay, all these reports were being relayed to Hardinge's staff at the Viceregal Lodge in Simla. Habibullah gave out orders to place the foreigners in Herat under close surveillance and, if it was confirmed that they were actually engaging in covert activity on behalf of Germany, to have them arrested and taken into custody.

Further distressing news for the British was relayed from across Afghanistan's border in Persia. Wild tales in Meshed's bazaars, spread by German agents, had it that Habibullah was no longer a friend of the British, that the amir had abandoned his neutrality and espoused the Turco-German cause in the war. Habibullah acted quickly to quash these stories by issuing a *firman*, or 'decree', denying the rumours. Closer to home, a deputation of tribesmen from the North-West Frontier arrived in Kabul at this time to seek the amir's sanction for jihad, as well as his assistance in the shape of firearms. In the city of Khost, less than 100 miles west of Peshawar, the tribesmen were eager to flock to the war banners and took to the streets where they heard the news that the amir soon intended to summon the faithful to jihad. Even in Kabul, posters appeared in public places, announcing such startling events as the imminent arrival of a German aeroplane to lead the assault. The *qazi*, or 'chief Qur'anic scholar', of Khost swore that he had received orders from Kabul to collect rations and arrange accommodation for Afghan troops. The entire country was gearing up for the coming holy war to liberate India. And there was more: Enver Pasha, it was assured, had crossed the Turkestan border at the head of an army of tens of thousands of Turks, which was assembling at Maimana in north-western Afghanistan.[2]

One did not have to look very far to spot the hand of Nasrullah behind the rumour-mongering. The amir's younger brother had never disguised his delight at the German presence in Kabul. He took it as an article of faith that the next step would be the creation of a tripartite Turco-German-Afghan alliance, culminating in the ouster of the British infidels from India. Nasrullah implored the amir to throw in his lot with the Germans, by arming the tribesmen and sending the mullahs to agitate among the frontier Pashtuns. When the frontier had burst into flames in the Great Pashtun Uprising of 1897, even the young cavalry officer Winston Churchill, who took part in the Malakand campaign, was convinced that the revolt posed a threat to the very survival of British India. It required a year of heavy fighting and thousands of British and Indian casualties to restore peace on the frontier. This time, Nasrullah and his fellow plotters reckoned, the British would not be capable of mustering a strong enough force to hold out against a full-scale revolt by the frontier tribes.

One of Roos-Keppel's spies in Kabul had spent some time sharing quarters with a court official who was privy to Nasrullah's machinations. In a
report sent a few days before the Germans were granted their first official
audience with Habibullah, this secret agent slipped out of Kabul and delivered to the chief commissioner in Peshawar a file on seditious activities
in Afghanistan. He revealed that Nasrullah had received a deputation of
Mahsuds and Waziris, two of the most warlike of the frontier tribes. The
tribesmen had been given a considerable supply of arms and were told that
the mullahs of the Mohmand region, another focal point of rebellion, would
receive a similar consignment.[3]

Enthusiasm for a great Islamic uprising was running at a high pitch. The
anti-British elements in Kabul fervently hoped that Persia would join the
war on the side of Turkey. The frontier mullahs were reinforced by those of
southern Afghanistan's Pashtun belt in urging the tribesmen to rise up in
the name of the sultan of Turkey and to take advantage of the drain on the
government of India's strength. The return of sick and wounded soldiers
from France gave rise to stories of German invincibility and, in consequence,
hundreds of Frontier tribesmen serving in the Indian army deserted their
ranks:

In 1914, there were nearly 5,000 trans-border Pashtuns in the Indian
Army, of whom about half were Afridis. By June 1915, over six hundred
Afridis had deserted, and there were many dismissals and discharges for
misconduct. In November 1915, all recruitment of trans-border Pashtuns
was stopped.[4]

Habibullah's only concession to the demands for war preparations was to
sanction the application of *hasht nafri*, a law requiring one man out of every
eight in each tribe to serve in the army. The Germans were aware of this
semi-mobilisation and they engaged in some covert sleuthing of their own.
After the first meeting with the amir they were granted permission to move
freely about Kabul. This privilege was given with some trepidation, for Afghan
chronicles of the 1838–42 First Afghan War had spoken with great vehemence
of the liberties that officers of the British Army in occupation of Kabul had

taken with Afghan women. Hentig discovered on one of his outings about the city that they were not the only Germanic Westerners in Kabul. He came across three Austrian officers and several soldiers lying sick in one of the city's guardhouses. These men had escaped from Russian prisoner-of-war camps and had trekked in horrendous circumstances over the mountains from Turkestan, led by one Captain Jakob Schreiner, whom Hentig found to be a dapper Austrian soldier with a gold pince-nez. The others were not in such a happy state as was their senior officer. 'They seemed a pile of fur and Austrian forage caps. The amir placed one of his English landaus at our disposal. They all looked emaciated so we took them back to our quarters.'[5] After their recovery, some of these Austrians were so wooed by the charms of Afghan women that they later converted to Islam to marry, although Hentig maintained that it was unlawful for a soldier in uniform in wartime to change his nationality. The amir gave his blessings to these unions and Hentig decided not to press his case.

The first encounter with Habibullah may have ended in deep disappointment, but Hentig and Niedermayer remained undaunted. Despite the amir's lack of enthusiasm for war, their days in Kabul were not spent in idleness. Niedermayer was actively making enquiries into Afghanistan's military preparedness, confident that sooner or later he would succeed in persuading the amir to abandon his neutrality and agree to take up arms against the British. The Germans had installed a wireless station in Kabul for the transmission of regular dispatches to Berlin. A lesser monarch might have buckled under this onslaught of political pressure from all sides, including from within his own family, or even fled the scene, which was the course of action his son Amanullah was to take 14 years later. Habibullah was not, like his father, an 'Iron Amir'. Nonetheless, to the Germans' frustration he stood his ground.

The government of India could deal with the hit-and-run attacks of Pashtun raiders of the frontier, but an all-out assault by tribesmen from across the border was a different matter. Years of gun-running through the Persian Gulf meant that many of the tribesmen were better armed than the frontier militia and even some regular army units. The extent of Afghan duplicity in this illegal import of arms was evident in the quality of the rifles sent to the tribesmen. From 1906 onwards the number of weapons smuggled into tribal territory through Afghanistan grew at an astonishing rate, rising from 15,000 in 1907 to almost 40,000 two years later. During the 1897 Pashtun Revolt only one in every ten tribesman was armed with a Martini-Henry rifle. By 1908 these weapons were the rule instead of the exception. The Ghilzai traders of Afghanistan were responsible for smuggling in guns by sea from Muscat through the Persian Gulf, then by camel caravan across Afghanistan to Kandahar and Ghazni, where the weapons were picked up by go-betweens in the pay of the frontier maliks, or 'headmen'. The Ghilzai merchants gradually acquired a monopoly on gun-running in the Persian Gulf and this became a flourishing enterprise, with annual sales amounting to £279,000 by 1907. This was until the government of India sent a Gurkha regiment to the region to intercept the shipments. A squadron of Royal Navy cruisers was also dispatched to the Gulf to engage the dhows, many of which were operating under French flags. This soon ceased to be a cost-effective business, with payment from the Afghan traders having fallen to a third of the value of their sailing vessels, which were frequently confiscated or blown out of the water by British warships. The Ghilzais also encountered growing hostility from the tribes on their main trade route in eastern Persia. The sultan of Muscat took a hand in stopping the arms dealers of his kingdom supplying the Ghilzais, for fear of provoking reprisals from the British, who assisted him in keeping at bay the hostile Bedouin tribes of the Muscat hinterland. Britain's intervention, however, came too late to stop modern rifles falling into the hands of some 150,000 Pashtun tribesmen of the North-West Frontier.

Niedermayer knew another course of action was open to them, one that did not depend on an Afghan initiative. A division of foreign troops, Turks or even Germans, could without much difficulty be marched into Afghanistan. He believed the sight of a disciplined, well-equipped force under the banner of Islam would be an irresistible incentive to put the Afghan tribes on a war footing, and one that the amir would be powerless to stop. This option would be kept in abeyance, pending the outcome of the next round of talks with the amir. Later, the Germans and Austrians in Kabul would come to exert a major influence on Afghanistan's military apparatus. British agents reported that 'according to the Mission, a war with England is inevitable. Officers are organising regular Afghan Army units and carrying out fortification works [...] and there is talk of a recently imported aeroplane.'[6] Niedermayer was effectively put in charge of organising Afghanistan's military, a task he worked on for months, almost up to the day the mission quit the country. The Kabul munitions factory eventually came under German supervision, and German officers were involved in training the army. Together with German, Austrian and Turkish auxiliary personnel, Niedermayer carried out an overhaul of the army. He improved the quality of the country's only officers' training academy and personally took charge of the staff college. Under German supervision, fortifications were built between Kabul and Peshawar on the strategic road that might one day carry an invading army into India. Niedermayer estimated the army's strength at some 50,000 men, of which perhaps 20 per cent were equipped with modern breech-loading rifles. He took steps to raise another 20,000 troops for military service, although the regular forces were very much a ragtag bunch which at best might be employed to provide support for the several hundred thousand frontier tribesmen who could be put into the field. With this in mind Niedermayer, using as intermediaries the Indian nationalists in his party, was in contact with leaders of some of the most belligerent tribes, namely the Afridis, Mahsuds and Mohmands, to plant the seed of a full-scale uprising in the British-administered territory of the frontier. The assumption was that if the Afghans embarked on an invasion and managed to fight their way to the Indus River – the Raj's main line of defence – the Indian population would at least remain passive, if not actually take up arms against the government. If Afghanistan was put on a war footing the amir, under the sway of Nasrullah and other seditious elements at court, could not resist being dragged along by the tide.

In any case, these measures were sufficient to disturb the British and, in spite of the continued assurance of friendship on the part of the amir, would force them to make greater military preparations on the North-West Frontier. We learned that roads and railways in that region were being completed, aerodromes established and large forces of white [i.e. British] troops concentrated.[7]

Niedermayer realised, however, that, apart from a telegraphic connection to Berlin, the mission was cut off from the outside world – hence success would depend entirely on their own resources and ingenuity. An Anglo-Indian force of 15,000 men and one Russian brigade blocked their contact with the West. There was no longer any prospect of importing weapons from Oman to arm the amir's troops. The Royal Navy's blockade of the Persian Gulf had put an end to that smuggling route. A harsh reality was staring them in the face: 'Unless financial assistance, arms and political guarantees could be secured from the Central Powers, the amir would not venture to come into open conflict with his powerful neighbours.'[8] Moreover, Niedermayer knew that their best hope lay in exploiting Habibullah's political conundrum. If the amir truly wanted to gain full independence for his country, the time to strike was now, when British India's defences were vulnerable, with the large deployment of troops to France and Mesopotamia. This was an opportunity for Habibullah's name to be enshrined as a heroic defender of Islam, for there was no doubt that his subjects sympathised strongly with Turkey's holy crusade. An Afghan declaration of war would undoubtedly also lead the Muslims of Central Asia to mobilise, and these khanates were only looking to Kabul for a signal.

In Niedermayer's opinion, in their next audience the Germans would have to put these arguments to the amir in the strongest possible terms, and at the right moment, for Habibullah's thinking was influenced by the course of events in Europe and he lived in dread of the British taking reprisals for his betrayal, should Germany turn out to be the loser. He knew this would cost him his throne, at the very least. Therefore, every setback the Central Powers took in Persia or the Far East caused him to hesitate. On the other hand, every advance of Britain's enemies, such as their successes in Serbia, the entry of Bulgaria into the war or the fall of the British garrison at the siege of Kut-al-Amara, was a step gained for the mission.[9]

In the Germans' encounters with Habibullah it became increasingly obvious that, unless a large force of foreign troops was seen to be massing on Afghanistan's border, there was little hope of Afghanistan declaring for the Central Powers. Persia would also have to join the Turco-German ranks in order to clear the British and Russians from their occupied corridors, thus securing unhindered passage to Afghanistan. While the mission contemplated its strategy for the upcoming second round of negotiations, Berlin spared no effort to push Persia into the German camp. The priority was to build up Persia's fighting capability, which for the most part consisted of scattered bands of nomadic tribesmen. October 1915 saw the alarm signals flash red in London's War Office. Intelligence memos coming in from spies in the field revealed a German attempt to purchase the allegiance of the unpopular and ineffectual Persian ruler, Ahmad Shah Qajar, by means of the offer of a large loan. This was to be granted on the condition that he agreed to put together a professional Persian fighting force. British observers in Tehran reported that the army was in a deplorable state and 'only has sufficient ammunition for two days at most'.[10]

Charles Marling, Britain's chargé d'affaires in Tehran, looked every inch the debonair diplomat-spy, with his monocle and neatly trimmed goatee and moustache. Marling had spent the month of October discreetly enquiring into Germany's stepped-up activity in Persia and was alarmed by what he learnt. 'Great quantities of arms and ammunition and, it is said, bombs are being imported, and the number of German agents has increased significantly,' he reported to Foreign Secretary Sir Edward Grey.[11] Marling put the number of Germans lurking about Tehran and elsewhere at 60 or so. There were about another 250 escaped Austrian prisoners of war, plus some 50 Turks and pro-German Indian nationalists, all of whom were engaged in suspicious activities. Together, these enemy agents had smuggled into Persia a formidable consignment of 80,000 rifles, seven or eight machine guns, bombs and other weapons, while at the same time lavishing money on disaffected elements in the press, the police and the Swedish gendarmerie. To the south, Wassmuss was doing his utmost to sabotage the British governor of Bushire and was having some success in recruiting armed tribesmen to the German cause. Griesinger, who was installed at Kerman, was operating as something of a common brigand, pulling off bank robberies, organising real as well as imaginary political assassinations of British officials – such as the tale of the British consul in Shiraz, who remained alive and well – and spreading rumours of an alleged violent dispute between the British and Russian ministers in Tehran.

It was only four months later, in February 1916, that Griesinger and Zugmayer departed Kerman, fired up with the intention of liberating Baluchistan from British rule. This operation revealed the farcical side of the German saboteurs and their common criminal activities. Six weeks after setting off with a small force of some 200 rifles, Griesinger's invasion plans ended in disaster: they discovered that the Baluch chieftains had little interest in being liberated and only wanted to make use of the Germans' firepower to settle scores with a few of their rival clans. 'It appears that we had been quite wrongly informed concerning Baluchistan. They must be the most incredible, impudent, most underhand, most mendacious and cowardly pack of cads, on a level with the beasts.'[12] So ended what can only be described as a ludicrous expedition to Baluchistan, Germany's one attempt during the war to invade British India.

The threat of Persia's entering the war on Germany's side was a matter of more serious concern. Marling in Tehran pleaded with London to put pressure on the Russians to reinforce their garrison at Kazvin, the largest city in north-central Persia, in order to shore up the country's defences against a German army incursion. Fears of a German–Persian alliance were running high, to the point that in late October 1915 US diplomatic sources in Berlin erroneously reported that Persia actually stood on the brink of declaring war. The British legation in Tehran heard from 'completely reliable sources' that Berlin was intending to send German officers to Persia, who would there take charge of three separate army groups. As for the desert tribes, Marling was told it would only require a small amount of imported cartridges to convince them to take up arms against the Russians, Persia's most hated enemy. Another 'thoroughly reliable source' reported that a special Persian–German convention was under negotiation in Tehran. Marling summed up his apprehensions in a telegram to the Foreign Secretary:

It is quite possible [...] that the Prime Minister of Persia may be forced by
the German party here to join the Germanic Alliance. If, on the other hand,
he should resist those influences, the Germans may use forcible means.
The only remedy is an immediate large reinforcement of the Russian garrison at Kazvin.[13]

Hentig still favoured diplomacy as the best way to advance Germany's interests in Afghanistan. It is instructive and not a little ironic that only weeks
after the mission's arrival in Kabul, Hentig was embracing a 'hearts and
minds' strategy, a tactic that nearly a century later had yet to be taken on
board by the combined military strategists of NATO. 'Our task there could
only be the foundation of a new and more efficient organisation of a state
laid out along modern lines.'[14] Hentig was convinced that putting an army
into Afghanistan, with the logistical and supply problems this would entail,
was entirely out of the question. 'It was a geographical impossibility to assist
the amir with troops. We had nothing to give and nothing to promise. Our
only policy was complete sincerity and the furthering of the interests of
Afghanistan.'[15] Hentig considered propaganda an integral part of this diplomatic offensive. One of the mission's members, Karl Ruhland, managed to
repair a small wireless receiver they had discovered lying abandoned in the
Kabul arsenal. He took it to the top of one of the hills outside the city, where
he was able to pick up bulletins broadcast from Peshawar and Delhi. News
items hostile to the Central Powers were supplemented with the German
version of events and published in Kabul's only newspaper.

The paper's founding editor, Mahmud Tarzi, was instrumental in spreading the doctrine of Islamic nationalism to Afghanistan's small but influential
reading public. Once war broke out in Europe, Tarzi began to come into conflict with the British. His anti-colonial and pan-Islamic articles were the cause
of considerable anxiety in India, to the extreme that Hardinge felt obliged
to bring it to Habibullah's attention: 'You may be sure that I have not the
slightest desire to interfere in any of the internal affairs of Afghanistan,' the
viceroy wrote, 'but I would suggest to Your Majesty, as a friend, the desirability
of taking steps, either to suppress this paper or to alter its present tone.'[16]

Habibullah gave his assurances that his son's father-in-law would henceforth refrain from publishing inflammatory articles that might endanger the peace of the frontier. But the appearance of the Hentig–Niedermayer mission in Kabul, bringing with it the hope of touching off an anti-British uprising, gave new impetus to Tarzi to renew his propaganda attack. Suffice it to say that Barakatullah was invited to do a stint as Tarzi's chief editorial assistant and that Pratap contributed signed articles to the paper in the months following the mission's arrival in Kabul. Hardinge found one of Pratap's articles to be so objectionable 'that we arranged for quiet interception of copies sent by post [to India] specially exempting those addressed to the amir's agents, so as to avoid publicity'.[17]

The mission held subsequent meetings with the amir in the weeks following the first formal encounter at Paghman. On each occasion, the Rolls-Royces would arrive at the gates of Bagh-e-Babur to take the foreigners to the amir's hilltop summer residence, and later in the year to the royal palace in Kabul. All the while, the Germans became increasingly frustrated by the tiresome and quite futile hours spent in Habibullah's company. The amir proved himself a skilled negotiator: before the next audience, which brought together all the leading figures of the mission, he arranged to receive separately and in private their chief representatives on three consecutive days. The first were Pratap and Barakatullah, then the Turkish envoy Kazim Bey, and finally Hentig and Niedermayer. It was a wily ploy, designed to drive a wedge between the mission's members, and one by which the amir made certain he remained the man in control.

The next meeting was an eight-hour affair at Paghman. The format of these encounters was always identical, starting with the usual elaborate preliminaries, seemingly designed to provoke Germanic exasperation. Niedermayer described these official audiences as 'increasingly difficult and nerve racking'. All they got from the amir was a sob story of how his hands were tied, morally and materially, to the all-powerful Raj. 'If the outlook cleared temporarily, heavy clouds soon gathered again, driven by a wind from Delhi or Simla.'[18] Habibullah regaled his guests with irrelevancies, about his health and daily life, not to overlook his sleeping habits, all this interspersed with servings of tea and sweetmeats. Hentig would wait for an appropriate moment to turn the conversation to the more pressing matters on the mission's agenda. Once again, was the amir prepared to switch allegiances and partake in the certain victory of Germany and her allies in the Great War? Would Habibullah, as ruler of the world's only independent Muslim country, apart from Turkey, join forces with the caliph and allow a Turkish army to cross Afghanistan?

Habibullah was given regular updates on the progress of the fighting in France and the Middle East. He was aware that the Gallipoli campaign was going very badly for the British and that the Entente had experienced other setbacks, such as when a British expedition to Baghdad was stopped, and of course the defeat at Kut-al-Amara. An Allied victory was by no means a foregone conclusion, judging by the first two years of war. But 1916 augured much better:

> The Russians had overcome their munitions crisis and the British were producing a land army. They were also financing the imports which were so vital for the Allied war effort. Chief of the German General Staff Erich von Falkenhayn could tell that time was not on Germany's side.[19]

For that matter, so could Habibullah: this was not a wise time to be laying odds on a German victory.

Gradually and with supreme astuteness, the amir disclosed his terms for agreeing to break ties with British India, demands which he must have known the Germans were unwilling and unable to meet. Afghanistan, he protested, was a poor country, lacking the military strength required to launch a serious attack on its neighbour. How could he enter the war without a supply of modern weapons and enough money to replace Lord Hardinge's handsome annual subsidy, which, by the way, the viceroy had just increased by 2 lakh rupees? The amir was able to produce a letter in which Hardinge said he was releasing the money 'as a token of appreciation of your [the amir's] attitude and in order to enable you to convince those of your advisers and people who question the wisdom of your present neutrality'.[20]

After the meeting, Niedermayer sent a message to Berlin explaining the amir's intransigence, a posture, he argued, which could only be overcome with a show of force. If Habibullah was to be won over, a thousand or so Turkish troops armed with automatic weapons would have to be amassed on the border, ready to march shoulder to shoulder with their Afghan brothers into India. Niedermayer also believed that news of a large body of Muslim soldiers coming to fight in the name of the caliph would touch off a rebellion in the Indian army, in which Muslims made up a third of the ranks. But Enver Pasha, Turkey's wartime leader, could not spare so large a number of troops for what amounted to a propaganda exercise, nor was there any hope of penetrating the Persian corridor that was kept under close surveillance by British and Russian army patrols.

The mission's hopes of securing Habibullah's allegiance were all but dashed in November 1915, when British intelligence intercepted a letter sent by the seasoned Persia hand Walter Röhr to Prince Heinrich Reuss, Germany's ambassador to Tehran. Reuss, a scion of the German nobility, took up his post in May 1915 and actively connived with Wassmuss to undermine British power in south Persia, with the aid of a spectacular £100,000 grant from Berlin to spread among the tribal chieftains. Röhr emphatically stated that the amir must be made to understand he was not without friends in the Muslim world, allies who stood prepared to fight alongside the Afghans. But, he added fatefully, if Habibullah remained adamant in his loyalty to the Raj, 'perhaps we shall find it necessary to begin by organising a coup d'état'.[21] In this, the Germans knew they had a willing accomplice in Nasrullah, who would have liked nothing better than to see the amir dethroned. Habibullah's brother, with the complicity with the pro-Turkish elements in the Afghan court, forged Habibullah's signature on a letter that was read out before the frontier Pashtuns, in which the amir allegedly asked the mullahs to prepare for jihad in the spring of 1916. This was supported by stories of German plans to send armies into Egypt, Persia and, eventually, Afghanistan.

The bogus letter was sent in the company of another from Niedermayer, in which he explained to the German minister in Tehran that the initial meeting with the amir had given little hope and that only a strong show of force by the Turks would swing him in the Germans' favour. Both letters were picked up by the British delegation at Meshed. Needless to say, Hardinge was delighted to be able to pass this priceless piece of propaganda on to Habibullah.

> I promptly wrote to the amir giving him full information of the contents of the intercepted letters and, as I knew him to be a man who would not run any personal risks, I expect he gave the Germans in Kabul a poor time in consequence.[22]

A further embarrassment lay in store for the Germans. Hentig sent a coded report updating Reuss in Tehran on recent events in Kabul, using as his courier a Persian whom he believed he could trust. The man was secretly in the pay of the Russians and so headed straight to their legation in Meshed. The letter was relayed to Petrograd, where it was decoded and passed on to the War Office in London and to Hardinge in Delhi. The document revealed the interesting fact that Hentig, the frustrated diplomatist, was beginning to appreciate the merits of the mission's sabre-rattlers. Hentig repeated the need for 1,000 or so Turkish troops, which might be enough to propel Afghanistan into the war. 'Then he added two elliptical sentences which caused the British authorities some consternation: "Perhaps internal revulsion of feeling is necessary here first. We are determined to go to any lengths." '[23]

Hardinge could scarcely believe this second stroke of luck. He lost no time in alerting Habibullah to the sinister intentions of the Germans in his midst. Hentig's letter quite obviously confirmed the existence of a secret plot to oust the amir, he told Habibullah. But *determined to go to any lengths* – that could only mean one thing: if necessary, the Germans would not hesitate to have the amir assassinated. Hardinge reassured his friend that he considered violence unlikely. 'At the same time, I think it right that you should know what manner of men are your present guests in Kabul.'[24]

The former US intelligence adviser Thomas L. Hughes had a meeting with Hentig in 1982, two years before the German diplomat's death. Hentig acknowledged that the British ploy was unknown to the mission at the time. Habibullah, however, was very much aware of the danger to his life and this uncomfortable thought kept him on his toes. In another meeting with Habibullah, Hentig recalled:

> Among the latest German technological marvels which we brought with us to impress the amir were pocket alarm clocks. One day while the amir and I were negotiating my alarm clock suddenly rang. He turned deathly pale, his jaw dropped as though paralysed, and he waited for the bomb to explode. I think he would have signed anything that moment, and in spite of my showing him how the alarm clock worked, it was one of our shorter sessions.[25]

The year 1915 was coming to an end, and with it came the approach of the Christmas season. After nearly three months in Kabul, the Germans found themselves no closer to achieving the mission's objective. To make matters worse, in spite of scouring the countryside around Kabul, the Germans and Austrians failed to find anything resembling a Christmas tree. They eventually settled on a green cut-out paper model, around which they gathered to sing carols. Habibullah tried to impart a festive air among the Germans by presenting them with a gift of some cognac that had been left behind more than 20 years previously by Sir Henry Mortimer Durand, who had led the delegation to the court of Abdur Rahman in 1893 to negotiate the border demarcation treaty. The Germans' stock of whisky had run dry in the early days of tedium while waiting to be summoned to the amir's presence. At that time some of the men had put their rudimentary distilling skills to use to produce an almost lethal alcoholic brew, with unhappy results. Two of the Austrians were found comatose in the street, to the horror of the Afghans who had never before witnessed the effects of extreme drunkenness.

In his meanderings about the city, Hentig had discovered a few other Europeans who had taken up residence in Kabul, apart from the Austrian prisoners of war. One of these, a German woman in her sixties, went by the Muslim name of Bibi Hanum, after the celebrated mosque in Samarkand.

She had arrived in Kabul in 1890s as maidservant to the wife of Gottlieb Fleischer, chief engineer of the Krupp arms manufacturer and the first German known to reside in Kabul. Fleischer himself had played an ambiguous role in Afghanistan and was assassinated in mysterious circumstances in 1904. Bibi Hanum stayed on and fell in love with an Afghan, and she converted to Islam in order to marry. She and Hentig would exchange German books and periodicals, and a few days before Christmas she handed him a 15-year-old copy of the Berlin weekly *Die Woche*, in which he was astonished to discover a portrait of his father. Pangs of homesickness, coupled with a sense of hopelessness, began to turn Hentig's thoughts to calling it a day on the Kabul mission, an option that began to come up in evening conversation at the Bagh-e-Babur.

December also brought new developments from the Indian nationalist camp. Mahendra Pratap, with his customary penchant for theatrics, invited the Turkish and German members of the mission to join him in his room on the night of 1 December to celebrate his 29th birthday. About ten people gathered in the chamber to listen to Pratap solemnly declare:

> Now, friends, we must tell you why we have given you all this trouble. We are going to establish this night the first Provisional Government of India. I am to take the oath of office as President and our honourable friend Moulana Barakatullah will be sworn in as Prime Minister.[26]

A third revolutionary, Maulavi Obeidullah, was appointed Minister for Home and Foreign Affairs. Obeidullah had arrived in Kabul in October 1915 with a handful of followers and had attached himself to the Pratap–Barakatullah faction of the mission. Born a Sikh, Obeidullah converted to Islam at an early age and became an ardent believer in the coming holy war to put an end to British power in India. It was not explained on whose authority and by what means this self-appointed government that was to rule 250 million people was to be established. These were mere minutiae for Pratap, who with growing fervour saw himself as a world revolutionary leader. The Indians presented their new government to Habibullah, along with a promise to appoint him king of India if Afghanistan joined the war against Britain. The amir declined their kind offer and wished them good luck. The Germans must have felt like guests at the Mad Hatter's tea party. Nonetheless, Niedermayer and Kazim Beg uttered a few words of congratulations, and then retired for the night. 'The influence of this government-in-exile was confined to the small group of exiles in Kabul and had no resources, as in the course of the journey through Persia all Pratap's luggage had been lost.'[27] In addition, on the desert crossing Hentig had been forced to leave behind almost all the letters of solidarity Hollweg had written to the rulers of India's princely states. The creation of this whimsical revolutionary government called into question Pratap's grasp of reality, if not his sanity. Lord Chelmsford, who succeeded Hardinge as viceroy, described Pratap as 'if not actually insane, very eccentric'.[28] General Sir Michael O'Dwyer saw him as an outright fool and a potentially dangerous agitator, 'evil minded but fatuous'.[29] One could take it a step farther and argue that Pratap was also capable of becoming a menace to his fellow revolutionaries, on one occasion with tragic consequences. The case in point was Pratap's dispatch of two colleagues with a letter of friendship for the Russian government, from himself as the President of the Provisional Government of India. The letter was sent when he came to realise the Germans were not going to achieve their objective of pushing Afghanistan into a war with Britain. Pratap thought he could seek support from Petrograd for his revolutionary cause, at a time of Russian military disasters and with the tsar's armies in a state of mutiny, with only a little more than a year to go before Nicholas II was toppled in the February Revolution. The two envoys never made it beyond Turkestan, where they were arrested and handed over to the British authorities, which had one of them hanged.

The mission's 'make or break' moment came in the final days of 1915. A glimmer of hope had suddenly made its appearance: Habibullah signalled to the Germans that after much deliberation and consultation with his advisers, he was now prepared to put a firm proposal on the table. What the amir had in mind fell well short of a declaration of war, despite rumours to that effect which had been circulating for weeks in Kabul. These stories were reported to Hardinge by his agent in Afghanistan and, it must be noted, they succeeded in setting the viceroy's nerves on edge. Once more, Hardinge dispatched a letter to Kabul reminding Habibullah of his commitment to neutrality. His latest missive brought the same semi-reassuring response: 'Don't mind what I say [...] but watch what I do.'[30]

Hentig was summoned to the palace one morning and asked point-blank if he was empowered to negotiate a treaty of trade and friendship. Could this be the long-awaited breakthrough? Hentig wondered. The news that Hentig brought back to the Bagh-e-Babur excited Niedermayer, who hoped this might be the first step towards a proclamation of jihad. Hentig eagerly replied in the affirmative, with the caveat that any treaty would have to be ratified by Berlin. The amir's offer came just in time to avoid a meltdown in German–Afghan relations. Niedermayer was fed up with Habibullah's dilatory tactics and on a number of occasions he threatened to withdraw the military component of the mission and return to Germany. Only the amir's entreaties of patience dissuaded him from pulling out. A sudden departure of the Germans would have cast Habibullah in a bad light, for it was important for him to placate Nasrullah and the other hawks in his entourage. This was quite the wrong moment for the amir to fall out of favour with the Germans and the Central Powers, certainly not when the British were taking an ignominious hammering from Turkish forces at Kut-al-Amara. It looked like Germany and her allies stood a reasonable chance of winning this war after all – and then what? It was inconceivable for a defeated Britain to retain control of her Indian empire, and that would mark the collapse of Habibullah's only ally, not to overlook the loss of handsome subsidies from Delhi. Given such a scenario, how long would it be before the dreaded coup implicit in Röhr's intercepted letter became a reality? Habibullah was palpably acting under pressure from Nasrullah, Amanullah and the latter's father-in-law, the newspaper editor Tarzi. Together, they made up Kabul's pro-German triumvirate, and the amir had good reason to fear these men.

Nasrullah had in fact confided to Hentig and Niedermayer that a treaty favouring Afghan national interests would be a strong incentive for join-ing the war on the side of the Central Powers. Whatever the risks involved, Habibullah was not to be rushed into concluding a pact with Britain's enemies, not while Hardinge occupied the seat of power in Delhi. The amir played for time, insisting that a bilateral treaty, especially one drawn up in wartime, was not something to be dashed off in a matter of days.

Hentig again showed himself to be ahead of his time in devising the most effective strategy for winning Afghan sympathies, a line of thought that was nothing short of anathema to Niedermayer. The idea was to avoid dragging Afghanistan into a possibly disastrous war. It was in both countries' interest to make Afghanistan a stable and independent nation. 'It was a geographical impossibility to assist the amir with troops. Our only policy must be complete sincerity and the furthering of Afghanistan's interests.'[31]

Habibullah was a wise enough ruler to know that the safest course of action was to keep all his options open. Whichever way the pendulum might swing on the battlefields of Europe and the Middle East, the amir's overriding concern was for his personal survival. He instructed his representative in India to liquidate his assets into cash and make it instantly available, should the need arise for a hasty retreat from Kabul. This and other signs of wavering on the amir's part were a matter of deepening concern to Delhi. In a rather inept ploy by British intelligence, a letter was brought to Kabul by a messenger claiming to be a German envoy. He was in reality a British spy. The letter attempted to convince Niedermayer and Hentig that they were wasting their time by concluding a treaty with the Afghans. The crudely worded German text spoke of Turkish army reverses in the Caucasus and urged the mission to depart Kabul immediately and return via Persia while this escape route was still open. It did not require an in-depth analysis for them to realise that the telegram was a ruse. The author had made obvious use of a dictionary to translate his message into German, with the result that the fraud was easily detected. His fatal mistake was to use the British spelling of 'amir' instead of the German 'emir'. This was disclosed to Habibullah, who had the messenger hanged on the spot.

The arrival of the new year saw the final drafting of a treaty, a document as unrealistic as it was unenforceable. On 24 January 1916, Habibullah and the mission's two German leaders signed a protocol consisting of ten articles, prefaced by the customary declaration of enduring friendship between Germany and Afghanistan. So far, so good, since the first part spoke of nothing more radical than Afghanistan's independence and the establishment of diplomatic relations with her neighbours. However, this diplomatic nicety failed to take into account one crucial factor: Afghanistan's foreign policy had been in British hands since the signing of the Treaty of Gandamak in 1879. If Habibullah broke with this agreement Britain might well consider it cause to march on Afghanistan to prevent the country falling into enemy hands. Most remarkable of all was Article Three, which contained a promise of elaborate German military aid. The co-signatories, Hentig and Niedermayer, of whom the former was to be accredited as the embassy secretary of the German Empire, pledged to supply the amir with 100,000 modern rifles (at its 1916 strength, this worked out to two rifles for every man in the Afghan army), 300 guns of different calibre, munitions and other war material, along with a personal gift to the amir of £10 million in gold bullion. If Afghanistan joined the war, the German government vowed to restore territories in India which Afghanistan had lost as a result of foreign – that is, British – conquest. No mention was made of whether this referred to the North-West Frontier tribal belt, the coveted city of Peshawar, or the vast lands beyond the Indus River stretching almost to Delhi, which in the eighteenth century were under Afghan dominion. The amir signed the treaty as 'The Lamp of the Nation and the Religion', while Niedermayer and Hentig pledged to recommend the treaty to the German government.

Habibullah was not to be taken in by the Germans' extravagant promises. For the time being, it made sense for him to placate his visitors, for in so doing he kept the wolves from the door, in the form of the pro-German faction led by his brother Nasrullah. In reality, the amir reasoned, Hentig and Niedermayer were but two low-ranking representatives of a country 3,000 miles away, while little more than a day's journey east of Kabul lay a vast and powerful empire which also extended the hand of friendship, and more. It was not surprising that even before the ink had dried on the treaty, on the evening of 24 January, Habibullah sent for Hafiz Saifullah Khan, the British agent at Kabul. When Saifullah arrived at the Kasr-i-Dilgusha palace the following day, he was ushered into a chamber by the amir's adviser, Ishaq Aqasi Mulki, who locked the door behind them. Habibullah informed Saifullah that he intended to hold another durbar on 29 January, at which he would reiterate his neutrality. The idea was to impress on the mullahs and village elders that firstly he was unperturbed by recent political upheavals in Persia, and likewise to make clear that 'the arrival and varying instigations of the Germans, Austrians and Turks [...] have not affected his sincerity and friendly attitude towards the British Government'.[32] The amir impressed on the British agent that he had no particular sympathy for Germany, Austria or any other power, but that his only source of anxiety was Turkey, which in his view had made a grievous mistake by entering the war against Britain and her allies. What caused him 'sleeplessness at night' was Turkey's

> great religious attraction in the common mind of the ignorant Muslims of the world in general, and of the rudest Afghan in particular, whose uncultured mind is easily capable of being deceived by the agitating German ministry at work everywhere, in secret and open.[33]

Habibullah offered the British representative a cigarette, and then, for a man who had never ventured farther beyond his borders than neighbouring India, he began to unfold a rather remarkable knowledge of the European political background that brought on the war. Among other things, he laid the blame for Turkey's hostility towards Britain on William Gladstone, the former prime minister, who as early as 1896 had openly condemned Turkish atrocities against the Armenians.[34] It was, the amir said, because Gladstone had failed to emulate the tradition of goodwill and friendship 'so well and wisely founded once by the golden policy of Lord Beaconsfield [Benjamin Disraeli] that Bismarck had succeeded in bringing Germany into friendly relations with Turkey'.[35]

The government of India welcomed Habibullah's protestations of enduring friendship and neutrality, but at the same time it was evident that the amir had been placed under great pressure to formulate the treaty. The uneasy balance of forces on the North-West Frontier was still threatened by Turkey's alliance with the Central Powers. Britain's war with Turkey also furnished influential leaders in the tribal areas with an opportunity to incite the local population to jihad. 'Hopes of a great Islamic renaissance were at once aroused. The anti-British elements hoped that Persia would join the war on the side of Turkey and that the amir, notwithstanding his present neutrality, would ultimately join Persia.'[36] There had been a fresh outbreak of clashes with the Mohmands, one of the most hostile of the tribes, which the army put down with customary brutality, usually involving the 'butcher and bolt' type of tactics. Tribesmen of the Swat district had also gone on the rampage. Roos-Keppel put this outbreak of violence down to 'sinister Afghan influences', suggesting that Nasrullah and his henchmen had seen the treaty as a signal to open hostilities with India. The Mohmand tribal leader who came to offer his submission to Roos-Keppel said his people would not launch any more attacks on their own account, but

> they can give no assurances that they will not join in a general attack if one is ordered from Kabul in the spring. A belief is growing [...] that the amir's resistance to his war party is weakening and that by the spring [1916] he will give in and give the word for a general jihad.[37]

Kabul and the frontier were awash with rumours that the call to jihad would come in April. That was when the Ghilzais, a confederation of nomadic Pashtuns who made up more than 20 per cent of the country's population, would be returning to Afghanistan. 'All believe that something big is going to happen in the late spring or early summer,' Roos-Keppel warned Hardinge, citing Britain's military setbacks in the Middle East as an incentive to attack India. 'Our repeated failures are shaking the confidence even of our friends in our ultimate success.'[38] Another alarming story was doing the rounds of the bazaars: Habibullah, it was said, was about to allow Turkish and German troops to occupy western Afghanistan, the same way in which the British forces had occupied Salonika in October 1915.[39]

Hentig and Niedermayer returned to the Bagh-e-Babur, taking daily rides on horseback around the Kabul valley, while contemplating what tactic to adopt if Habibullah failed to take military action. The amir's strategy was to play for time, and this he achieved with supreme cunning. His main task was to ensure Hardinge of his friendship, which meant he must display no signs of wavering from his avowed neutrality. As for the Germans and their draft treaty, Habibullah rightly pointed out that it could not be put into effect until it had been signed by the kaiser. The Central Powers and the Triple Entente had been at war for nearly a year and a half, the amir reflected. The coming months would most surely determine the outcome, and if Britain and her allies were the victors, Afghanistan had nothing to gain and everything to lose by siding now with Germany. 'Habibullah's judicious manoeuvring continued all spring. He kept everyone guessing. He did not want to find himself on the losing side.'[40] The Germans, not content to remain idle, turned up the heat on the amir. Niedermayer had a letter sent, with the amir's forged signature, to the frontier tribal leaders, urging them to prepare for jihad. News of this mysterious letter reached Delhi as well as Kabul. An angry and worried Habibullah could guess where the letter had originated and he totally approved of Hardinge's response. This was to gather several thousand tribal elders and maliks at Peshawar, where they were suitably awed by a display of air power, and then given the glad tidings that their loyalty was to be rewarded with increased subsidies.

Niedermayer was still hopeful that with proper inducements the amir could be persuaded to launch an attack on India. He said as much in his communications with the military authorities in Berlin. The amir would not make a move on the basis of promises alone: guns were immediately required, along with £1 million (sterling) in initial funding. Niedermayer informed the German Foreign Ministry of undertakings he had allegedly received from the amir, to the effect that 'war begins at once as soon as 20,000 to 100,000 German or Turkish soldiers arrive in Afghanistan'.[41] These foreign troops were to protect Afghanistan's rear against Russian intervention, while the amir's army and the frontier tribesmen would open hostilities against India. There is no written evidence to support Niedermayer's claims, which were founded largely on widespread rumours of a call to jihad that would be issued in the spring. He passed this information on to his military superiors, citing April as the most favourable month for action.

A secret report dated 23 March 1915, relayed by a British agent from Petrograd to Delhi, added a touch of heightened drama to the situation. According to Russian sources, Habibullah intended shortly to issue a *firman* containing a declaration of war. The telegram makes mention of Nasrullah, who would send the *firman* to Afghanistan's major cities, from Kabul to Herat via Kandahar. The message stated: 'Chiefs of tribes on Indian frontier ordered to look to their arms because war against English will be declared in March.'[42] A note scribbled in the margin by an officer of the War Office in London says that according to a statement picked up from the governor general of the oasis city of Ashgabat, now the capital of Turkmenistan, jihad had already been declared on 15 March. The handwritten memo adds with scepticism: 'with no confirmatory evidence from India, we do not at present place reliance on these reports, which have so far emanated from Russian sources – and possibly inspired by Germans.'[43]

It had not been a particularly severe winter. Snow had fallen in Kabul only in the middle of January, and by mid-March the temperature had risen quickly, coaxing out the first pink and white blossoms on the fruit trees of the Bagh-e-Babur gardens. The whole of the Kabul valley around glowed with a greenish-yellow tint, against the gleaming white backdrop of the mountains behind Paghman, where a dusting of snow still lingered. During the night, the Kabul River became a raging torrent that flooded the surrounding countryside. Perhaps unconsciously, this sudden change in weather instilled uneasiness in Hentig and Niedermayer. They came to realise that the time for decisions might be at hand, while the roads were still passable or, what was of greater concern, before their route out of Afghanistan was blocked by enemy forces. The Russians were closing in on Tehran and advancing in the direction of Isfahan and Kermanshah, cutting off communication with their agents in Persia. Fritz Seiler, one of the mission's members who had remained behind in Persia with Griesinger and Zugmayer, reported having spotted British patrols around Neybandan

1. Werner Otto von Hentig, whose diplomatic efforts to bring Afghanistan into the war on the German side ended in failure. Hentig nonetheless showed himself to be decades ahead of his time in understanding the need for a 'hearts and minds' approach to winning Afghan friendship.

2. Oskar Ritter von Niedermayer, one of the leaders of the mission to Kabul, in 1917 as an officer in the Great War. Niedermayer later served in the Wehrmacht during the Second World War, commanding a division of Muslim troops.

3. Habibullah Khan was amir of Afghanistan during the First World War. His neutralist policy was instrumental in enabling British India to release Indian Army troops to fight in Europe and the Middle East.

4. Nasrullah Khan, Habibullah's younger brother, was one of the key leaders of the anti-British faction in Kabul. His efforts to stir up rebellion against British India met with no success and he ended his life in prison after attempting to usurp power from his nephew, King Amanullah, in 1919.

5. Kaiser Wilhelm II supported the mission to Kabul in the mistaken belief that the Afghans could be persuaded to launch an invasion of India. The Germans put about a fanciful rumour that he had converted to Islam, hoping to rally the Muslim world to enter the war on the side of the Central Powers.

6. Mahendra Pratap, a visionary Indian revolutionary, accompanied the Germans to Kabul but never played a significant role in the negotiations with the amir, although he considered himself the mission's leader. His impact on the Indian nationalist movement was minimal, before and after the war.

7. Enver Pasha was Turkey's war minister and the architect
of the Ottoman–German alliance. He personally supported
Niedermayer as leader of the military side of the mission, although
he envisaged it as a Turkish-led enterprise. The Germans opposed
this idea and Pasha withdrew Turkish military support.

8. Oskar Ritter von Niedermayer in his Wehrmacht uniform
during the Second World War. Niedermayer detested Hitler,
whom he considered a vulgarian and a demagogue, and on several
occasions he found himself in hot water with the Gestapo.

9. Wilhelm Wassmuss was known as the 'German Lawrence'. He was the epitome of the romantic desert adventurer, who spent the war stirring up the tribes of Persia to rebel against the British.

10. Frederick John Napier Thesiger, Lord Chelmsford, who succeeded Charles Hardinge as viceroy in 1916, was determined to keep Habibullah in the neutral camp and spared no effort, in stern warnings as well as lavish subsidies, to achieve his objective.

11. Charles Hardinge, Lord Hardinge of Penshurst, had a major influence on India. As viceroy he presided over the 1911 durbar to celebrate King George V's accession, the reunification of the two parts of Bengal that had been partitioned in Curzon's time, the transfer of the capital from Calcutta to Delhi, and India's involvement in the crucial first two years of the Great War.

12. King Amanullah inherited the throne after the assassination of his father Habibullah. He sought to ingratiate himself with the religious and military hardliners and launched an invasion of India in 1919, which became the Third Anglo-Afghan War.

13. Horse-drawn wagons in the flatlands of Mesopotamia in June 1915, en route to Afghanistan. The mission travelled by every conceivable means of transport, from rail to riverboats and camels, as well as on foot.

14. The mission's leading figures pose for a group photo. Seated from left to right are the Turkish representative Kazim Bey, Werner Otto von Hentig, the Indian revolutionary Mahendra Pratap, Oskar Ritter von Niedermayer and the radical Indian Muslim Maulavi Barakatullah. Standing from left to right are three of the mission's German members, Walter Röhr, Kurt Wagner and Günter Voigt.

15. Amir Habibullah Khan presiding over a jirga, or 'council', of Afghan notables. These assemblies were convened to hear royal pronouncements and to debate matters of state.

16. *Niedermayer adopted a convincing disguise on his return journey to Berlin, with great attention to detail, to the point of removing a gold crown he had had fitted to a tooth in Germany.*

17. The expedition to Isfahan, where Hentig and Niedermayer joined forces for the march to Kabul.

18. The Emperor Babur's 500-year-old burial garden, the Bagh-e-Babur,
stands on a 27-acre site near the Kabul River. It was in this splendid palace
that the mission was quartered during their stay in Kabul.

19. The imposing Bala Hissar hilltop citadel was once the residence of Afghan rulers. There is little left today to evoke its former grandeur.

20. A caravanserai was a rest stop, generally a walled enclosure serving as a guest house for travellers on commercial routes from south-eastern Europe to Asia.

21. The Kabul bazaar was one of the largest in Central Asia until it was destroyed by the British in the First Anglo-Afghan War in 1842. Today it has once again become a thriving hub for shoppers.

22. The Khawak Pass, a 12,625-foot gap between soaring mountain peaks in Afghanistan, was the invasion route followed by Alexander and Tamerlane and crossed by the mission on the homeward-bound journey.

23. Part of the Turco-German caravan crossing the Persian
desert near the historic south-eastern city of Kerman.

district, well north of their southern corridor limits and uncomfortably close to the Afghan border.

While Niedermayer and Hentig, on the one side, and Habibullah, on the other, pondered their next moves, the arrival of a new viceroy brought a change of players to this version of the Great Game between Germany, Afghanistan and British India. Lord Hardinge had not had an easy four years in office. The start of his viceroyalty came close to ending in tragedy in 1912, while he and his wife were making their state entry into Delhi on an elephant. A bomb was thrown at them by an Indian fanatic and this resulted in the newly appointed viceroy spending his first weeks in India laid up in hospital. In July 1914 his wife died after undergoing surgery, and a few months later his son was killed on the Western Front. In the Mesopotamian campaign Hardinge was responsible for the transport and maintenance of troops in the Persian Gulf. The abysmally poor care of the sick and wounded in that campaign became the subject of a parliamentary enquiry. Although responsibility technically fell to Hardinge, the viceroy was exonerated from blame, which was laid more directly on the Indian military authorities. As a gesture of the government's confidence in Hardinge, in the summer of 1915 Prime Minister Herbert Asquith requested him to stay on in India another six months. Hardinge returned to London in December 1915 to take up his former post as permanent under-secretary at the Foreign Office, and at the conclusion of the war he arranged for the peace conference at Versailles.

Hardinge's successor was Frederic John Napier Thesiger, Viscount Chelmsford, a quiet and retiring intellectual. Chelmsford was a classical scholar, a product of Eton and Magdalen College, Oxford. He had gained his Indian experience before being appointed viceroy, having served as a Territorial captain nearly at the age of 50. It was somewhat ironic that Hardinge had designated the man who was to be his successor to take a mission of enquiry to the Persian Gulf, and there to report on the scandalous medical mismanagement of British casualties. Chelmsford's appointment was officially announced in early March 1916, while he was on this assignment. He had in fact the letter of confirmation from the Secretary of State for India in his pocket, when his colonel told him he ought to be doing something better than commanding a company.

Lord Chelmsford had too much on his plate in India to allow himself to be distracted by German machinations in Afghanistan. The new viceroy was obliged to deal with 'the anarchical and revolutionary movement in Bengal, whose Muslim majority, it must not be forgotten, came directly under the influence of anti-British propaganda spread by their co-religionists across the border'.[44] Managing the Indian nationalist movement was becoming a massive political headache, mostly due to a lack of agreement among the three parties involved – the government of India, the India Office in London and the government of Bengal – on the measures required to tackle the crisis. But Afghanistan could not be set to one side while the government of India concentrated on its internal troubles.

Chelmsford was an untested commodity in Kabul, where a nervous amir was anxious to reassure him of his loyalty to British India. In early September 1916, Habibullah once again received the British agent Hafiz Saifullah Khan, alone and behind locked doors, where he hastened to make clear:

> You know that the German Mission visited this country and tried their best to persuade me to join their cause. But I declined and totally disapproved of their objects and aims, which seemed to me to be based not on reasonable grounds but on selfish and wicked motives.

Habibullah then gave Saifullah Khan his solemn oath that

> nothing has shaken the firm determination which I have held from the first to maintain neutrality and my friendship with the British Government to the last, at my cost, and I will continue to preserve this policy to the end.[45]

Chelmsford was pleased and more than a little relieved to have these reassurances, but he was not totally taken in by the amir's effusions of loyalty.

He knew full well that up to now Habibullah had been biding his time, waiting to see which way the winds of war would blow. From his hilltop summer residence at Simla he wrote to the amir saying that, provided relations between both powers remained unaltered, the government of India would make him a gift, at the end of the war, of the 44 lakh rupees that he had drawn in advance from his allowance to meet the expenses of maintaining neutrality. That was the carrot. The stick followed when Chelmsford cautioned Habibullah that the government was not prepared to allow the German visitors to make use of Afghanistan to hatch conspiracies against India. The viceroy 'would venture to impress on Your Majesty the desirability of issuing stringent orders to prevent Afghanistan becoming a base for intrigues of this kind'.[46]

Several months later, after these pledges of mutual friendship had been conveyed by runners back and forth along the 700 miles of hill country that separate Kabul from Simla, Hentig and Niedermayer, going their separate ways, were embarking on adventures that were to prove far more punishing than anything they had endured on the journey to Afghanistan. In May 1916, 18 months after Niedermayer and the first contingent had set out from Berlin, the failed German mission was rapidly and not unexpectedly falling to pieces.

5

To Berlin the Hard Way

Habibullah's apparent enthusiasm for the draft treaty should have raised hopes for the mission's success, yet the signs were that morale in the German camp was on the decline. Their spirits were brought low by news of reverses in the Middle East theatre of war, for Niedermayer and Hentig knew that only German and Turkish victories could prise the amir from British India's grasp. They waited in vain for news of Turkish victories to deliver to Habibullah. Meanwhile, in the Arabian Peninsula an alliance was being forged between the Entente powers and Grand Sharif Hussein, guardian of the holy city of Mecca, whose aim was to drive the Turks from Arab lands. This became the embryo of the Arab Revolt, the campaign in which legendary figures like T.E. Lawrence and Gertrude Bell played leading roles. In mid-February 1916, the Russians dealt the Ottomans a severe military blow as well as a loss of prestige when the tsar's imperial army captured the strategic city of Erzurum in eastern Turkey. The Ottoman Empire, which for the Germans in Kabul served as a key propaganda weapon, in less than two years' time would cease to exist, and the fatal cracks were beginning to show. In a word, there was no longer any hope of Turkish troops reaching Afghanistan. These military defeats also knocked Persia out of the picture as a staging ground for a Turkish advance on Afghanistan. 'General Colmar von der Goltz abandoned his plan to lead German-officered Persian volunteers against India and the German role in Persia itself rapidly declined.'[1] The idea of raising a Persian army was, in fact, a complete German failure.

Von der Goltz summarised the position in his notes for February: 'Anarchy in Persia, nothing to be done. Dust, cupidity and cowardice. Vast expenditure and no return.'[2]

One morning in early spring 1916, Niedermayer and Hentig, with a few other members of their party, were out on one of their daily rides in the Kabul countryside. Trotting along a road east of the city, Niedermayer spied in the distance what looked like a large caravan moving slowly in their direction. These were the Ghilzai nomads on their yearly post-winter return to the Afghan uplands from the steaming plains of the Indus Valley. For these people there existed no border, no Durand Line. They moved unhindered between both countries, and had been doing so since time immemorial. Niedermayer contemplated their approach with a pang of despondency, reflecting on the many months he and his companions had been living like virtual prisoners behind the walls of the Bagh-e-Babur palace, while these free souls roamed the vast spaces of Asia. The Ghilzais had been the first to convey news to India of the Germans in Kabul the previous year. Now they brought back reports of developments in British territory, where the military authorities had substantially reinforced the frontier defences to deter any attempt of an Afghan invasion.

By 1916 India was again strong in military resources, with the return of Indian army brigades from the Western Front and the Middle East. John Ewart, an officer with the Indian police in Peshawar, described India's preparedness in florid, albeit accurate prose:

> Masses of white tents convinced the boldest that we had more troops than we could house. The drone of aeroplanes in the sky and the hum of motor transport on the roads were an impressive novelty and, above all, the steadfastness of India's great benefactor in the war, Amir Habibullah, checkmated the efforts of those who would have made cat's paws of the tribes by tales of the coming again of one of the old-time invasions from the north and west.[3]

The Ghilzais pitched camp a few miles from Kabul and invited Niedermayer and the others to join them for tea inside their black felt tents. In the following days, the Germans returned several times to the nomads' camp, taking sweetmeats to their ragged children and relaxing in the company of these unassuming, free-spirited wanderers. 'Yet all the time, there was our longing for our own freedom, for intercourse with other people and for fresh action.'[4] Far from assuaging the Germans' sense of loneliness, contact with these independent tribesmen only sharpened their longing to escape their alien environment. In a word, they were homesick. Niedermayer took the view that it was not in his interest to remain in Kabul merely to spend his time training the amir's troops for a campaign that was increasingly unlikely to get off the ground. 'It was therefore imperative to ascertain whether the amir actually intended to take measures which, in our estimation, would inevitably lead to conflict with Great Britain.'[5] As the mission's military commander, Niedermayer reasoned that Delhi's awareness of their presence in Kabul might be an unsettling factor and force the British to reinforce the frontier garrison. But this in itself achieved precious little with regard to Germany's war aims in India.

To Niedermayer's mind, their only tangible success in all these months was to have forced the government of India to deploy reinforcements to the gates of India. It was shortly after the surrender of Kut-al-Amara to the Turks that the Germans learnt of fresh troops having been dispatched from the Punjab to guard the gates of India. This preventive action took the pressure off Germany and her allies in Mesopotamia. Now was the time to take their case to Habibullah in a last-ditch attempt to win over his allegiance to the Central Powers. The amir must take a decision on which side he stood and, if he resolutely spurned the Germans' petitions for him to abandon his neutrality, the mission would have no choice but to strike camp and head for home.

Habibullah knew why Niedermayer and Hentig had requested an urgent audience in early May. The amir had carefully prepared for this encounter, knowing it would probably be the last time he and his German guests were to meet face to face. Habibullah was also aware that Hentig and Niedermayer were just that – guests in his country, under the protection of the Pashtunwali code of honour.[6] By allowing the Germans to enter Afghanistan and granting them sanctuary in his country, and moreover by accommodating them and their entourage in regal style, Habibullah had put in jeopardy his long-standing friendship with the government of India. There was no need for contrition on the amir's part: he held the moral high ground and he intended to stand firm. Without the dispatch of Ottoman and German troops and weapons for his army, an invasion of India was out of the question. But it went beyond that. As far as Habibullah was concerned, this amounted to a classic win–win situation. If the Germans were that eager for him to attack India, he had nothing to lose by raising the stakes beyond what was stated in the draft treaty. When Niedermayer and Hentig came to see him, they would be confronted with a set of fresh demands. For one thing, with regard to payment, Habibullah wanted 4 million German marks a month for the duration of hostilities. Germany must also deploy 5,000 troops and provide weapons and training for 80,000 Afghan recruits. The amir's boldest gambit was to demand the annexation from India of the Punjab and especially the coveted province of Baluchistan, which would give his landlocked country an outlet to the Arabian Sea. If, as was more than likely, the Germans were unable to comply with these terms and departed for home, Habibullah would be regarded by Chelmsford as a trusted friend who valiantly refused to let himself be drawn into the enemy camp.

Habibullah knew that his neutrality had been the single most important factor that had enabled the government of India to free up Indian army troops for service in Europe and the Middle East. He conveyed this message, rather boastfully, in one of his regular meetings with the British envoy Hafiz Saifullah Khan:

It is I who has caused India to be swept away of its armies to be able to fight in France and in Egypt. Had it not been due to a trust laid on me by the Government of India, there would have never occurred such total army-sweeping [i.e. redeployment] and, hence, I deserve thanks from His Excellency the Viceroy Lord Chelmsford.[7]

Posturing aside, Habibullah was of course absolutely right in his assessment of Afghanistan's strategic role in the Great War. After this pronouncement, the amir took up a firing position, aiming an imaginary rifle like a soldier in combat, which caused Saifullah Khan 'to laugh uncontrollably'.[8]

The mission's two German leaders alighted from the Rolls-Royce at the palace gates with a sense of foreboding that this meeting was to be a mere formality, in all likelihood a farewell visit. Their thoughts were more on arranging a smooth and safe exit from Kabul than trying, yet again, to convince the amir to mobilise his army and the frontier tribesmen.

> But now that they [the Germans] had reached their final goal and the best of their achievements seemed, as to conflagrations, to go no farther than the scraping of matches, they looked back over the hundred wastes over which they had wretchedly crawled, they began to shoulder the huge burden of their failure. They had started from Germany with dismal pre-monitions, they had seen them fulfilled, and now they were left, almost without resources, with the problem of returning.[9]

Hentig and Niedermayer once more pleaded their case to Habibullah, urging him to give an answer as soon as possible; both of them embold-ened in their demands by the certainty that the mission had come to an end. When the amir continued to drag his feet, Hentig angrily came out with a request for permission to start off immediately on his own. To this Habibullah replied that if they chose to depart it could only be as a group, otherwise they would be obliged to remain in Kabul at the amir's pleasure. Niedermayer found Habibullah's tone decidedly icy, and this caused him some anxiety about their future movements in Afghanistan. The talks on that day and in the few subsequent meetings that followed were of a strained nature. 'It soon became evident to me that we should not be in a position to induce the nervous monarch, who did not clearly read the signs of the times, to assume an openly hostile attitude towards India.'[10] By mid-May 1916, Niedermayer and Hentig had definitely made up their minds, and the only questions remaining were how soon they could leave and the choice of the safest way home. And the sooner the better. Now that the tide in Persia had clearly turned in favour of the British and Russians, there was a growing danger of this route home being cut off. The decision to quit Afghanistan was communicated to Habibullah. As a gesture of their continuing friendship, Hentig bestowed on the amir the Order of the Red Eagle, an ancient decoration of the Kingdom of Prussia, albeit one notch below that of the Black Eagle. In return, with his penchant for dandyism Habibullah made Hentig a gift of a silver glove buttoner and a scarf pin with an Afghan ruby.

In what was to be the last interview with Habibullah, Niedermayer made a final desperate plea for Afghan intervention on the side of the Ottomans and in the name of the caliph and Islam. The anti-British clique in Kabul was celebrating the news of the Turkish victory at Kut-al-Amara on 29 April 1916. Did this signal event not kindle the flames of war in the amir's heart? 'Habibullah turned his eyes upon Niedermayer, inviting him to read an answer there, and indeed they were very large. Niedermayer then declared that the party would like to return to Persia.'[11] He told the amir his intention was to remain in Kabul a little while longer, while Hentig would depart with a group of Germans. Habibullah caught the scent of treachery, suspecting that Niedermayer might vanish into the shadows to conspire with Nasrullah, Amanullah and Tarzi to overthrow the amir and mobilise their forces for an attack on India. Habibullah replied that the mission was welcome to stay on, if they so wished, but he reiterated that if they chose to go it must be as one group. This remark was directed at the 'brains' of the mission, Niedermayer, Hentig and their closest associates, for many others did stay behind for a while, including the Indian radicals and most of the escaped Austrian prisoners of war. There was no accurate count of how many Austrians had sought refuge in Kabul, but their numbers were estimated at roughly 100, a great deal more Westerners than the city had ever previously had in its midst. However, the amir judged their presence innocuous compared with that of the Germans.

Nasrullah was one of those most unhappy at losing touch with the Germans, for in Hentig and particularly in Niedermayer he thought he had found valued allies to counteract his brother's pro-British persuasion. In last-minute meetings with the Germans, Nasrullah begged them to reconsider, but to no avail. His parting gesture was to hand Hentig a letter for the German chancellor, Theobald von Bethmann-Hollweg, in which he appealed to the Reichskanzler to commit his government to the terms of the January bilateral draft treaty. Hentig, as befitted his status, took the view that to save face and prevent future difficulties the diplomatic option was to leave at the earliest possible opportunity. The war's outcome was looking uncertain and, if Germany were to be defeated, he might find himself in a precarious situation in Kabul.

> I considered it better to leave while I was still highly honoured than to one day be pushed aside as being as useless as a squeezed lemon. The second part of my task was to go back to Germany, to inform the Foreign Office of the result of the Mission, and to serve my country elsewhere.[12]

Habibullah was keen that upon their return to Berlin, the Germans did not report the ruler of Afghanistan to be a British toady. He showered Hentig and Niedermayer with farewell gifts, while at the same time affirming his wish for the continued friendship of both countries, whatever the war's outcome. The amir promised to scotch the rumours that had already begun to spread, alleging that the mission had been instructed by him to pack up and leave Kabul. In a meeting one afternoon, he drew Niedermayer aside to one of the windows overlooking the city and pointed to the ruins of the once-magnificent hilltop Bala Hissar. The implication, which coincides with a widely held but erroneous belief, was that the citadel had been reduced to rubble by invading British forces over the years.[13] In spite of his assurances of friendship, mistrust of the British was embedded in Habibullah's DNA. In 1839 his grandfather, Amir Dost Mohammed, was humiliatingly deposed by a duplicitous governor general,[14] Lord Auckland, who had sent an army to Kabul to install the amir's deadly rival, Shah Shuja, on the throne. A little more than 50 years later, in 1893, Habibullah's father, Amir Abdur Rahman, was cajoled by Viceroy Lord Lansdowne's emissary, Sir Henry Mortimer Durand, into accepting what became known as the Durand Line, which demarcated an artificial and still-disputed border between Afghanistan and British India. As Habibullah explained to Niedermayer:

You consider me a friend of Great Britain. The people who left us this token of remembrance cannot be regarded as a friend by any Afghan. As to my action [i.e. his maintained neutrality], you must believe me that I was unable to do otherwise. It is possible that the verdict of History will be against me.[15]

Niedermayer later stated, wrongly, as history was to prove, that this was most likely to be the case. He then went to take his leave of Nasrullah. It was a cordial, albeit sad, occasion, for the Germans' leaving deprived the amir's hardline brother of his best hope of seeing his ambitions fulfilled. Nasrullah stressed that he was in total opposition to his brother's pro-British politics. He accompanied Niedermayer to the door of his palatial residence and bade him farewell, neither man suspecting how Nasrullah would years later be made to suffer in the web of Afghan political intrigue.

If the decision to throw in the towel had been an onerous choice for the Germans, even more difficult was working out the logistics of their voyage home. Niedermayer and Hentig were justifiably worried about the details of their journey being leaked to enemy agents lurking about the city. If word got out of their leave-taking, there would be no chance of such a large party eluding British and Russian military patrols lying in wait beyond Afghanistan's borders. The mission stood a much stronger chance of establishing contact with friendly troops and reaching home if they broke up into a number of groups, each crossing the Afghan frontier at different points. In the lead-up to their departure on 21 May 1916, Hentig and Niedermayer spent evenings at the Bagh-e-Babur palace formulating the different routes each would follow on the homeward journey. Niedermayer's adjutant, Günter Voigt, had no previous experience of overseas service. The most practical plan was to send him to a safe destination to await orders. He would take a few of the Indians with him and make for the fortress town of Ghazni and Kandahar to the south, then eastward to the Afridi tribe's homeland of Tirah in the mountainous border region. The South-West African veteran, Wilhelm Paschen, would cross the border west of Herat, not far from the spot where the mission had entered Afghanistan. From there he would be left to his own devices to make his way across Persia by whatever route he deemed feasible. That left

Niedermayer and Hentig. The two leaders and Hentig's personal companion, Walter Röhr, along with Kurt Wagner, another South-West African soldier, and Josef Janosch, one of the escaped Austro-Hungarian prisoners of war, decided that the least risk of detection lay in taking a northerly direction which led across the towering mountains of the Hindu Kush.

Habibullah provided the Germans and their men with an escort to guide them to the border. The troops were selected from those the amir believed he could trust to keep a confidence. There was no way to stop all of Kabul bearing witness to the foreigners' departure, but it was crucial to keep their route and destination a secret. Once across the Hindu Kush into Afghan Turkestan, the party would separate into smaller groups. Hentig and Röhr were to head north-east, crossing the Pamir range for what they correctly anticipated would turn into an epic round-the-globe trek. Wagner's route lay south-west from Mazar-i-Sharif, aiming to reach Herat and await the signal to move out across the Persian desert. Niedermayer's plan was to break away from his party once he had made it across the mountains and crossed the Russian–Persian frontier on his own. This way he could travel faster, with a lower risk of attracting enemy attention.

Despite the Germans' efforts to keep their plans under wraps, the enemy's whereabouts did not escape the vigilant eyes of Viscount Chelmsford's spies in Kabul. Less than a fortnight after the party rode out the gates of Kabul, the viceroy was able to cable the Secretary of State for India, Austen Chamberlain, giving him chapter and verse of the mission's movements: 'Confirmation has been received that German members of original Mission, with possibly three exceptions, were dismissed by the amir in presence of sardars ['noblemen'] Nasrullah and Inayatullah and left Kabul on 22nd May.'[16] The Indian army Afridi deserters and Austrian prisoners of war who had escaped confinement in Russian territory remained behind in Kabul. They were, in fact, detained at His Majesty Habibullah's pleasure, albeit with a certain amount of freedom to move about the city. The amir had no wish to have large groups of foreigners roaming the Afghan countryside, possibly stirring up trouble among the Pashtun tribes who awaited the call to jihad. The British espionage network had been able to gather detailed intelligence on the mission's whereabouts: Chelmsford was told of the two

Germans heading towards Mazar-i-Sharif and Kandahar, Wagner and Voigt respectively. The viceroy urged Chamberlain to pass on this information to the Russians, on the off chance that one of the groups might attempt to make for Russian Turkestan. The British military outposts in eastern Persia, at Meshed and Seistan, were alerted be on the lookout for Germans on the run.

Hentig and Niedermayer never displayed any view of racial superiority towards the Muslims or Indian Hindus who formed part of the mission – unlike Griesinger, who to the end ranted hysterically against every non-German he encountered on his travels in Persia.[17] Of the six Afridis who were recruited from Germany's Halmondlager prisoner-of-war camp for the mission, one of the tribesmen, Sayed Ahmed, was taken on as Hentig's cook. Over the months the two men struck up a close friendship and travelled together through the Pamir Mountains on the return journey. Ahmad was the only Pashtun of the group who was not a deserter from the British army but had been legitimately captured. Through the good offices of Swedish and British missionaries they encountered on the way, Hentig was able to negotiate Ahmad's safe passage back to his native Buner district within British territory. Hentig also awarded another of the Pashtun volunteers the Prussian Order of the Crown, while the rest were honourably released from service and remained behind in Kabul. Niedermayer's affinity with 'non-Aryans' was noted by the German General Staff, to the extent that in the next European war he was promoted to the rank of major-general in charge of the 162nd Turkmen Division, one of the Muslim units recruited into the Waffen-SS. It could be argued that while the mission failed in its primary objective of prodding Afghanistan into war, one of its most notable aspects was to have treated their hosts with respect. The two European leaders, Hentig and Niedermayer, never showed the slightest arrogance towards their Afghan hosts, quite a departure from the contempt shown by the British and Russians during the frenzied rivalry of the nineteenth century, when both imperial powers regarded Afghanistan as nothing other than a barrier between giant adversaries. The British Empire held a very strong magnetism for certain of its Indian subjects, one of whom was the author and diplomat Ikbal Ali

Shah, whose loyalty to Britain was sealed by his marriage to a Scotswoman. In his writings, Ali Shah expressed this very same view of Afghanistan as a political puppet. 'The amir's [Habibullah's] anxieties regarding the defence of his kingdom should be and, as a matter of fact, are shared by all those in the British Empire who realise the importance of maintaining Afghanistan as a buffer state.'[18] Even in the reign of Zahir Shah, the British had no qualms about affirming an imperial policy towards Afghanistan.

> The policy reaffirmed in [Cabinet policy] in 1928 is, briefly, that the pres-
> ervation of the independence and integrity of Afghanistan as a strategic
> buffer state between Russia and India is of so great importance to Indian
> and Imperial interests that any substantial Russian encroachment into
> northern Afghanistan must be treated as a *casus belli* in the last resort.[19]

The Germans' deference, on the other hand, was not lost on the Afghans and it paid them handsome dividends in future years, when Germany came to be held in the highest regard by Afghanistan's rulers and ordinary citizens alike.

In the early hours of Sunday, 21 May, the day the mission set off on its final Afghan adventure. Niedermayer recalls that he rode up the hill to Jakob's grave to pay his last respects. During the arduous months spent in Kabul, negotiating with the amir while trying to organise his army and the country's defences, Niedermayer had on many occasions almost expressed an envy of his former adjutant's state of peace. After a few moments of reflection he mounted his horse and rode off on a northerly course, chatting for a short while with several of the Austrian officers who rode alongside for a few miles, then returning to look after their men in Kabul. Once left on his own, Niedermayer spurred his horse to catch up with the main body. Ahead stood the Hindu Kush, its permanent snow gleaming white in the morning sun against the backdrop of a sparkling blue sky. Beyond the mountain passes lay dark perils such as the travellers could scarcely anticipate.

Mahendra Pratap was the most prominent of the mission's members to stay behind in Kabul. The bespectacled Indian revolutionary had taken this decision with the conviction that where the Germans had failed, his provisional government could succeed in rallying the Afghans and his Indian compatriots alike to rise up against the government of India. This was wholly in keeping with his starry-eyed vision of political realities, for by now it should have sunk in that Berlin's war aim was not to help the Indians to gain their independence. Leaving propaganda rhetoric to one side, the kaiser preferred to deal with Britain's 'jewel in the Crown' through his cousin King George V, rather than with a band of native insurrectionists, who could just as easily turn on Germany as they aspired to free themselves from British domination. By all means, the kaiser reasoned, let the Afghans force the British enemy to tie up divisions in India, thereby reducing the number of troops available for combat on the Western Front. If the Afghans could serve as a tool in this endeavour, by harassing the Indian army and stirring up trouble on the North-West Frontier, so much the better. As this fact of political life became more apparent to Pratap and his henchmen, relations between the Indians and the Germans began to cool in the months leading up to the mission's withdrawal. Pratap's pride was wounded, for much as he styled himself as the mission's head, it was clear to all that Hentig and Niedermayer had taken the lead in talks with the amir. There is, in fact, no evidence that Pratap or Barakatullah were ever consulted in the process of framing the Afghan–German draft treaty.

Mahendra Pratap spent close to another year as the amir's guest in Kabul. This suited the British, who could thus keep tabs on Pratap's whereabouts and seditionist activities. By March 1917, however, Habibullah had had enough of this troublemaker, with the thought in mind that his presence in Kabul was not conducive to harmonious Anglo-Afghan relations. For Pratap's part, all hopes had been dashed of using Afghanistan as a launch pad to free India from the British yoke. Pratap's version of his decision to leave Kabul was this: 'Becoming convinced that no decisive political step of advantage to India was to be expected from Amir Habibullah, I, too, at last decided to leave Kabul.'[20] The British, who were keeping Pratap under close surveillance through their agent in Kabul and other listening posts, saw things differently. The British consul-general in Kashgar, Sir George Macartney, sent this memo to his Russian counterpart, Prince Meshchersky: 'It may be presumed that the amir of Afghanistan intends to evict Mahendra Pratap.' Macartney reckoned the Indian fugitive, as he was shortly to become, had two possible escape routes. 'Once in Badakhshan [north-eastern Afghanistan] Mahendra would, I imagine, try to escape into Chinese territory, by going either across the Russian Pamirs [...] or via Afghan Wakhan.'[21]

The government of India had already put a 5,000-rupee bounty on Pratap's head, now described as 'an enemy agent of quiet and mournful manners'.[22] Pratap had, as suspected, followed the Wakhan Corridor escape route up the remote valleys of this finger of land that protrudes from north-eastern Afghanistan, pointing at China. Before quitting Kabul with a small party of Sikhs and an escort of 12 Afghan soldiers, Pratap sent a letter to the tsar, which was etched in English on a thin tablet of pure gold, requesting in all seriousness that Nicolas II break off ties with Britain and instead enter into an alliance with Afghanistan. After waiting a suitable time for a reply, which never came, Pratap set off on his journey to Europe, taking with him a message of friendship from Habibullah to the sultan of Turkey and the German emperor.

Pratap crossed the Pamir Mountains to find himself walking straight into the Russian Revolution, with British agents hot on his heels all the way to the border. The Foreign Office in London accurately surmised, in a coded telegram to Sir George Buchanan, Whitehall's representative in Petrograd, that 'the revolution in Russia may very possibly encourage him [Pratap] as a revolutionary to seek refuge there. It would be well to impress on the new Russian Government the great importance we attach to the capture of this man.'[23] Pratap was well aware that the British were determined to take him into custody, which is why from that time onwards he lived the life of an insurrectionist on the run. He made it safely to Petrograd in March 1918, just in time to partake in the first-anniversary celebrations of the Bolshevist coup and proclaim his call for Indian freedom to a stadium filled with 11,000 well-wishers. He met with Trotsky and invited him to join in the movement to rid India of its British masters. The Marxist leader, who at the time was preoccupied with organising the Red Army to fight the pro-tsarist forces, praised Pratap's anti-colonial struggle and put him on a train to Berlin, where he arrived on 28 March. Pratap gave Habibullah's letter to the kaiser, taking advantage of the meeting to propose raising an international socialist army to march on India. Wilhelm suggested he take his idea to the German General Staff, where he was given short shrift and departed the city in despair. He decided there was nothing more to do but take Habibullah's letter to the sultan of Turkey and retire to Budapest to immerse himself in spiritual life. He returned to Afghanistan in 1919, where the new amir, Amanullah, granted him Afghan citizenship.

As an itinerant preacher of revolution, Pratap spent the next few years wandering the globe, from Switzerland to China, Mongolia, Nepal and finally to Japan, where he sat out the Second World War, vowing, 'I will die travelling and will not return to India until she is free.'[24] But he went back on his word: in the run-up to independence the government of India reasoned that at this juncture, Mahendra Pratap's presence on Indian soil could do no harm and in fact might serve to diffuse some of the tensions between the government and the more radical pro-independence agitators. Pratap was given permission to return to his homeland and in August 1946 he docked at Madras, exactly one year before the partition. From that day until his death in 1979 at the age of 93, Pratap carried on working tirelessly as a political activist. Now that his country had achieved its freedom, his mantra became a campaign for social justice in post-colonial India.

The Ghadr movement ceased to pose a serious threat once the government of India had crushed the 1915 Christmas Day Plot and arrested the chief plotters. However, Maulavi Obeidullah remained in Kabul until the end of the 1919 Third Anglo-Afghan War, where he continued to conspire against the Raj. Obeidullah was an alumnus of the Deoband Theological School in India, a hotbed of Muslim militant teachings with heavy overtones of the fanatical Wahhabi sect of Saudi Arabia. While Pratap was diligently working in Russia and Germany for India's liberation, Obeidullah focused his seditious activities on raising what he designated as an 'Army of God', to be associated with the provisional government of India, in which all founder members were to receive military titles. The headquarters was to be in Medina, with secondary centres in Constantinople, Tehran and Kabul. Obeidullah designated himself 'Officiating General'. This army's object was to liberate not only India, but all Islamic countries under infidel rule. There is no indication that the Germans ever took this secret army seriously, and with good reason, for by late 1916 Obeidullah's most audacious escapade had been unmasked and the movement held up to ridicule. That was when General Sir Michael O'Dwyer, Lieutenant General of the Punjab, discovered an attempt by Obeidullah and his associates to communicate with sympathisers in India by means of a plot known as the Silk Letters Conspiracy. It had the trappings of a chimerical, almost childish ploy, though the potential repercussions were taken seriously enough for the British authorities to step in and break up the conspiracy. Memories of the previously mentioned scheme the German government had executed, and on which the silk letters were based, were still fresh. Using Indian agents, the Germans had addressed letters in Urdu, sumptuously bound and signed by Chancellor Theobald von Bethmann-Hollweg, to the leading Indian princes, promising them great rewards if they took up arms against the British. Many of these letters were intercepted en route across Persia to India and those that got through had no effect on the rulers of India's princely states, who were already drawing handsome subsidies from the government of India.

Obeidullah contacted a Muslim agent and sent him disguised as a pilgrim on his way to Mecca. The messenger had secreted in his coat letters written on folds of yellow silk for the sultan of Turkey, bearing news of the formation of the Army of God.

It was designed to unite all the forces of Islam, the Turks, the Arabs under the Sherif of Mecca, the Afghans, the Frontier tribes, and the Mohammedans of India, in a combined effort against British rule. This was to take the form of an attack by the Frontier tribes, incited by the Hindustani Fanatics [...] supported by a general Mohammedan rising in India. It was hoped that the revolutionary Hindus and the America-returned Sikhs would at once join in.[25]

The conspiracy was aborted on the agent's journey from Kabul to Mecca, when Obeidullah's messenger was forced to show the letters to a Muslim former Indian Army officer, whom he thought to be trustworthy, but who turned out to be an acquaintance of O'Dwyer's. The retired soldier cut the letters out of the agent's coat and, while thinking them pure nonsense, he nonetheless took them to the commissioner of the division, who sent them on to O'Dwyer. 'I did not grasp their full meaning at first [they were written in Persian], but understood enough to satisfy myself that they revealed a plot with wide ramifications.'[26] The courier was arrested and O'Dwyer passed the letters on to the Criminal Intelligence Department (CID), where the chief of Indian intelligence, Sir Charles Cleveland, speedily unravelled the whole mystery. The letters described the plans of the provisional government and the constitution of the Army of God movement in Kabul and India. The result was the exposure of a great number of Army of God militants of rank up to 'field marshal'. This enabled O'Dwyer to take preventive measures, with the internment of a dozen or so militants in the Punjab who were known to be the most pro-Turkish seditionists. Thus, by 1917 the British could congratulate themselves on having suppressed all seditious movements directed against India from outside its borders.

By now the Germans knew that their plans to subvert Britain's Indian Empire had failed miserably, and that their only real success had come through the work of Wassmuss in Persia. And what of the elusive Wassmuss? That question was preying on the minds of British intelligence officers the length and breadth of Persia, from Kermanshah to Shiraz. Once a fortnight the Intelligence Branch of the General Staff issued a map showing the distribution of the enemy's forces in the Eastern theatres of war. Across one whole corner of this map there appeared, printed in red ink, the word 'Wassmuss'. The area covered by this one word equalled several times that of England. By 1916 Wassmuss, like Niedermayer and Hentig, had realised that in spite of his achievements, which some claimed included having helped in the Turkish victory at Kut-al-Amara, Persia was not going to declare war against the Allies. He had spent nearly two years among the Tangistan tribesmen, and towards the end of the year he left Bushire on the Persian Gulf for Kazerun, a city 40 miles inland, west of Shiraz. The years of hardship among the desert tribes had taken their toll on Wassmuss's appearance:

> He was thin and his hair had gone quite white. He had grown to look so like a Persian that he no longer feared to be seen by an Englishman, and he had reason to suppose that there might be a few Englishmen in Kazerun.[27]

The message was soon driven home that unlike his British counterpart, T.E. Lawrence, Wassmuss had little hope of raising the tribes to revolt. He spent several months, from the winter of 1917 to March 1918, the last year of the war, travelling across Tangistan, doing his best to inflame the tribes, pursued all the while by the British. Things could not be said to be going well. One night he and his party were attacked by bandits and Wassmuss took a knife-thrust to the leg that left him with a permanent limp.

In November 1918 Wassmuss received a letter announcing the Armistice. He was told the British were prepared to offer terms: if Wassmuss gave himself up within seven days he would be repatriated to Germany. If he refused and was captured, he would be treated as a prisoner of war. He sent a reply stating that any attempt at capture would constitute a breach of Persian neutrality. His next move was to make a break for it, along with his German companion, Helmut Spiller, and six tribesmen, hoping to reach safety in Turkey. Once past Shiraz, Wassmuss removed the tribal robe he had worn for three years and changed into European dress. The German master of deception, who slipped with ease from one character to the next, was to take on another new identity. Wassmuss now gave out that he was an English geologist in the Anglo-Persian Oil Company. He assumed the name of Mr Witt, and spoke Persian with an English accent.[28]

For the remainder of that year and into early 1919, Wassmuss led his pursuers a merry chase across Persia. The British intelligence services all but gave up hope of apprehending the evasive German, fearing the worst: that he had crossed into Turkey undetected. Wassmuss's luck ran out in Kashan in central Persia, as he was travelling west towards the Turkish border. In this dusty, once historic pottery-crafting city, he was finally betrayed by a sharp-eyed Armenian telegraph operator. The excited Armenian caught the scent of a reward and quickly alerted the authorities. Wassmuss and his party were caught in a trap laid by a Persian gendarme patrol, from which all managed to escape, save for Wassmuss, Spiller and their companion, Sultan Ali. The prisoners were escorted to Tehran, then on to Qasvin north-west of the capital, where they were kept under a light guard – a mistake that was to cost the captors their prey, for the ever resourceful Wassmuss managed to make yet another daring escape by slipping past the unsuspecting sentries. He trekked in secret back to Tehran, penniless and in rags, where upon his arrival he walked into the German legation to demand repatriation home. He and Spiller were driven to the Turkish border, then on to Constantinople and put on a ship bound for Germany, where Wassmuss took up a position at the Foreign Ministry in Berlin, a city his free and adventurous spirit led him to detest.

Wassmuss's later years were not a happy time. In 1924 he gave up his job and returned to Persia, where he bought a plot of land near Bushire, hoping – with an admirable sense of honour – to raise enough money from farming to pay the tribesmen the reward they had been promised for having sheltered him and having risked their lives fighting the enemy. Four years later the farm failed and Wassmuss found himself deep in debt. He returned to Berlin in 1931, a poverty-stricken, broken and all-but-forgotten man, and died a few months later.

One of the greatest tributes a soldier can hope for is praise from the enemy. The Allies could not help admiring Wassmuss's ingenuity and determination, even when this led to heavy losses on their side. The British expression 'It's not whether you win or lose, it's how you play the game' could have been conceived with Wassmuss in mind. After the war the Daily Mail, a newspaper that was often accused of harbouring pro-German sympathies, heaped great praise on this 'German Lawrence'. The paper extolled Wassmuss's soldierly abilities, saying he stood for

all that is skilful, cunning, thorough and dangerous in the German system of Eastern penetration [...] In November 1914 we tried to capture this young gentleman but, like the Goeben, he escaped, and a human Goeben he was destined to remain throughout the war, a constant menace, a political force to be reckoned with, and one which served to immobilise thousands of British troops. The state of military preparations in India, the disposition of our forces in Mesopotamia, and the dispatch of troops to other theatres of war – all became known to him, and the information was duly forwarded on.[29]

6

West to Berlin

Niedermayer embarked along a line which to any casual map-reader would have looked like the only logical way back to Germany. He would later have cause to question the wisdom of his chosen route. Niedermayer's tactical decision to split the mission into smaller groups, while taking himself on a northerly course, seemed to make perfect sense. But by the middle of 1916 the westward route across Persia was shaping up as a more hazardous undertaking than the previous year's march east to Afghanistan. The German agitators were taking a beating and had lost Shiraz. Zugmayer and Griesinger fell into British hands after their escapade in Persian Baluchistan. In August 1916, Paschen was captured by the Russians during his attempt to break through from Herat. Niedermayer had instructed him to make for Baghdad, but once across the Afghan border he was arrested and taken in for interrogation by the Russians, in the presence of British intelligence agents. Paschen revealed that in the proposed German–Afghan treaty Habibullah had placed at the top of his demands, after achieving full independence for Afghanistan, a call for an Arabian Sea outlet at Makran on the Baluchistan coast. This was greeted with amusement by Paschen's British interrogators: if the Germans could do no better than to send a couple of bunglers like Zugmayer and Griesinger, who were both in custody, to 'liberate' Baluchistan, there was little cause for concern on that front.

*

Niedermayer and Hentig were following the path taken by Alexander the Great more than 2,000 years previously. They set out from Kabul in a north-easterly direction into the Panjshir Valley, a broad, fertile expanse sheltered by the towering walls of the Hindu Kush, famed for its emerald and silver mines. Niedermayer, with his military eye, noted in his diary that the mountain range formed a barrier so immense 'that even now it may be regarded as an almost impassable military frontier. Any Power which could succeed in establishing itself on these heights would dominate both lowland countries' (that is, the plains of Afghanistan to the south and Tajikistan to the north of the range).[1] Niedermayer's appraisal of the Panjshir as an impregnable redoubt held true, in the past, at the time of the 1979–89 war against the Soviets, as well as during the Taliban period, when the predominantly ethnic Tajik forces of Ahmad Shah Massoud saw off the Taliban's attempts to over-run the valley. Habibullah had seen to it that his departing guests were well looked after, providing supplies and an escort for the time they remained on Afghan territory. Nasrullah and his confederates were displeased to see the Germans go, and it would have put the amir in a very tight spot had any mishap befallen them on their homeward journey. Habibullah sent along with Niedermayer and Hentig his mehmandar, or chief of the royal escort, Shuja ud-Daula, who treated the party with kindness and always managed to find food and shelter in one of Afghanistan's most sparsely populated regions.

As they rode at a slow pace along the rocky path, following the northward course of the Panjshir River, the mission's failure weighed heavy on the minds of all, but at least they had taken a resolute decision to put an end to the tiresome weeks of idleness in Kabul:

> Having been so long familiar with the mode of life in this country, we made no great claims, but were glad to be once more in the saddle and to be moving on. We preferred to endure bodily hardships, rather than to remain inactive in one spot and wearing out mind and body in vain efforts.[2]

After two days' march they reached the junction of three valleys, the rivers of which cascaded with a mighty rush of water on a south-easterly course to the Kabul River. German engineers had identified this as a potentially major centre of hydroelectric power and it must have given Niedermayer and Hentig a pang of irony to pass one of the electric power stations, which was still under construction. From this point the mission turned to the north-east, carrying on up the Panjshir Valley, now through terrain narrowed and cut by deep gorges, which led to a vast highland plateau.

Four days out of Kabul took them to the small mountain hamlet of Dasht-i-Rewat, little more than a speck on the map, which straddles the Saricha Road leading to Tajikistan. The village is situated in the uplands along a riverbed, in a narrow sector of the valley. It was there that Niedermayer and Hentig decided to part company, each going their separate way to Germany. Niedermayer planned to travel in a north-westerly direction, taking with him the larger part of the caravan on a route he knew would expose him to the enemy's attention.

Niedermayer's task was to lead his party over the Hindu Kush into the remotest reaches of Afghanistan. This entailed a crossing of the snow-covered Khawak Pass, a 12,625-foot gap between soaring mountain peaks, the invasion route followed by Alexander and Tamerlane. Niedermayer had his men break camp after midnight in order to negotiate the great snowfields that lay ahead before the heat of day left the snow too soft for the horses and pack animals. The caravan route was well marked by animal tracks, but each time a horse wandered off the trail it sank up to its saddle and had to be unloaded and pulled out of the snow. Niedermayer was drenched in sweat by the time he climbed to the top of the pass. The descent took them into the homeland of the Turkmens, a people of nomadic origin, where they rested for three days before following a line of march almost directly westwards for three days towards Bamyan.

Niedermayer relished the journey ahead which led to some of the world's most fabled historic sites: Khulum, the great trade centre between Turkmenistan and India, and Balkh, the former Bactria of Alexander's day, reputed to be the most ancient city in the world and also said to be the birth-place of Zoroaster. Despite the need to press on and avoid the Russian patrols which were keeping a sharp lookout for the caravan, Niedermayer could not resist the temptation to pitch his tents in one of Balkh's shady gardens. He spent three days at this spot taking photographs of the ruins of early Islamic and Buddhist buildings. Those days spent in and around Balkh rekindled Niedermayer's lifelong passion for geography, the subject he took up in the postwar years as a PhD candidate at the University of Munich. A few years after leaving the army in 1921, he was appointed Lecturer in Geography at the University of Berlin, a post he retained until re-enlisting in the army in October 1939 with the rank of colonel.

As they moved westwards they soon reached Sheberghan, the main trading post for nomads coming down from the northern steppes, where they were received kindly by the governor, who happened to be a relative of Habibullah's. 'Here I again allowed one day's rest, and then moved on slowly in a south-westerly direction to Sar-i-Pul, at the foot of the mountains. I wished to gather strength for the hardships now facing me.'[3]

At this stage Niedermayer weighed up the prospect a crossing of the Karakum Desert to the west, a daunting enough undertaking during the cool winter months, but nothing short of madness in the height of summer. The desert, whose name translates ominously as 'black sand' in Turkic languages, is more than twice the size of England, a 135,000-square-mile expanse covering most of Turkmenistan, and a truly desolate corner of the Earth, where human habitation averages one person per 2.5 square miles and rainfall never exceeds six inches in a year. Niedermayer concluded that the enemy could scarcely expect to have found him using this hellhole for his escape route. Before taking his leave of Sheberghan, he changed into Turkmen dress, shaved his head and dyed his hair black. Determined to spare no pains to stay out of enemy hands, he yanked the gold crown from one of his teeth and stitched it into the lining of his felt tribesman's cap. Such modern dental procedures as crowns were unknown to the nomads of the Central Asian steppes. If in spite of these elaborate artifices he were to be unmasked, the only weapon he carried was a small Browning pistol, which he tucked into his woollen tunic. Before leaving, he dispatched Wagner to Herat with the Austrians. They carried with them all the expedition's luggage, apart from what Niedermayer and his guide would require for their journey.

On the night of 23 June 1916, Niedermayer spurred his chestnut mount on the first leg of the trek towards the desert and the vast expanse of the Turkmen steppes. The following day he rode into a small village to pick up the guide who had been arranged for him by the governor of Sheberghan. Their party consisted of eight men: six well-armed Turkmens, Niedermayer and his personal servant. The group was compact and could move at a fast pace, but was unfortunately not small enough to escape the attention of Russian army patrols. At their evening campsites in the desert Niedermayer encountered a grisly reminder of the previous year's crossing to Afghanistan. Animal life in this wasteland was sparse, with only the odd lizard, jerboa and other rodents scampering about the barren landscape. But there were also immense tarantulas on the ground, clusters of them, as well as deadly spotted snakes. These loathsome creatures

> dogged one's footsteps and made the short night's rest in the sand very disagreeable. We often had to use our whips, held in readiness for this purpose, to kill tarantulas or venomous snakes which came too close to us. We were obliged to examine carefully any place at which we intended to rest.[4]

As they rode along in single file on a long, narrow track through the sand, under a burning heat that sent the thermometer soaring to 122 ° F, Niedermayer had a foreboding that something was amiss with his Turkmen escort. They repeatedly called a halt to the march and would try to induce him to lie down and nap. Often they lost their way, and soon Niedermayer discovered the reason for this strange behaviour: his escort, to a man, was comprised of opium addicts, unable to function coherently without stopping at intervals to light their pipes. To make matters worse, they were now out of water and plagued by thirst. The men slumped in their saddles and the group began to break up, as one by one they dropped to the ground from exhaustion. Presently one of the Turkmen on a ridge gave a shout – water-holes had been spotted beyond the crest. They stumbled down the hillside to the pools, where to their dismay the water turned out to be so brackish that even the horses refused to drink.

Niedermayer treated their cowardly behaviour with the contempt one would expect from a battle-hardened German army officer. Turning their backs on the half-drugged Turkmen, he and his faithful servant Abdul Wahab spurred their horses on north-west to the Panjdeh region, which Niedermayer knew to be occupied by Russian troops. This is where in 1885 Russian Army units had staged an incursion into Afghan territory and taken control of the oasis fortress. Scarcely had they abandoned their bewildered escort in the desert, when the Turkmen came galloping up behind to demand payment for their services. Niedermayer handed them their pay and promptly turned the tables on them by offering their leader a handsome fee to accompany him and his servant as far as the Persian frontier.

The three travellers now came upon an unguarded railway line. With no Russians in sight they crossed the line and almost to Niedermayer's disbelief, they shortly found themselves at the border, where they crossed into territory he and Ernst Diez had explored in 1913. A blessed sight lay before him: a river, which offered the prospect of his first bath since Kabul. The second-hand Turkmen garb he had acquired in Sheberghan was infested with vermin, and he spent hours sitting by the riverbank, picking lice out of his tunic. He gave up after counting 400 of the creatures, with patches still crawling with lice, which he estimated to number up to 2,000. The Turkmen guide had been as good as his word, so Niedermayer paid him off and he and Abdul Wahab continued on their trek into Russian-controlled northern Persia. He knew that the Persian spies in this region were almost as numerous as the lice embedded in his clothes, and a good deal more treacherous.

> Hitherto the whole affair had been excellent sport, but I was forced to renounce everything which our culture values, from the point of view of a European and a soldier. I was obliged to become a rogue to outwit other rogues.[5]

When Niedermayer and Abdul Wahab joined the main road to Meshed, they came across a party of Baluchistan traders who warned them that a troop of Cossacks had recently been through the area, asking questions about a German traveller. This piece of news suited Niedermayer's plan: he was confident that the last place he was likely to be hunted was Meshed, the Russian military headquarters for East Persia with its 600-strong garrison. That decided it: Meshed was to be his destination. Niedermayer sent Abdul Wahab ahead to obtain an entry permit under a false identity for his German companion. Niedermayer then slipped quietly into town shortly before dawn. So far, it looked like he had managed to escape detection, but his luck ran out on the second day. As he wandered through the bazaar, bargaining for a set of vermin-free Afghan clothes, a pair of Russian soldiers were questioning the proprietor of Niedermayer's caravanserai about two unknown travellers who had arrived the previous day. One of them did not have a very convincing appearance as an Afghan. Abdul Wahab dashed into the bazaar with alarming news of trouble at the caravanserai and from that moment until they reached Tehran Niedermayer and the Afghan were on the run.

Niedermayer mounted his horse and at a gallop the two men cleared the chain barrier strung across the town's West Gate, dashing off into the desert night. This put paid to Niedermayer's original idea of driving to Tehran in a wagon, under a burkha to disguise himself as a woman. Six hours of hard riding found them in Kurdish territory, where more trouble awaited. When they reached the main road they were challenged and pursued by a gang of robber tribesmen, firing their rifles as they chased after the two strangers. With the whistle of shots still ringing round their ears, Niedermayer and Abdul Wahab pulled up at Safi-Abad, a few miles north of the main road to Tehran. This was the residence of the district deputy governor, who received this somehow odd-looking Afghan and his companion with suspicion and apprehension. These were bad times, he explained to his guests, with Russian troops roaming the countryside and spies everywhere on the prowl. Niedermayer immediately recognised his host and smiled to himself when in the course of conversation, the Persian official spoke of two foreigners, Germans as he recalled, who had passed through his outpost a few years previously. He had been impressed by their astronomical observation equipment and the splendid camera they carried with them. The two Germans in question were, of course, Niedermayer and Diez on their 1913 expedition. Niedermayer took his leave of the deputy governor without bothering to reveal his identity, amusing though that might have been.

They reached Damghan, a town famed for its pistachios and almonds but more importantly, given that their horses were by now almost reduced to skeletons, a staging post for the mail coach to Tehran, 213 miles to the west. Niedermayer had to tread cautiously, for he was travelling as an Afghan and the people of Damghan kept in their collective memory the sacking of the city by Afghan warriors in the early eighteenth century. Abdul Wahan booked two seats on the evening coach to Tehran, which was a road journey of three to four days. Much to Niedermayer's dismay, he found himself sitting across from a little Frenchman, a diplomat attached to the French Foreign Ministry, whom he had met in Tehran the previous year on his way to Kabul. The Frenchman began throwing quizzical glances and questions at Niedermayer, who feigned illness. When he refused to answer, the Frenchman turned his attention to Abdul Wahan, who soon became confused and gave contradictory replies. Niedermayer was forced to join in the conversation with his unwelcome travelling companion, who claimed to be an avid collector of plants, gemstones and antiquities. He extracted a book of sketches from his satchel, but Niedermayer pretended not to understand the pictures, asking if the leaf he was shown was for smoking or eating. After thirty hours on the road, the Frenchman had become so suspicious of Niedermayer's identity that he tried to rouse their fellow passengers against him. Finally, at a rest stop Niedermayer decided his best option was to reveal his identity and throw himself on the Frenchman's mercy, at least as a fellow European in alien territory, if not an ally. To the German's relief, the Frenchman embraced him and kissed him on both cheeks, promising to keep his enemy's secret and offer him assistance in Tehran.

On 26 July 1916 Niedermayer arrived in Tehran, after thirty-one days of sand, blistering heat and perilous encounters on the trail, starting almost from the day they left Sar-i-Pul. Of course, no sooner had they alighted from the coach than the Frenchman betrayed Niedermayer to the Persians as well as to enemy authorities, obliging the German to shift quarters seven times during his stay. His first night was spent with his fellow coach travellers in a house in the bazaar. The next day he went directly to the US Legation to call on Rudolf Sommer, Germany's chargé d'affaires and the only German diplomat remaining in the city. In November 1915 all the representatives of the Central Powers had abandoned Tehran ahead of the Russian advance. By the spring of 1916, the Allied forces, closing in from the north and south, had managed to wipe out all the German positions in the provinces. Only a few agents, Wassmuss notable among them, were still holding out in the countryside. Niedermayer had spent more than a month in a news blackout. He now learnt to his dismay of German defeats in France and Russia, as well as of the retreat from Persia. It was this dispiriting news that drained him of his last shred of physical stamina. He collapsed in a raging fever and was evacuated to Derband, a nearby mountain village north of the city where in a peasant's hut he lay, prostrate but safe, on a cot teeming with bedbugs. For three days he was unable to move, until the filth and the stench became so unbearable that he dragged himself outside to a mountain stream. There he wallowed for hours, his naked body wrapped in a sheet. The cool water brought down his fever and he was gradually restored to health. 'It was indeed a marvel that I had not been ill before, since I had lived like a Persian fakir, had drunk water from any possible source, and slept among riff-raff and filthy surroundings.'[6]

Tehran had become a dangerous place for Niedermayer to show his face. Spies in the pay of almost everybody, Germans, British and Russians alike, skulked about the diplomatic legations, the bazaars and caravanserais. Nobody could say when the Turkish Army would strike but if it did, the ensuing battle for the capital would be of ferocious proportions. Niedermayer had no wish to be caught up in the fighting – his thoughts were focused on getting himself safely back to Germany and being reunited with those of his comrades who had made it home from the trenches. He paid off his faithful servant Abdul Wahan and on 17 August 1916, after a three month sojourn in the Persian capital, he negotiated his way onto a caravan heading south-west 230 miles to Hamadan, the oldest city in Persia, pleasantly nestled in the green foothills of the holy mountain of Alvand. The city lies roughly halfway between Tehran and the Mesopotamian frontier, which he expected to reach in a march of two to three days.

It was on the approach to Robat Karim, a desert settlement a day's journey from Tehran, that Niedermayer had his closest brush with death on the
road from Kabul, or indeed since leaving Berlin. Without warning, his large
caravan of sixty camels and many donkeys came under attack by brigands as
it passed a caravanserai. The robbers blocked the road, brandishing rifles
and cudgels. It was quite dark and all Niedermayer knew was that they were
suddenly surrounded on all sides and caught in a trap. On Niedermayer's
instigation, they made the fateful mistake of trying to force their way through
by firing a few shots from the few weapons in their possession. This was the
signal for the brigands to open fire and almost instantly the groans and cries
of the wounded and screams of the animals were heard on all sides. With
men and animals dropping all around him, Niedermayer tried to shelter
behind the walls of the caravanserai, where the attackers caught him and
knocked him unconscious with blows to the head from their rifle butts. He
regained consciousness moments later, to find himself in the midst of a
melee of stampeding camels and men scattering in all directions. The dead
and wounded had their possessions looted, while those who were not killed
were taken off, bound and gagged and thrown down in a heap. Niedermayer
was forced to lie on his back in the middle of this mound of prisoners where
he managed, unobserved, to unfasten a small leather belt, which contained
a few gold coins. By using his fingernails he was able to bury the money
under the ground behind his back.

When this pillage was completed and all the animals had been rounded
up, the men were driven off into the desert to the accompaniment of curses
and blows from their attackers. Now there would be more time for a leisurely
and thorough search. The caravan was a rich prize for the thieves, for camels
travelling without loads meant that it was a so-called 'money-laden caravan' on its return from market, where goods had been exchanged for cash.
Niedermayer and a few others who had been badly wounded were allowed
to ride donkeys to a spot where they were placed in a circle and ordered to
keep their heads bowed. One by one, they were pulled out of the circle and
searched. Those who could produce no valuables stashed in their clothing
were beaten and accused of hiding their money. 'If this procedure failed,
they were thrashed until one heard bones crack. There were, moreover, the

pitiful cries of the men so treated and the moans of the wounded: it was not a scene for weak nerves.'7 When all the loot had been collected and the strongest of the camels picked out, the gang of robbers disappeared into the desert night.

Niedermayer dug up his buried money sack and staggered on to Hamadan. On 1 September 1916 he walked into Turkish Army headquarters in Ottoman-occupied territory, a physical wreck, unable to move his head or left arm and with some bone fractures which were discovered later. His feet were blistering and swollen from marching barefoot over the prickly plants of the steppe and the hot, sharp stones. When he gave his name it was some time before anyone believed it was really him. The duty officer, a Lieutenant Wiech, who was attached to the Turkish staff, gaped in astonishment when Niedermayer addressed him in German. To his delight, Niedermayer learnt that his brother Waldman was still alive. Two days later he was driven in unimagined luxury by motor car to Kermanshah where more good news awaited: Paschen had found his way safely to Hamadan and later, in December, to his great surprise Seiler made his appearance in Kermanshah after escaping from his Russian captors. Niedermayer listened with a sense of outrage to Seiler's tale of their mistreatment by their British captors in Shiraz. The citadel that served as their prison was held by a detachment of Indian Army soldiers under the command of British officers. In March 1917 the prisoners were taken to Isfahan, chained hands and feet, on the orders of General Percy Sykes, who warned them they would be treated as brigands and shot if they attempted to escape. Seiler had previously hatched several escape plans, each one of which was foiled by the British. He was lucky to avoid execution but this did not stop him trying: he at last succeeded in breaking out, retracing almost the exact route the mission had taken two years previously, and finally reached safety in Kermanshah.

Seiler's journey was an epic, albeit on a smaller scale, to rival that of Niedermayer, who had crossed roughly the same territory on his way to Kermanshah. In November 1917 Seiler and his Persian escort were in Khorasan, where Wassmuss had been active. They rode into Faradonbeh in western Persia and reached the town of Kariz the following morning, stropping only to refresh themselves and their mounts. They travelled on towards Isfahan, tantalisingly close to the safety of Kermanshah and the Mesopotamian border. The whole region around Isfahan was held by the enemy and it was not long before they came under fire from Cossack troops crouching behind a cluster of rocks on a hillside. From what Seiler could make out, there were only two stray soldiers who were more than likely as terrified of the approaching caravan as were Seiler and his men of being ambushed on an open road. After a brief skirmish, one of the Cossacks decided to make himself scarce and in a few moments his companion was captured, stripped of his weapons and set free. Seiler had had no more than three hours' sleep for nearly as many days, but there was no question of resting. They were now only a few hours' from Isfahan, in the midst of hostile territory. Reaching the northern road to Isfahan, they picked up the unwelcome sound of a caravan slowly heading towards them.

Seiler and his men scattered to take cover behind rocks on higher ground. He soon realised that on this occasion fortune had smiled on them: he and his men wielded superior firepower, which made the caravan ripe for the picking. Even better, it turned out that the caravan was carrying supplies for the British in Shiraz. Seiler's men pounced on the unsuspecting camel herders and made off with their loads of wheat, woollen cloaks, grape juice, bread and, for good measure, a donkey to carry the booty. After suffering through two night marches of freezing temperatures and a lashing east wind, they reached the gold-mining district of Muteh. In late November they came out from the biting cold mountain country to descend to a plain near Sultanabad (now known as Arak), less than two hundred miles east of Kermanshah. The Turks, Persians and Russians were engaged in fierce fighting for control of Sultanabad. Seiler took a quick decision to turn his party south-west when they observed Russian troops bringing up machine guns. Seiler noted that he was greeted warmly along the way by villagers who took them to be reinforcements of Persian troops. But he recognised this more as war-weariness than an outpouring of loyalty to their own people: 'Probably, however, had the Russians passed this way, the peasants would have received them with equally deep, or even deeper, salaams, much as they hated them in their hearts.'[8] On the last day of their journey to Kermanshah they became so impatient to reach their destination that they covered the fifty miles from Sahneh in a single day, although their mounts were so exhausted they were forced to urge them on using whips made of willow twigs. Seiler and his weary men rode into Kermanshah in early December. 'We marched through its dark, narrow streets to headquarters, and the first German to greet us was our leader Captain Niedermayer.'⁹

Wagner stood by his post in Herat for longer than was prudent, as his later misfortunes on the road westward were to prove. The deteriorating military situation in Persia and Mesopotamia made this city the Germans' crucial link to Afghanistan, where the mission had left Wagner in charge of most of their baggage and valuables. As the tide turned in the Allies' favour, Habibullah deemed it prudent to restrict the movements of the few Germans remaining on Afghan soil. Wagner realised the futility of staying on, with no hope of obtaining help from his comrades who were themselves struggling to reach Germany. He and a handful of Austrians packed up and left Herat in late 1917, roughly following in Niedermayer's footsteps towards Khorasan. Like Niedermayer, they had their own encounter with brigands on the road. With armies fighting for control of Persia, whatever semblance of law and order that had prevailed was rapidly disintegrating, providing the ideal climate for rampant banditry. Wagner and his party were surrounded and attacked south of Khorasan, where one of the Austrian officers was killed and most of the others captured in a gunfight. Wagner himself was able to escape, taking the northern route across the Dasht-i-Kavir to Tehran and Turkey, where he arrived safely in early 1918.

Niedermayer spent several weeks in Kermanshah, a safe haven which remained securely under Ottoman occupation until 1917, filing reports to Berlin, dispatching messengers to Wagner up to his departure from Herat, and to his men imprisoned at Shiraz. He also kept up regular wireless communication with Wassmuss, who was still holding out at his rebel base in Tangistan. Niedermayer does not make mention of the exact date of his return to Berlin in his memoirs. We know that he left Kermanshah on 15 January of that year for Baghdad, and from there he travelled to

Constantinople, where he boarded a train for Berlin on 10 May. It can safely be assumed that he reached the German capital between 12 and 14 May 1917. In mid-May he wrote to Hentig's father, mentioning that he expected to be sent back to the front in around ten days' time, after being received by the kaiser.

7

East to Berlin

Hentig's departure from Kabul had not been a particularly joyous occasion. It came on the day before his 30th birthday and the most momentous event of his career had just collapsed in abject failure. For whatever Hentig's progressive views on the mission's social accomplishments, in the eyes of the German Foreign Ministry and the General Staff, the almost nine months spent in Kabul amounted to just that: failure to meet their diplomatic and military objectives. It did not bring Hentig much birthday cheer to have been transformed in a single day from an honoured envoy of the German emperor into a fugitive on the run. Nor was there much comfort in the knowledge that the shrewd Habibullah had extracted a maximum of profit from the mission's stay in Kabul, with a minimum of personal commitment.

Not only were the energetic Niedermayer and his companions advising him on how to modernise and train his troops along the latest Prussian lines, but also Habibullah was thus able to keep a close watch on what they were up to. 'Furthermore, as the Germans were only too uncomfortably aware, when the right moment came they would make a valuable gift from the amir to the Viceroy of India.'[1] Niedermayer and Hentig split up in northern Afghanistan, with the idea of reducing the risk of being spotted by British and Russian patrols that were abroad in their pursuit. An old caravan route extends from the south over the mountains into northern Asia. These trails are the same ones that were used to transport Alexander's armies on their path of conquest. Niedermayer had followed this track on his westward trek to Persia. Hentig was denied this route, which would undoubtedly be under close enemy surveillance. He instead took his large, noisy group, comprised of 120 animals, cooks, assorted servants and his fellow European, Persian and Indian companions, on a zigzagging course over steep passes and disused tracks, aiming to cross the Pamir Mountains into China.

Hentig called a halt on the fifth day out of Kabul, after riding through wild terrain rising relentlessly towards the snow-covered massif that forms the junction of five mountain ranges across as many countries. The Pamirs, or the 'Roof of the World' to the Tajiks, in whose territory they now found themselves, were penetrable through the Wakhan Corridor, Afghanistan's north-eastern appendix which is so narrow in places that the Russians and British could stare into one another's faces across the gorge of the Oxus River. Hentig sent the main body of his party ahead on an old caravan route while he, along with Röhr and several of the others, numbering 30 in all, turned north-east into a small, half-hidden valley.

Hentig's plan was to quick-march his party into the Pamirs, for he was acutely aware that they were still on Afghan soil. Their absence from Kabul was no longer a secret to anyone who might wish to do them harm. Hentig's youth and his extraordinary physical fitness gave him the strength to race ahead of the rest, moving mainly by night when the hardened snow made it easier going for the pack animals. At one point, they were hit by a snowstorm of such ferocity that it became impossible to distinguish a body two feet in front of the animals. When the gale-force winds tore the clouds away, Hentig turned to gaze in exasperation on the dotted line of the caravan struggling up the snowfield below.

They reached the top of a frozen pass to be confronted by a most remarkable sight: a fakir arose from the snow, a man with a wild, dark face, wearing only a loincloth. He was an Indian holy man who had made the pilgrimage to Mazar-i-Sharif and from there to the mountains of the east. Hentig did not linger to exchange pleasantries with this spectral creature – he needed to take his group to lower altitudes in all haste or face the risk of losing men to frostbite and hypothermia. The descent proved treacherous on the glassy slope, but once below 10,000 feet they began to breathe deeply, and Hentig was relieved to see smiles break out on the men's faces.

On they went to Badakhshan, the region that covers the extreme north-east of Afghanistan and the south-eastern corner of what is today Tajikistan, a mountainous land enclosed on all sides by the Hindu Kush. The path rose steadily higher and became rougher as they climbed into the rarefied air, causing the weary animals to stumble on the rock-strewn trail. As they approached the settlement of Faizabad, almost at the mouth of the Wakhan Corridor, they came across some friendly villagers who provided them with food and shelter for several days. Hentig found out from a Kyrgyz merchant that the enemy net was tightening around them, thanks to the help of a widespread intelligence web. The Chinese *amban*, or 'district officer', in Tashkurgan to the north-east, had sent word that Hentig's movements were now known to the British consul in that Uyghur city, via reports sent from Peshawar and as far off as Peking, and that consequently the Russians were concentrating troops in the region. The *amban*, no friend of the Russians, offered to send troops to escort them through the Tagdumbash Valley into neutral China. Hentig declined the offer, which would have made their presence all the more obvious. The Kyrgyz proposed guiding them to Kashgar, a four- or five-day march. It was a tempting destination, for Hentig knew there was a telegraph post in the city which would allow him to contact the German legation in Peking and arrange for safe conduct across China. But the risk of falling into a Russian trap in that region was too high – Yarkand, on the southern rim of the Tarim River basin, was instead to be their objective. Hentig ordered his men to discard anything that might slow their crossing of the Pamirs. He hired two Kyrgyz guides in exchange for $15 and three lambs and started off, from an altitude of 15,000 feet, across the mountains, the entire group disguised as caravan travellers.

Hentig was not one to go slinking feebly back to Berlin without putting up a fight. Starting from Yarkand, the centre of an ancient Buddhist kingdom on the Silk Road, 'Hentig planned to make as much mischief as possible for the British and Russian communities in this isolated region.'[2] Hentig was understandably distressed over the mission's lack of success, and even more so at the prospect of another arduous journey through the wilds of Asia, struggling all the while to evade his country's foes. The diplomat-soldier tactician in him concocted schemes to whip up the local tribes against the British and Russians as he travelled through Muslim lands. In a small way this might force the enemy to divert troops to the region, thereby taking some of the pressure off German armies engaged in distant battlefields. Hentig did his utmost to spread rumours about German victories in Europe and the arrival of German army units in Afghanistan. In Yarkand he began spreading anti-Russian propaganda to stir up a rebellion. His efforts brought some measure of success when some local tribesmen staged a revolt in several districts and murdered a handful of Russian settlers. It required only some small detachments of Chinese troops to suppress the movement, in which a large number of insurgents were killed and captured. Whether or not Hentig's tales of Germany's invincibility were believed, the Muslims by and large did not respond to his agitation, and the one certainty was that he now needed to get on with his march eastwards. For the moment, other challenges loomed on the track through the mountains and into the Middle Kingdom. Hentig declared in later life that this part of the journey remained etched in his memory as one of his worst experiences. 'I shall never forget the marches that followed. It was a black and stormy and cold time, in which we travelled into a foodless, treacherous, forbidding wasteland.'[3] The Kyrgyz guides rode a few paces ahead of the caravan, leaning into the icy wind in which every so often a sharp and terrifying crack was heard, as new crevasses opened up in the glacier. They moved ahead in darkness, praying to be spared instant death from the boulders that broke loose and came crashing down from the hillsides above the trail.

A few days into the march, at the first light of dawn, Hentig spotted a Russian outpost. He drew his pistol and made a quick reconnaissance of the area, but found the little fortification to be abandoned. The next night he discovered the reason why: the garrison had moved on to another fort alongside the road, and as the travellers had no choice but to carry on, it was only the howling wind that saved them from detection. However, their luck was to run out the following day when a scout pulled up to warn them of a 40-strong Cossack cavalry patrol riding hard in their pursuit. Hentig and his party needed to descend and penetrate a deep gorge which was their only possible escape route. They at last emerged battered but safe into a broad valley, having lost two mules in the river that cut through the ravine. For the next four days they wound their way eastwards, constantly criss-crossing the river to keep to the path, on one day as many as 30 times. They found themselves in neutral Chinese Turkestan, on the edge of a vast salt flat which took them to Yarkand, where they holed up in an old abandoned palace outside the city walls. Hentig spent his time debating the wisdom of embarking on the easy and short ride north-west to Kashgar to make contact with German officialdom. He reminded himself that in spite of his wretched state he was a diplomat attached to the Foreign Ministry, and as such it was his duty to report on how far British and Russian influence had penetrated the western part of China.

Hentig decided to take a chance on the journey to Kashgar, but as events were to prove, it was not a wise decision. Marco Polo had passed through this desert city in the thirteenth century. Tamerlane ravaged it a century later, and since that time Kashgar has been the scene of continual conflict between rival Chinese dynasties. It was a volatile and unpredictable place for a European. Hentig mounted his horse and spent several hours riding back and forth through the bazaar until he was satisfied that any enemy spies had been thrown off his track. He slipped out one of Yarkand's many gates, leaving behind Röhr and the Hungarian József Honvéd. Hentig made the usual seven-day journey to Kashgar at breakneck speed in two nights and a day. In that short time he found it necessary to escape a party of Chinese troops who wanted to force him back to Yarkand, as well as a raucous pack of Mongol horsemen who circled him menacingly, shouting their war cries. Once Hentig had broken free of this mob a Chinese official appeared to tell him the taotai, a kind of district commissioner, awaited him at his residence, where he was invited to spend the night. So far, so good, but at a late hour Hentig received an unexpected guest. A Swedish missionary burst into his room in a cold sweat. He warned Hentig of a stormy argument that had taken place that afternoon in the palace, between the taotai and his host, the local amban,[4] who was for all intents a Russian agent. The amban, reeling about in a drunken state, was calling for Hentig's execution by firing squad. The argument began to heat up. The taotai demanded that Hentig be given up to his own soldiers and, to emphasise his point, he threatened the *amban* with a loaded rifle. This settled the dispute. Hentig sat in his room, pondering his melancholy fate, unaware that a detachment of the *taotai*'s troops was on its way to liberate him.[5]

Hentig had taken into account the threat of treachery when he reached Kashgar and had boldly put about a tale of a great number of armed horsemen in the hills outside the city walls, waiting for the signal to attack at the first sign of trouble. This ruse succeeded in instilling fears of a massive German reprisal if any harm came to their leader, so, responding in haste, Hentig demanded unhindered passage through the twisting bazaars to the city gates, along with a safe-conduct pass for his onward journey to Peking. Before departing Kashgar, Hentig telegraphed Röhr in Yarkand, instructing him to proceed to Maralbexi (now called Bachu), a town to the north-east, roughly equidistant from both cities. After their rendezvous a few days later, they carried on across the northern rim of the notorious Taklamakan Desert, heading for Urumqi, once a major hub on the Silk Road. They marched for more than two monotonous, almost eventless months, on a trail that in no way held the horrors of the Persian desert crossing on their way to Afghanistan. When low on water or provisions, they would stop at one of the numerous oases or caravanserais along the route, until they reached one spot where Hentig thought the heat had finally gone to his head. They came upon a small wooden church inhabited by a Flemish missionary of the Order of the Sacred Heart of Jesus, a friar in a long brown robe and wearing a flowing red beard, who refused to shake the hand of an 'enemy', a reminder that a war still raged thousands of miles to the west. An even stranger encounter waited a few days later, when they were confronted with a solitary Englishman who, for reasons unknown, was staying in a village. He greeted his European visitors in a friendlier manner than the Flemish churchman. 'We are Germans,' Hentig said apprehensively. 'That is excellent,' the Englishman replied. 'Very pleased to meet you. Won't you come over for tea with me?'[6] Their host had good reason to be cheerful. He gave Hentig the news that the Austrians had been defeated on the Carpathian front, where 200,000 prisoners and more than 200 guns had been taken. Hentig listened, somewhat disheartened, but after more than three months of hard marching across Central Asia and China, his thoughts turned to the butter and jam laid out on the table before him.

On 24 December 1916, after 130 days spent in the deserts of China, Hentig came within sight of a railway bridge across a river at a town which he referred to as 'Mientsche', today's Mianchi. The road ahead was jammed with caravans and vehicles. Camels brayed and men shouted at the beasts, and at one another, to clear a passage in the narrow road. Most unexpectedly, a Lutheran church stood nearby. Hentig had reached civilisation as well as his first bed and bath since his departure from Kabul seven months previously. This was thanks to the generosity of the church pastors, the Ringberg family, Swedish missionaries who took Hentig to attend a Christmas service where he spent an emotional evening singing familiar Lutheran hymns.

Hentig's Afridi companion Sayed Ahmed, who had accompanied the mission to Afghanistan, remained in Mianchi and was later taken back under escort to his home in the North-West Frontier. That was the last Hentig ever heard of his cook, who had been his travelling companion for 17 adventurous months. Hentig and Röhr boarded a train to Hankow, one of the three cities that merged to form present-day Wuhan, where they arrived two days after Christmas. The city bustled with foreigners, including British officials and agents of various ilk, people who had been chasing Hentig since he had stepped foot across the Persian border in July 1915. He made his way cautiously to the telegraph office to send a message to Admiral Paul von Hintze, the German minister in Peking. Hentig asked for permission to carry on to the Chinese capital and from there to book passage to the United States, which had not yet entered the war. To his astonishment, Hintze turned down his request on the grounds that Hentig was too valuable an asset to the Auswärtiges Amt to allow him to leave Asia. Hentig was having none of it. He constructed an elaborate route for the return journey to Berlin, which entailed circling half the globe and could best be described as a highly imaginative scheme. The idea was to sail from China to Japan and from there to Mexico, then on to neutral Spain, where he planned to get a lift on a German submarine for the final leg back to a German port. To avoid revealing his nationality, and with his command of the accent of southern France, he decided to travel as far as Spain disguised as a native of that region.

Hentig had had the foresight to telegraph ahead to the German consul in Hankow and was therefore provided with comfortable accommodation and the luxury of a clean Western suit of clothes, in exchange for regular briefings on the mission's activities in Afghanistan and the political situation in the Chinese regions they had crossed. Twelve weeks into his stay in Hankow, with no word on his request for an onward travel permit, the news that China had severed diplomatic relations with Germany on 14 March 1917 came as a release from the daily tedium of city life. That day the flag was lowered on the German legation, and exactly three months later China declared war on the Central Powers.

In the scramble to evacuate German nationals from the country ahead of the declaration of war, Hintze's orders for Hentig to hold fast in China lost their validity. Hentig booked passage from Shanghai on the Dutch ship *Rembrandt*. He took his leave of Röhr, but this was not to be their last encounter, for after returning to Germany Röhr married Hentig's sister. To throw pursuers off his track, Hentig took the steamer as far as Nanking, where he planned to make his way by train to Shanghai. 'He chose to travel by train, thinking that as the railway was under English supervision, the vigilance would not be as strict as on the steamers, where those wishing to escape the control of the Allies were more likely to be found.'[7] Hentig was in an optimistic frame of mind the morning he boarded the train for the 170-mile journey to Shanghai. The German consulate, which was in the process of being evacuated, had urged him to proceed in all haste, as his onward travel papers were now ready. It was at most a matter of weeks before China would become an uncomfortable place for a German officer.

His high spirits were deflated within hours of docking at the bustling Chinese seaport. The British authorities, though inexplicably failing to recognise whom they had in their grasp, nonetheless refused him a visa for the very reason that he was a German army officer. Hentig produced his diplomatic credentials, but to no avail. He stormed out of the British legation, determined to lodge his petition for an exit permit with the French authorities. The French, working hand in glove with their British allies, took note of his request and never bothered to send a reply. He tried the Japanese, who responded with a stalling tactic, claiming they first needed to forward an enquiry to their embassy in Peking. Finally, in utter frustration Hentig took his case to the neutral US consulate where, to his relief, Consul-General James Cunningham told him he had been instructed by the US ambassador in Peking to grant him a visa.

Hentig's tribulations were finally over, or so he thought. A few days later he was summoned back to the US consulate, where Cunningham sheepishly broke the news that fresh instructions had come in from Peking: he could only be granted exit papers with the express agreement of the British and French authorities, who were of course shortly to be fighting alongside US troops in the war against Germany.

> I looked him up and down and told him politely but coldly that I was not hitherto aware that the American Government took its orders from the English and the French in the execution of its international duties, and I left his office.[8]

Hentig went into hiding in the rabbit warren of Shanghai's back streets, fearful that, having shown his face to the enemy, it would not be long before the penny dropped and orders went out for his arrest. He spent the next few days trying to track down information on ships departing Shanghai. He had made his whereabouts known to the German ambassador, who advised him not to travel on the *Rembrandt*, the steamer that the ambassador himself was taking for his homeward journey. Hentig had now lost his last diplomatic safety net. He decided to make his escape, with or without papers, on board the American ship SS *Ecuador*, which was due to sail from Shanghai on 1 April 1917. In so doing, he adopted some peculiar props to camouflage his getaway, by first securing a US Navy shirt and a second-hand suit, both of which could serve as disguises if the need arose. A friendly Swede he had stayed with on the journey across China had provided him with a missionary's long coat, which he now wore to avoid raising awkward questions about an undocumented and baggage-laden European lurking about the harbour. Most importantly, he purchased a passport belonging to a Norwegian subject of ill-repute, and this later saw him safely aboard a steamer to Bergen on the final leg of his journey. A Japanese bargeman agreed for a price to take him out to the ship on his flat-bottomed boat. Once on board he immediately pretended to be asleep, again hoping to prevent enquiries by the authorities. This ruse served him well in one uncomfortable moment, when two British officers in the Chinese customs service came alongside, taking no notice of the sleeping bundle. The barge chugged through the harbour, passing the German and Austrian steamers that the Chinese had interned, and after some hours they reached the open sea at Woosung, a port town located 14 miles downriver from Shanghai.

Hentig took a cautious look over the barge's bow once they had sailed a safe distance from shore. He caught sight of one of the Empress liners of the Canadian Pacific shipping company and, moored alongside, his vessel to freedom, the SS *Ecuador*. The plan at this stage was to lay low in the barge while the steamer's cargo was being taken over her side. Before stealing his way on board, he scrutinised the crew and passengers as they boarded the ship. They consisted for the most part of a handful of officers of the countries of the Central Powers who were being repatriated, US diplomatic and military personnel and Chinese travelling on assorted business matters. Through an intricate network of connections that had been arranged in Shanghai, Hentig was on the lookout for the ship's barber, to whom he had obtained an introduction through one of the members of the Shanghai orchestra, who was in turn a former steward on the same ship as the barber. Once the passengers and crew had boarded, Hentig slipped out of the barge and onto the dock. He shouldered his large bundle of personal effects to board the ship, pretending to be one of the loading crew. The first person he dared to approach was the boatswain. He turned out to be an Irishman who, out of hatred for the British, expressed his sympathy with Hentig's plea for help to travel as a stowaway. The boatswain was more than happy to help a fellow enemy of Britain, but deemed it too risky to try and pass him off as a crewmember. Hentig stole his way along the deck as inconspicuously as possible until the ship weighed anchor. If he were to be challenged and sent ashore for travelling without papers, he would almost certainly end up in a cell. He stopped at a cabin door, hearing German voices coming from inside. He cautiously knocked, to be greeted by two equally anxious Austrian officers who were travelling with false papers. As a fellow officer and ally, they told Hentig he was welcome to hide in their cabin for the crossing, and this was easily arranged by slipping the Chinese cabin boy the equivalent of 100 yuan in the gold coins he was carrying.

Once underway, their first port of call was Kobe, a cosmopolitan city on the southern coast of Japan, 720 nautical miles east of Shanghai. Despite the Japanese having entered the war in alliance with the Entente, Hentig felt he could at last relax, confident that he was on his way home, a free man soon to be reunited with his Foreign Ministry colleagues. This was, at least, until he heard an announcement over the ship's Tannoy that they had docked in an area infected by a smallpox epidemic. A disinfectant team, accompanied by police officers, would be boarding the ship to carry out an inspection. No sooner were the voices of officialdom heard at the cabin door than Hentig concealed himself inside a small wardrobe. There he remained, locked in darkness and suffering Hades during the interrogation of his Austrian comrades who, in his own words, 'were sweating blood'.[9] Once the police had gone, Hentig emerged from the wardrobe to find the ship underway, bound at last for Honolulu, where they docked a little more than a week later. Some distressing news awaited him: on 7 April 1917, the US had declared war on Germany. Hentig now found himself back on enemy soil.

It would have been pointless to attempt an escape by mixing with the ship's disembarking passengers, for there was not a hope of him slipping past Immigration. Had Hentig been able to produce an official Chinese exit permit, he would have been detained, interrogated and in due course sent home to Germany. Without papers, he was headed straight to an internment camp for enemy aliens. But this time Hentig had prepared himself for such unforeseen snags. Friendly sources had briefed him on a getaway plan. It was a risky gambit to say the least, but it had to be that or face the even worse risk of falling into US hands, with the prospect of no consular support from his own country. Waiting until nightfall, Hentig gathered his personal belongings into a large bundle and lowered himself over the side of the ship. He was a champion swimmer, but even his stamina was tested to the limit by what followed: the plan called for him to swim out of Honolulu harbour towards the open sea to elude harbour patrol boats, circle the outermost buoy and make his way back over the reef, bundle and all, weighing nearly one hundredweight in its saturated state. Pushing the bundle ahead of himself, he constantly had to dodge the searchlights that swept the harbour, until he passed two smokestacks which had been previously described to him. Reaching this spot, he crawled ashore, his face, hands and stomach lacerated by debris after two and a half hours immersed in water. He still needed to clamber over security fences and cross several fields, shouldering his bundle, until he came to the first street, which he followed to the harbour's shipping offices.

When morning came he made himself look as presentable as possible in his waterlogged circumstances. Still holding a pocketful of the mission's funds, he approached several steamship lines to book passage to Europe. None of the companies would issue him a ticket without a visa. He had prepared himself for this hitch, heading straight for the consular office of neutral Spain, the country that represented German interests in the US, where he made himself known to the consul. With much regret, the Spanish consul told him he could not offer any help to an undocumented alien, but he did agree to make an appointment for Hentig to plead his case to the attorney general. Later that day, the US official listened attentively to Hentig's remarkable story and informed him that he did not believe half of it. Nevertheless, he arranged for Hentig to be sent to San Francisco, where upon docking he was escorted off the ship and interned on Angel Island, the immigration bureau that also served as a detention centre for prisoners of war. He was subjected to a vigorous cross-examination by US immigration officers, who showed a keen interest in two points: whether he was an accredited staff member of the Auswärtiges Amt, and how he had managed to get away from Shanghai. Seeing that a good deal of lying was getting him nowhere, he decided to provide his interrogators with a fairly accurate account of his escape from China, 'under the belief that two of his compatriots had given him away'.[10] The British found it extraordinary that Washington should have agreed to grant Hentig a safe-conduct pass, after the same authorities at Peking had refused the concession. The Directorate of Military Intelligence Section 5 (MI5) expressed outrage in a memo to the

Foreign Office: 'It looks as though the Americans so admired Hentig's pluck that they were anxious to do all they could to help him.' The agents were now aware of who had cleverly slipped through their net, but they were less well briefed about Hentig's future movements. Once it was clear that Hentig was free to make mischief and conspire to his heart's content, British intelligence began to regard him as a kind of Scarlet Pimpernel. 'The outcome [of Hentig's return to Germany],' the memos stated,

> cannot but be regarded as unfortunate, as Hentig is now at the head of another Mission on its way to Afghanistan, if he has not already arrived there. In the present state of affairs in Central Asia there does not seem to be much hope that the amir will this time be able to resist the persuasion of the mission to abandon his neutrality.[11]

This follow-up German mission to Kabul is unknown to history. Another report had Hentig drawing up a two-inch scale map of India for the Germans, who were now engaged in working out an invasion plan of that country. This is indeed imaginative intelligence gathering, for the German General Staff had little time for thoughts of an Indian campaign after the defeat at Verdun, the effectiveness of the British naval blockade and the entry of the US into the war.

But that is getting ahead of the story. There was still a German consular official in San Francisco and through his offices arrangements were made for Hentig to cross the US to New York under police escort, where he was taken to the city's immigration department and met by Secret Service agents. Hentig feared the worst, so one might have expected a look of delight to cross his face when his interrogators told him a safe-conduct pass had been approved for his repatriation to Germany aboard a Norwegian steamer. But Hentig was physically and mentally worn down since having departed Shanghai in a state of deep anxiety. Once in Allied hands, he expected at any moment to spend the rest of the war in a US detention camp. He had received no news of what future awaited him in Berlin or which, if any, of his comrades had survived the trenches. 'I had no special feeling of joy. After the past twenty-six months, joyous sentiments seemed unattainable.'[12] Once

underway, everyone on board the ship heaved a sigh of relief after passing though the heavily mined waters around Halifax, their last port of call
before embarking on a very choppy Atlantic crossing to Europe. Hentig went
through his final interrogation at this Canadian port city, of which he voiced
no complaints, except for some 'uncalled for observations made by a ship's
officer'.[13] Hentig's diary entries speak of an uneventful docking at Bergen in
neutral Norway, where he boarded another ship bound for Hamburg. From
there it was a short railway journey to Berlin and the Wilhelmstrasse, where
he was to give a full account of his exploits.

8

My Enemies' Enemy is Germany

The Allied victory in the First World War had been a close-run thing, and Habibullah was aware that even in defeat Germany was a power to be reckoned with. By uniting Britain and Russia in a common cause against the Central Powers, the war also, albeit temporarily, put an end to the political and military antagonism in which Afghanistan had figured as the centrepiece for nearly a century. For now, the two great empires would not manipulate Afghanistan as a pawn in their struggle for supremacy in Central Asia, and Habibullah knew he had Germany to thank for that. Conversely the Anglo-Russian alliance signified that the amir could no longer use these two powers' mutual antagonism for personal gain, which usually meant exploiting British India's fears of Russian aggression in order to extract arms and substantial subsidies from Delhi.

It was therefore logical for Afghanistan to look to Germany, although vanquished in the Great War, as its closest European ally, one that would act as a balancing force to prevent Russia or Britain from gaining a dominant influence in the country or forcing Afghanistan back into its role as a political cushion between these two rival imperial powers. Germany had surrendered, but before doing so she had defeated tsarist Russia, a country now critically weakened and engulfed in turmoil under Bolshevik rule. Britain had emerged victorious in the Great War, but at so terrible a cost in human lives and economic resources that she had no choice but to grant Afghanistan full sovereignty, or at least that was how Habibullah's son and heir, Amanullah, interpreted the outcome of the Third Anglo-Afghan War of 1919. Germany's defeat in the Great War vindicated Habibullah's neutralist policy. The amir could congratulate himself on having stuck to his guns in the face of almost overwhelming pressure from within his household, with his younger brother Nasrullah and his third son Amanullah, and Amanullah's mother Sarwar Sultana Begum (one of Habibullah's five wives), in the forefront of the war party. Less than two months after the signing of the Armistice in November 1918, the amir judged the political atmosphere calm enough to go off on a shooting holiday in the Laghman district, not far from Jalalabad. A few weeks into his trip, in the early hours of 20 February 1919, a lone gunman crept into the amir's tent and put a bullet though his head. Inexplicably the assassin was not challenged by the royal guard on approaching the tent or, even more puzzling, as he made his escape.

The motives for the amir's murder pertain to the realm of speculation. It was quite obvious that Nasrullah and Amanullah were unhappy over Habibullah's refusal to take up arms against British India. Anti-British anger could have emanated from any number of nationalist politicians, religious leaders or army officers, in particular the rapid nationalist commander-in-chief, Nadir Shah. A few weeks before the assassination, Habibullah's highest-ranking advisers wanted him to petition the viceroy to have the issue of Afghanistan's full independence put on the table at the Versailles peace conference. Lord Chelmsford turned down the request, for the same reasons that Afghanistan was not granted a seat at the conference. Despite the crucial role the country had played in preventing an attack on the Raj, or at least the threat of an invasion, Afghanistan had not taken part in the war and therefore was not entitled to join the peace negotiations at Versailles.

In the days of turmoil that followed Habibullah's death, Nasrullah lost no time in stepping in to make a grab for the crown. The court had decamped to Jalalabad for the winter season and it was in that eastern city where Nasrullah proclaimed himself amir, a title he held for all of one week. Inayatullah, the heir apparent and a supporter of his late father's policies, was nonetheless compelled to acknowledge the accession of his more powerful uncle. But Nasrullah had underestimated his nephew Amanullah, who was officiating as governor of Kabul during his father Habibullah's absence. Being in charge of the capital meant that Amanullah also controlled the royal treasury and the arsenal, as well as having command of the Kabul garrison. This enabled him to win the short-lived power play with his uncle, Nasrullah. While Nasrullah, a devout Muslim, represented the religious and conservative elements in the country, Amanullah – young, ambitious and popular – represented nationalism and progress.[1] It was to Amanullah that the nation now turned for a leader.

Amanullah's first step as amir was to tie up the loose ends surrounding his father's assassination. He had his uncle arrested and imprisoned for attempting to usurp the throne, a move that set the ultra-conservative clergy against the new ruler. Nasrullah died a year later in a Kabul prison in unexplained circumstances. On 13 April 1919, Amanullah presided at the trial of the military men who had been arrested and accused of complicity in the regicide. General Nadir Shah and 21 others were set free. Amanullah still needed a victim to bring the case to a neat conclusion, so the young Colonel Shah Ali Reza Khan, who was the officer in charge of the royal guard on the night of the murder, was convicted on the flimsiest of evidence and executed by bayoneting. His involvement in the assassination was never proved and to this day the true killer's identity remains a mystery. In the eyes of many, Amanullah himself is the prime suspect. Sir Hamilton Grant, chief commissioner of the North-West Frontier Province and Britain's chief delegate at the peace talks which followed the 1919 war with Afghanistan, took the view that Habibullah had undoubtedly, by his 'ungovernable temper', estranged certain officials of his entourage. His murder, Hamilton maintained, was probably due to private revenge and not connected with politics or dynastic conspiracies. 'But it was never safe to prophesy about Afghanistan for a longer period than twenty-four hours.'[2]

Amanullah's aptitude for sensing trouble was more acute than his father's, for no sooner had he ascended the throne than the new amir – or 'king' as he was to style himself – recognised the need to quell discontent within the armed forces. Amanullah first acted to secure the allegiance of the troops by raising their pay. He smoothed the feathers of the higher-ranking officers by appointing the popular Saleh Mohammed as commander-in-chief, while Nadir Shah was removed to the remote eastern garrison of Khost. This set the scene for Amanullah's greatest exploit in the decade he sat on the throne: the Afghan was engaged in secret preparations for the long-awaited attack on British India. In May 1919, Hentig's and Niedermayer's ambitions were fulfilled, though with an outcome different to what they might have anticipated. On his accession to the throne Amanullah sent a letter to the viceroy, proclaiming his enduring friendship and eagerness to enter into treaties from which both countries might derive commercial benefits. In so doing, Amanullah ironically set the scene for an armed confrontation with Britain. 'The action of Amanullah in condemning his uncle, the champion of the mullahs [...] alienated alike the mullahs and the army.'[3] Discontent spread among these disaffected factions, with the result that the khutba, or 'public prayers', were not read that month in the king's name, a deliberate affront to his royal authority. Amanullah was left desperately seeking a means to gain support from his people and his generals. He found the answer in the time-honoured expedient of waging war on an unpopular neighbour.

Britain's third Afghan campaign was an inglorious affair, in many ways more of a month-long skirmish than something that could properly be called a war. On 3 May 1919, a party of 150 Afghan regulars occupied the village of Bagh in the Khyber Pass. The presence of Afghan troops in British territory constituted an act of war, hence three days later general mobilisation was ordered and war was declared on Afghanistan. The course of the war falls outside the remit of this narrative, but suffice it to say that Amanullah had misjudged Britain's ability to raise a formidable fighting force, which was otherwise weakened and exhausted after four years of trench warfare in Europe. In spite of the almost overwhelming difficulties that confronted the army in India, British arms were victorious. Nadir Shah inflicted a setback on British forces in the Kurram Valley, which was celebrated in Kabul by the erection of a column with a chained lion, representing Britain, at its base. After witnessing in horror the aerial bombing of his palace in Kabul, on 28 May Amanullah sued for peace. Three months later an armistice was signed in Rawalpindi. This was to all effects a face-saving agreement for both belligerents. In the somewhat ambiguous document that emerged from the talks, Britain recognised Afghanistan's full independence, while at the same time unceremoniously putting a stop to all subsidies and arms shipments to Amanullah.

If for no reason other than geographical proximity, British India, and Russia as well, would continue to exercise a considerable degree of political clout in Afghanistan. But there was now a third European power steadily gaining traction in Kabul, and that was Germany. Had not Germany shown itself to be Islam's only true friend among the Western powers? Was it not well known, even to the illiterate frontier tribesmen, that the kaiser was a great admirer of Islam, a convert to the faith, in fact, and that the German mission and their Turkish comrades had come to Kabul bearing letters of friendship from Wilhelm II as well as the caliph?

Once Afghanistan was granted complete independence to conduct its own external affairs, one of Amanullah's first tasks was to give substance to his country's new status by inviting foreign governments to open legations in Kabul and, moreover, to persuade them that Afghanistan was truly the master of its own destiny. The man regarded as Afghanistan's most distinguished political and military figure, General Mohammed Wali Khan, an uncle of the future king, Mohammed Zahir Shah, was sent off on a tour of Western capitals to establish relations with Europe's most important countries, as well as the United States. To the British government's irritation, Mohammed Wali's first stop in 1919 was Moscow, where he hoped to secure a commitment of Soviet support against the threat of any future British military intervention. Mohammed Wali planned to travel to Paris in the hope of securing for his country a seat at the Versailles peace conference, but the viceroy, Lord Chelmsford, saw to it that permission was refused on the grounds that Afghanistan had not been one of the belligerents.

Two years later, in 1921, the general's mission achieved its aim of signing treaties of friendship with the Soviet Union, and also with Turkey and Persia, through the good offices of their diplomatic representatives in Moscow. Securing diplomatic recognition from Germany was to prove a thornier issue:

> Although it was relatively simple for Afghanistan to establish relations with a number of European countries, it was quite difficult to do so with Germany. Germany had lost the war and was therefore unable and unwilling to challenge Britain in a sensitive area.[4]

The terms of the Treaty of Versailles imposed tight restrictions on Germany's diplomatic aspirations. In March 1921 Mohammed Wali and his delegation made their way from Moscow to Berlin, where they met for talks with two Foreign Ministry diplomats: Fritz Grobba and none other than Werner Otto von Hentig, the skilled Afghan hand. The Afghans made their pitch for German diplomatic recognition, coupled with a request to have German engineers and technicians sent to Kabul. Berlin listened sympathetically to Afghanistan's need to upgrade its infrastructure and arms industry, and German mining interests had their sights set on the country's vast, untapped mineral resources, whose value the US Geological Survey today estimates to be in excess of $1 trillion. Nonetheless, Berlin was at this stage reluctant to risk a confrontation with Britain. Despite the provisions of the 1919 Treaty of Rawalpindi, the Raj was still regarded by the European powers as the de facto custodian of Afghanistan's foreign affairs.

In 1923 Germany joined Britain, Turkey, Italy and France in granting full diplomatic recognition to the sovereign kingdom of Afghanistan. In that same year Grobba, one of the Weimar Republic's more colourful diplomats, arrived in Kabul to take up his post as chargé d'affaires in Kabul. Grobba was without doubt the best-qualified person the Abteilung III – the Foreign Ministry's Middle East section – could put forward for the job. Born Arthur Borg in Brandenburg in 1886, he changed his name (inverting Borg to Grob and adding 'ba') to disguise his identity, when General Erich Ludendorff sent him on a covert intelligence mission to the Middle East. By that time Grobba had converted to Islam and taken a Syrian wife. In Kabul he could offer the unique advantage of being able to converse with Amir Amanullah in Turkish, a language in which both were fluent.

Under Grobba's energetic nationalism, less than a year after his arrival the Germans had become the largest colony of foreigners in Afghanistan, numbering more than 70 technicians and businessmen, not counting families. To their surprise, they discovered that they were not the only German-speakers living in Kabul. Nearly 100 Austrian escapees from Russian prisoner-of-war camps had fled to Afghanistan while war was still raging in Europe. In

Kabul, most probably out of sheer lack of purpose, they formed a military unit which was pompously designated The Royal and Imperial East Indian Detachment. These Austrians were not attached to the Afghan armed forces and performed no military role, but this was not to say their presence in Kabul was without its use. Some imparted their manual skills to Afghan apprentices and others were employed on various urban-improvement projects. Those who held officer rank took advantage of the freedom of movement they enjoyed to maintain contact with Kurt Wagner in Herat, the only German to remain behind when the mission departed Kabul in 1916. Wagner kept alive the channels of communication with former mission members, a few of whom made a brief reappearance in Kabul after 1920.

> Some came in search of their belongings or buried money that they could not take with them when they left Afghanistan through British-controlled territory. Others were emigrants who left an impoverished and defeated Germany in search of employment and new careers.[5]

By 1924 Afghanistan was importing German factory equipment and cement for Amanullah's ambitious national modernisation enterprises. This was arranged through the Deutsch-Afghanische Compagnie (DACOM), a trading company set up in Bremen for the express purpose of developing commercial ties with Afghanistan. The Hentig–Niedermayer mission's footprint was very much in evidence in DACOM's Kabul branch office, where Kurt Wagner had arrived from Herat to take up a post as one of the company's five full-time employees. There was never much love lost between Wagner and the arch-hawk Grobba, who had little sympathy for what he considered a failed mission, and least of all for Hentig, whose brand of soft diplomacy he detested. That same year Germany blatantly defied the restrictions of the Versailles treaty by selling 6,000 rifles and 250 machine guns to the Afghans. The arms were shipped via Riga across Russia to Kabul.

In Amanullah, Germany had found a true friend as well as an ardent enthusiast of her technological skills. The amir saw himself as Afghanistan's great moderniser, the ruler who would bestow upon a backward tribal society the blessings of a sweeping programme of social and economic reforms. To Amanullah's way of thinking this was the only guarantee of his country's independent future, now that the Ottoman Empire had been consigned to the proverbial dustbin of history and Muslim countries such as Afghanistan were left to their own devices for political survival. It goes without saying that the amir's plans for turning Afghanistan into a modern European-style nation played nicely into Grobba's hands.

The US was a great but distant power, one whose foreign policy took scant notice of Afghan affairs, apart from keeping a watchful eye on Soviet expansionism in the region. Washington did not even open its first official Kabul legation until 1942. As for France, it had never been a major player in Afghanistan, and Amanullah was disdainful of a country that, despite being among the victors of the recent European war, had been so easily and devastatingly overrun by Germany's military machine. France was also disliked at the Afghan court because of its role in the break-up of the Ottoman Empire in 1920, when the League of Nations granted Paris mandates over Syria and Lebanon. Italy had ruled itself out as a force in Afghanistan, even after Rome offered to supply Amanullah with weapons and machinery. The Italians suffered a major diplomatic setback in 1924 when an Italian resident in Kabul shot dead a policeman, sparking a row that eventually ended messily with the Italian's execution by hanging and Mussolini's going into a rage over the affair, after which there was a steady winding down of Italy's presence in Afghanistan.[6]

Historically Britain had always been the most influential foreign power in Afghanistan, but not always under the most congenial of circumstances, having fought three wars with the Afghans in a period of 80 years. British India was still the natural conduit for trade and commerce with its neighbour. In the 1920s, however, Delhi was preoccupied with the more pressing problem of a growing Indian nationalist agitation, with the added worry of tribal violence on the North-West Frontier and the threat of the closure of the Khyber Pass, the traditional trade and military route between India and Afghanistan. Amanullah's most promising partner in this bold venture to bring enlightenment to his country was therefore bound to be Germany.

In 1923 the king inaugurated Afghanistan's first foreign-language schools, to offer the children of Kabul's elite and middle classes an education in French, English and German, of which the last grew to become the largest of the three. The Goethe-Institut of Afghanistan continues to thrive in Kabul to this day.

Britain may have been reluctant to mentor Afghanistan into the modern world, but London was equally hostile to Amanullah's plan to seek military aid from the Soviets. Officially the Great Game had become a historical anachronism. In reality, however, British officialdom still viewed with great suspicion and deep apprehension any move that might draw Afghanistan into the Soviet Union's sphere of influence. Whitehall kept an ever-vigilant eye on Soviet intentions regarding Afghanistan throughout the 1920s and 1930s, until Hitler's invasion of Russia in 1941 turned Moscow's attention away from Central Asia. In 1932 Prime Minister Ramsay MacDonald's government informed Zahir Shah in no uncertain terms that in the event of an unprovoked Russian attack, Britain would consider itself obliged to break off relations with the Soviets. In even stronger language, undoubtedly intended for Soviet ears, the message came with a warning: 'His Majesty's Government have noted that the Defence of India Committee of 1927 [...] assumed that Russian action of the kind in question would in fact in the last resort be followed by a declaration of war against that Power.'[7] So the Great Game was still very much alive and kicking around the corridors of Whitehall. If further evidence of Britain's belligerence was required, an extract of a January 1928 meeting of the Committee of Imperial Defence spelt out the details:

The material consequences of any substantial Russian encroachment into Afghanistan would be no less dangerous to India, and no less disastrous to our general interests in the present time than they were in the past. [...] The deliberate crossing of the Oxus [...] by Russia would be the violation of a frontier which we are bound to defend.[8]

Amanullah had already opened talks with Moscow which were aimed at procuring military hardware to upgrade his armed forces, whose woeful deficiencies had cost Afghanistan the 1919 war with Britain. That brief conflict left no doubt in the king's mind that Afghanistan needed an air force of its own, for it was this new and devastating tactic of aerial bombing that had brought the country to its knees. However, the last thing Delhi wanted was to find Afghanistan building a capability to challenge British air supremacy, least of all in the borderlands where postwar bombing campaigns against tribal raiders were proving highly successful. There was another side to this coin, articulated by Sir Francis Humphrys, the British minister at Kabul. Humphrys was eminently qualified to brief the government on this matter, having served as an RAF pilot in Europe during the Great War. He pointed out that Article 179 of the Treaty of Versailles, which prohibited Germany from entering into arms deals with foreign powers, was, a decade after its ratification, to all effects a dead duck. That said, Humphrys argued that bending the rules could work in Britain's favour. 'The employment of German personnel, both as military instructors and also in the Afghan air force, would obviously be a valuable counterpoise to the Russians, and might lead to a gradual displacement of the latter.'⁹

The theory espoused by Humphrys and a few other British Russophobes of using Germany to neutralise Russian influence in Afghanistan was met with little enthusiasm in Whitehall. The Great Game cast of mind still dominated the thinking of Britain's policy makers, in London as well as Delhi. The Russian Revolution had thrown the Muslim khanates of Central Asia into a state of turmoil. The breakdown of Russian control in northern Persia made it much easier to communicate with Afghanistan from Constantinople, Germany's favoured nest of Middle Eastern intrigue. These factors pointed to even greater instability in a region festering with political volatility. Even before Amanullah sent his troops across the Khyber Pass in 1919, British intelligence continued to worry about Afghanistan's avowed neutrality. A British secret agent identified as 'C', a code name for 'Chief', reported on a radically changed picture from Habibullah's point of view, with the virtual independence of Muslim khanates like Bokhara, Khiva and Baku straddling Afghanistan's northern frontier. 'C' also made reference in one of his dispatches to a second wartime Turco-German mission being discussed in Constantinople, with aims along the same lines as the Hentig–Niedermayer expedition. This mission was to start out in late October 1918, but there is little evidence of German involvement in this plan. Nonetheless, the reports in themselves were sufficient cause for alarm.

Another top-secret memorandum from the Department of Information of the Intelligence Bureau in London's Victoria Street reveals the unremitting fear of German activities directed at Afghanistan:

> All these pieces of evidence point to a new organised attempt to create trouble for us in Afghanistan [...] Even if Amir Habibullah is personally unwilling to embark on an anti-British policy, the arrival of the new Mission, reinforcing the existing propaganda, may force his hand.[10]

With the outbreak of the Second World War, while Hentig discussed such issues as diplomatic recognition and commercial deals with Mohammed Wali, officials at Berlin's Ministry of Defence were listening to an impassioned appeal by Niedermayer, the implacable militarist, on turning Afghanistan into the staging area to bring down the government of British India: 'On an attached map, Niedermayer sketched in detail the steps towards an attack on India from Afghanistan. A crucial factor was the water supply for the troops.'[11] The difficulty of keeping an army supplied with food and water on a march across Afghanistan, from Herat to the west, the southern city of Kandahar, or across the Hindu Kush, was always going to be an enormous challenge to any invader marching to India. Niedermayer believed this problem could be overcome by German engineering, as demonstrated by his own brother Richard, 'who was engaged in building a water supply system for the Afghan city of Kandahar'.[12]

Niedermayer pressed on, trying to mobilise support for eventual military action, which as always centred on using Afghanistan as a spearhead for an attack on India. At the same time, he did not rule out the possibility of a Russian-led invasion from the Hindu Kush, a thrust that would require building a road suitable for the transport of heavy armour across the mountain passes. Niedermayer summoned his former mission colleague, Günter Voigt, to Berlin, and instructed him to proceed to Kabul via Moscow to forge a tripartite alliance between Germany, Russia and Afghanistan. The initial objective was to incite revolutionary activity by Indian nationalists, with the longer-term aim of winning over Amanullah to the idea of mobilising his army for another attack on India. The possibility of the Russians' taking the military initiative was contemplated and discussed at the Kremlin, but Voigt's efforts got him nowhere: the Soviets laid down conditions that were considered unacceptable to the German, while at the same time Germany's Turkish ally, Enver Pasha, as well as Amanullah, began to distance themselves from Moscow and the Soviet regime's atheist ideology. Berlin had failed to appreciate Islam's deep-rooted abhorrence of godless communism.

With or without Afghanistan's material support, Germany and the Soviet Union still shared a common aspiration to bring about a gradual destabilisation of British India. They were happy to leave it to the Indian revolutionaries to deliver the *coup de grâce*, with one important caveat: as was the case in the Great War, and now under the Weimar Republic, and of course with the Nazi regime that was lurking a few years down the road, from the standpoint of Germany's strategic thinking the idea had always been to put British India on the back foot without actually bringing about the downfall of the Raj. Cripple the British Empire, yes, but the last thing Germany wanted was for the government of India to fall into Indian hands. Amanullah, a staunch supporter of the Kabul war party at the time of the Hentig–Niedermayer mission, could be relied upon to stand on the sidelines and hopefully to encourage the frontier Pashtun tribes to harass British towns and outposts. Niedermayer played an active role in the Russo-German alliance. General Hans von Seeckt, who organised the Reichswehr defence force after the war, the only army command Germany was allowed under the Treaty of Versailles, appointed Niedermayer as envoy to Moscow, where he travelled under the code name 'Dr Neumann'. It was Niedermayer who signed a contract with the Russians to assemble 300 German Junkers aeroplanes per year in a factory outside Moscow. The Junkers aircraft company was also granted the right to use Soviet airspace for commercial flights to Afghanistan.[13]

Mistrust of the Soviets was running at fever pitch in London. This was based on Russia's geographical proximity to Afghanistan and the collapse of Russian control over the Muslim territories lying between both countries. In defiance of British wishes, Amanullah had no misgivings when it came to welcoming German participation in his country's development programmes. German engineers were in fact nearly always at the forefront of these projects. The most ambitious undertaking was the construction of a European-style royal palace at Darulaman, 6 miles outside Kabul, which was built with the assistance of German designers and craftsmen. The Afghans acquired three small steam locomotives from German transportation-equipment manufacturer Henschel of Kassel. The railway line was used to carry the royal family and court officials between the new palace and the city centre, and for years it was the only railway in existence in Afghanistan. Apart from Germany's reputation for engineering excellence, Amanullah perceived another advantage in employing German workers. With the Indian rupee pegged to sterling, hiring British personnel offered no cost advantage over inflation-ravaged Germany, which could supply labourers for a quarter of British wages. For this same reason, Germany was also invited to provide experts and equipment to work on the modernisation projects of Kandahar and other cities.

Just when Afghan–German relations were beginning to look like a marriage made in heaven, in late 1925 things took a sudden turn for the worse. The incident that sparked Amanullah's wrath was the shooting of an Afghan by a young German, Gustav Stratil-Sauer, who had arrived in Afghanistan on a geography research trip. On his journey, Stratil-Sauer's motorbike collided with the horse of a camel-caravan driver. A fight broke out between the two men, in which the German pulled out a gun and shot the Afghan dead, allegedly in self-defence. Grobba helped Stratil-Sauer to slip out of Kabul disguised in Afghan dress, but he was captured on the road and taken back to Kabul, where he was put on trial for murder. Amanullah had no wish to upset the goose that laid the golden egg, and he most certainly lost little sleep over the death of a camel driver. But the king's progressive reforms were coming under fire from Islamist quarters in the clergy and armed forces. He needed to appease his reactionary enemies while also treading cautiously to avoid alienating his German partners. The king settled on a face-saving gesture by having the German geographer sentenced to four years' imprisonment for manslaughter. A month later he granted him a royal pardon, covering his back at the same time by announcing that Grobba was to be sent home to Berlin, where shortly after his arrival he took up a post at the Abteilung III bureau, with responsibility for Afghanistan, Persia and India. Grobba's adventurous spirit was incompatible with a desk-bound life at the Foreign Ministry. His relentless, quite thuggish demand for Arab jihad against the British and French brought him into conflict with a number of his more polished colleagues, in particular his bitter rival Werner Otto von Hentig. After four years on the desk Grobba persuaded his superiors to appoint him ambassador to Iraq, but he was forced to flee Baghdad in 1938 after he was found to have engineered the blowing-up of a British oil pipeline by Arab nationalists. Following a series of adventures and narrow escapes in Syria and Nazi-occupied Europe, Grobba was eventually taken prisoner by the Soviets and held captive until 1955.

Germany's commercial relations with Afghanistan suffered a seven-month derailment as both sides grappled to find a solution to the Stratil-Sauer affair. The impasse was finally broken by the arrival of August Feigel as envoy to Kabul in June 1926, an appointment that smoothed the way for a renewal of German activity in Afghanistan. Feigel was a lawyer by training with 25 years' experience in the diplomatic service, just the man to negotiate a friendship treaty between the two countries. During his three-year posting to Kabul, Feigel played a key role in ensuring that German companies were awarded the lion's share of contracts for power stations, roadworks, irrigation systems and other major engineering projects in Amanullah's reform programme.

> In the German high school, seven German teachers together with Afghan educators were training some 400 students [...] Two hospitals were super-vised by Germans, the German Junkers aircraft manufacturing firm was given the exclusive right to establish and maintain air service between Germany and Afghanistan via Turkey and Iran [direct flights were to come later] on to China. This line was not to touch either Russian or British soil and was thus meant to free Afghanistan's air communications from control by her neighbours.[14]

Amanullah had sown the seeds of his own downfall by underestimating the impact his European tour was to have on the powerful clique of reactionaries gnashing their teeth back in Kabul. The king either failed to hear or chose to close his ears to the outcry from the ultra-conservative mullahs, who were incensed over Queen Soraya's failure to wear a veil and, what was far more scandalous, to have appeared at a banquet with her shoulders bared. Amanullah shared the common failing of most absolute rulers by ignoring the obvious warning signals. His haughtiness led him to the hitherto unthinkable extreme of announcing a plan for the compulsory education of women and demanding that 'tribal leaders shave their beards and don top hats and tails'.[15] This unfortunate belief in his own invulnerability can be traced back to 1924, when he had successfully put down a tribal revolt with the help of German pilots and aircraft mechanics. That same year saw the start of organised resistance to Amanullah's reforms, and the first shots were fired in Khost, a small town in south-eastern Afghanistan. What had begun as a localised rebellion soon took on the dimensions of a civil war. The insurrection had been provoked by measures that adversely affected rural taxpayers, the low clergy and some of the tribes. Amanullah shrewdly dismissed the rebel leaders as traitors in the pay of the British, a ploy which was trumpeted by the press and Amanullah's supporters, who produced as proof the sudden appearance in Afghanistan of Abdul Karim, a claimant to the throne, who had been biding his time in exile in British India. The British denied any connivance in his escape and in turn pointed the finger at the Russians, marking another twist in the never-ending Great Game.

Feigel was recalled to Berlin in 1929, when it was obvious to all but the king himself that his fundamentalist enemies were spreading the call to armed rebellion. In that year Afghanistan once again slipped into political chaos and there was no longer any point in promoting German business for projects that had been shelved, along with the man who had conceived them. This time there were no German airmen to suppress a full-scale revolt across the country. Amanullah had pushed his reformist zeal too far. An uprising in Jalalabad culminated in a march on the capital. Despite Amanullah's efforts to rally support from the army to put a stop to the protests, most of his troops deserted and the king was forced to flee from the same reactionary forces that had murdered his father. One of the more intriguing anecdotes to emerge from those turbulent months was the alleged involvement of T.E. Lawrence in Amanullah's downfall. Lawrence had been serving at a base in British India at the time and was hastily sent back to Britain when rumours began to circulate of his espionage activities on the North-West Frontier and in Afghanistan. The conspiracy theorists believed that Lawrence, a seasoned practitioner in stirring up revolts, was sent to help the insurrectionists organise their attack on Kabul. The rationale was that it suited the British to have Amanullah, their former enemy, put out of the way. London considered the king untrustworthy, especially given his cosy relationship with Germany, which was secretly preparing to rearm in defiance of the Treaty of Versailles. There is no documentary evidence to substantiate this speculation, but it is very much in keeping with the Lawrence legend. In May 1929 Amanullah escaped over the Khyber Pass in his Rolls-Royce, clutching his favourite caged canary, with his erstwhile loyal subjects in hot pursuit. Following in the footsteps of several of his forebears, he went into exile in British India. Amanullah and his family later travelled from India to settle in Italy, recalling that on his visit to Rome King Victor Emmanuel III had invited him to consider the country his own. He decided to take up Victor Emmanuel's offer. Amanullah handed over power to his brother Inayatullah, who ruled for all of three days before he was forced to abdicate.

Amanullah's ouster was followed by one of the most bizarre episodes in modern Afghan history. On 17 January 1929, with the uprising in full swing, an illiterate and fanatical Tajik warlord Habibullah Kalakani, known as Bacha-i Saqao (literally, 'Son of a Water Carrier'), suddenly seized power. This was the first and only time a non-Pashtun was to sit on the throne of Kabul, and not for very long at that. Nine months after his coup Bacha-i Saqao, whose brutal and savage rule has been likened to that of the Visigoths in ancient Rome, was himself deposed. Nadir Shah, a member of another branch of the royal family and the general who had commanded the Afghan forces in the Third Anglo-Afghan War, had left his country to go into exile in British India after falling out with Amanullah. When the revolt erupted and Nadir Shah was told that the army was refusing to back the king, he crossed the border into Afghanistan with the connivance of the British and led the troops in a march on Kabul, which they captured and sacked. With Amanullah out of the picture and Nadir Shah hailed as a national hero, there now stood only one obstacle between him and the throne: Bacha-i Saqao, a man who was not even a Pashtun and who ruled more by terror than consent. Nadir Shah decided to dispose of his rival by inviting the Tajik to attend peace talks, at which he seized Bacha-i Saqao, put him on trial and had him hanged, along with 17 of his cohort.

The German chargé d'affaires during Bacha-i Saqao's brief reign was Baron Leopold von Plessen, the dapper mirror image of a 1930s film star. This was Plessen's first major foreign posting, yet he spent less than a year in Kabul before Berlin decided there was no point in keeping a diplomatic presence in a country that lacked even a semblance of stability. Given the potential threat to foreigners, in the summer of 1929 Plessen, along with most other Western diplomats, abandoned Kabul. Germany was without diplomatic representation in Kabul for two years until 1931, when Berlin dispatched in quick succession two envoys to Kabul. The first, Kurt Ziemke, was replaced in 1937 by Hans Pilger, who served as the Nazi regime's ambassador during the Second World War.

Nadir Shah did not share the almost evangelical zeal for modernising that had characterised his predecessor Amanullah: he was too wary of the role of the reactionary clergy in the uprising against the monarchy. Most of Amanullah's social reforms were cast by the wayside, though Nadir Shah can be credited with having established Kabul University, which admitted its first students in 1932 and later became one of Central Asia's most prestigious institutes of higher learning. His principal initiatives were concerned with improving the country's defence system, the construction of the Great North Road through the Hindu Kush and the transformation of a ragtag militia into a reasonably coherent and well-equipped 40,000-strong fighting force.

Nadir Shah was anxious to repair bridges with the West, mainly with the Germans. Relations with Berlin had been badly damaged in the nine months of chaos from the anti-Amanullah revolt to the overthrow of the nefarious Bacha-i Saqao regime. The new king expressed great sympathy for Germany, which he considered the only European power destined to build long-term commercial ties with Afghanistan. However, a number of stumbling blocks still lay in the path between Berlin and Kabul. Nadir Shah was uneasy about the close ties Germany had maintained with Amanullah. The Germans had been awarded many succulent contracts for projects which Nadir Shah had no intention of implementing, mindful of those powerful elements that had violently opposed these same schemes. Could the Germans, he wondered, secretly be hatching a plan to restore Amanullah to the throne and thus re-establish their commercial supremacy in Afghanistan? On the matter of contracts, many had been torn to shreds with the change of regime and Nadir Shah was keen to know the whereabouts of money that had been paid to German contractors. The German's counterclaim centred on the issue of a loan Berlin had granted the Amanullah government but which remained outstanding.

The commercial disputes between both countries were aggravated by an atrocity that took place in June 1933. In November of the previous year the king had captured one of his chief rivals, Ghulam Nabi Charkhi, a Tajik fighter who had fomented a short-lived uprising in the south, with the objective of restoring Amanullah to the throne. Nadir Shah's order to have Charkhi executed provoked a fury among Afghanistan's Tajik minority, which was to have grievous repercussions for the king. Seven months after Charkhi was hanged, Nadir Shah's brother, Mohammed Aziz, was gunned down in a retaliatory attack in Berlin by one Sayyid Kemal, one of the first group of Afghan students to be sent to Germany in the 1920s. The attack took place in the Afghan embassy, where Aziz was serving as minister. The diplomatic row that erupted as a result of this murder was settled to the Afghans' satisfaction in 1935 when the killer, a Charkhi adherent, was convicted and hanged. Agreement was eventually reached over contract payments to Germany and the part repayment of Amanullah's debt. But the happy ending came a bit late for Nadir Shah. In November 1933, when the king was hosting an awards ceremony for students from the German school in Kabul, a 16-year-old boy leapt from the crowd and shot Nadir Shah dead. The incident, as well as the assassin, was disposed of quickly, so the story that the killer was Ghulam Nabi Charkhi's son was never confirmed.

Within hours of the regicide Nadir Shah's son, the 19-year-old Zahir Shah, was enthroned as king of Afghanistan, the country's last monarch. It was one of Afghanistan's rare unopposed transitions of power, and even more noteworthy was the fact that Zahir Shah presided over a nation at peace for 40 years, until his ousting in 1973 by his cousin Mohammed Daoud, who proclaimed Afghanistan a republic and himself president. Zahir Shah had benefited from an international education in France, where he embraced the ideals of European enlightenment which later shaped his policies as a young Minister of Education. Guided by his two powerful uncles, who for years stood as the real power behind the throne, in 1934 Afghanistan's international profile received a significant boost when the country became a member of the League of Nations and obtained formal recognition from the United States.

In this new period of stability, Afghanistan began to put out commercial feelers to the outside world. The focus of this initiative was the future Axis powers of Italy, Japan and Germany, with emphasis on the last of these. Zahir Shah was not particularly enamoured of Nazi doctrine; however, he had been warned to tread cautiously in any approaches made to Russia and Britain. It was feared the two great imperial powers might have designs on Afghanistan, to prevent the country becoming a base for pro-German propaganda and espionage in the next European war. The argument that prevailed in the Great War applied equally to the mid-1930s: Russia and Britain hovered uncomfortably on Afghanistan's doorstep, but Germany was thousands of miles distant.

Germany lost no time in exploiting her advantage to become once again a major player in Afghanistan, both commercially and as a defender of the country's independence in the face of perceived Russian and British threats. The German community in Kabul doubled in number in the early years of Zahir Shah's reign. Berlin's new envoy to Afghanistan, Georg Ripken, was a seasoned career diplomat attached to the Foreign Ministry's Middle Eastern desk. He arrived in Kabul in 1934, shortly after becoming a member of the Nazi Party. Ripken set about gathering intelligence on the Afghan government's plans to seek economic assistance from abroad. He reported back to Berlin on the prevailing political currents within the power elite and the strategy of each regarding Afghanistan's foreign policy. 'They were represented [...] by pro-German, pro-British, pro-Soviet and isolationist parties.'[16] Ripken possessed a formidable amount of information on the government's inner workings, on a level rivalling that of British agents who had been keeping a watch on Afghanistan for decades. One of the strongest of groups was led by the Minister of Commerce, who was against having to rely on foreign assistance from any quarters. The Foreign Ministry circle favoured closer ties with the Soviet Union, as a bulwark against the long-standing threat from Britain. In opposition to this group stood three key Cabinet ministers, who believed British India was still potentially Afghanistan's greatest benefactor. Zahir Shah himself presided over the majority faction that acknowledged the need for foreign aid, so long as it did not come from Britain or Russia. In other words, here was Germany's opportunity to notch itself up from third-power status to pole position in Kabul.

> Representatives of this coalition told [Ripken] that they favoured exclusive cooperation with Germany and wanted to know whether Germany was prepared to assume sole responsibility for the modernisation of Afghanistan, which would require substantial credits to provide the means for Afghanistan's development.[17]

Afghanistan's geographical remoteness held another advantage, for it implied that Germany had no political interests in Central Asia. Kabul assumed that Berlin could be trusted not to interfere in Afghanistan's domestic affairs, hence few restrictions were put on the movements of German engineers and other experts engaged in projects in various parts of the country. Unhampered access to Afghanistan and other parts of Central Asia encouraged the Nazis to embark on some of their more hare-brained expeditions in this mysterious corner of the world. In 1935 a party of German researchers arrived in the remote valleys of Nuristan, whose blond-haired, blue-eyed people are believed by some to be descendants of Alexander's soldiers, in search of the original source of wheat. Then in 1938 Reichsführer-SS Heinrich Himmler dispatched a party of scientists to Tibet, hoping to discover an imaginary race of Aryans which he believed to be the ancestors of Teutonic Germans. Madcap schemes were but an insignificant part of the more serious build-up of Germany's presence in Afghanistan. Germany was adding to her stock of raw materials by tapping into Afghanistan's huge mineral resources, which include gold, nickel, copper and asbestos. German machinery and bridging material was in the process of erection, the great engineering firm Siemens opened an agency in Kabul, 'and houses and furniture of hideous German design were increasingly in evidence'.[18]

By 1937 Germany's heavy-industry exports to Afghanistan had far out-stripped those of the United Kingdom, hitherto Kabul's major trading partner. German steel shipped to Afghanistan was valued at 2.8 million rupees, com-pared with 38,600 rupees for Britain. In the same year, Afghanistan imported 3.2 million rupees' worth of machinery from Germany, more than twice what was purchased from British manufacturers. The British government could not afford to remain indifferent to this steady escalation of Germany's commercial hegemony of Afghanistan. The thought of the Nazis establish-ing a power base on India's doorstep, with another war on the horizon, was the stuff of nightmares. In July 1938 the seasoned Afghan hand Sir William Fraser-Tytler, who was serving as British minister in Kabul, sent a lengthy report to Foreign Secretary Viscount Halifax, giving what he believed to be the reasons for Germany's popularity among the Afghans. The soldier-diplomat identified three factors behind the rise of German influence and prestige in Afghanistan. On the one hand, Berlin was prepared to advance loans of up to £2 million for the purchase of arms, in flagrant violation of the Treaty of Versailles, which Hitler had repudiated in a speech in 1935. The loans were repayable over several years in £600,000 worth of raw materials and the balance in cash. It was believed that Siemens and a German steel company had granted another £1.5 million for machinery orders. Secondly, more than 80 German technicians and experts in various fields, who were prepared to work for a moderate wage and in conditions of extreme discom-fort, were now resident in Afghanistan. Fraser-Tytler also cited the strong German bias of Abdul Majid, president of the Afghan National Bank, who happened to have a German wife.

The Germans were happy to go the extra mile, as it were, to gain the admiration of the people they were trying to woo, even if this meant taking a loss with regard to some of their commercial initiatives. Such was the case with the Berlin–Kabul air service, which carried no post or cargo and only four passengers per flight. Its sole object was in its propaganda value as the one direct link between Afghanistan and Europe, giving the impression that Afghans would find their warmest welcome in Berlin.

> On the social and cultural side of the picture, the revival of the German School in 1935 has had a powerful and lasting effect on a proportion of the rising generation. Two years ago [in 1936] the Olympic Games at Berlin gave an opportunity to a number of young Afghan athletes to see something of German organisation and efficiency, and the tales they brought back of their experiences in Germany as compared with the hospitality they met with elsewhere in Europe lost nothing in the telling. These are all matters which have had and are having an effect on the young intelligentsia of Afghanistan, among whom admiration and respect for the rising power of Germany is widespread.[19]

In Afghanistan there was always a certain amount of pro-German sentiment, springing not unnaturally from the Afghan experiences of the 1930s. The Olympics reinforced these views, having made a deep impression of German efficiency, discipline and power, engendered by the games.

After the outbreak of hostilities in September 1939, officials of the Asia desk at the Auswärtiges Amt began to see the situation in Afghanistan as a rerun of the First World War. Berlin's hopes of tying down troops in India in the face of a threatened Afghan attack had been dashed by King Zahir Shah who, although often wavering, adhered to a policy of neutrality throughout the war. It was not an easy policy to justify to the anti-British factions within his government. Like Habibullah in the Great War, a series of signal defeats inflicted on British forces made it look like the king was perhaps backing the wrong horse. The pressure mounted on Zahir Shah to change course in February 1942, when some 85,000 men, the remainder of the British troops in Malaya, gave themselves up to the Japanese in Singapore. The final surrender was the culmination of a disaster as complete and dramatic as any that has befallen British arms anywhere in the world. In the East there had been nothing like it since the annihilation of a British army in the gorges of the Kabul River just 100 years before.[20] That calamity had a tremendous impact on the Raj, seriously damaging British prestige and undermining British claims to military prowess. But the king faced down his opponents, confident of ultimate Allied victory, and thus the government of India was able to deploy troops from its 2.5-million-strong force, the largest volunteer army in history, to fight in Europe, Africa and Asia.

Hitler never expressed an interest in toppling the Raj: he abhorred the very thought of working hand-in-hand with Indians against the British. As early as 1933, when the leading Indian nationalist Subhas Chandra Bose went to Berlin to meet the newly installed Nazi hierarchy, his first question was when Germany was going to strike at Britain, 'so that we might take up arms simultaneously against the British'.[21] The Germans coolly dismissed him, saying they had no thoughts on this and that they hoped for a compromise. When Bose returned to Berlin in March 1941, the Nazi leadership was preoccupied with more pressing matters. Hitler had already decided on the invasion of Russia, which was to start in June, and his army was now committed to rescuing the Italians in Libya. Hitler's views on Afghanistan, if that country occupied his thoughts at all, concerned its usefulness as a tool for putting Britain on the defensive and tying down troops in India. The prospect of India falling under Indian rule flew in the face of the Führer's racial policies. Indian demands for independence suited Nazi policy in the same way that the Arab insurgency served as a natural ally against the British. The raising of a war party in Afghanistan would strengthen the forces hostile to Britain in India. The strategy was to interrupt Britain's lines of communication from India and to tie down troops and shipping at the expense of other theatres of war. This was the thinking behind Hitler's decision to go to the support of the rebel government of Rashid Ali in Iraq, and it is why Germany needed an anti-British leader in Afghanistan. Having dealt with Axis aggression in Iraq, Britain made the logical assumption that Germany's plans for India went beyond a campaign of border harassment. Fears of a German invasion are still in evidence in the rusted tank traps that straddle the Khyber Pass between Afghanistan and what was British India.

Zahir Shah officially proclaimed his neutrality on 6 September 1939. The king was desperate to obtain military assistance from Britain to defend himself against a Soviet attack, alarmed as he was by the Russian invasion of Finland, another of its small neighbours. His fears were well founded, for at the start of 1940 General Walther von Brauchitsch, commander-in-chief of the German ground forces, proposed sending Russian forces to Afghanistan and India under the auspices of the Nazi–Soviet Pact. A military campaign against India would stir up the tribes of the North-West Frontier and prevent Britain sending troop reinforcements from India – a replay of the Hentig–Niedermayer strategy of 1915. As the Axis pincers were closing in on the Middle East the Afghans became more and more explicit in their overtures to the Germans and Italians. The Afghans indicated that they were ready to fight on the side of the Axis, but only after the termination of the German campaign in the Caucasus and Middle East, and only if the Axis powers were prepared to carry on the campaign into India. Second, the Afghan offer was based on the understanding that that the Axis powers did not intend to subjugate fellow Muslims but, on the contrary, to liberate them.

> Finally, because of the permanent threat of being invaded by the British and Russians, the Afghans insisted that it was imperative for them to behave with utmost caution until the very moment when Axis troops were close enough and ready to render assistance.[22]

The terms laid down by the king bore the hallmarks of what had transpired a quarter of a century before in Kabul. At that time Habibullah had likewise played a cautious hand, endeavouring to keep himself in good graces with both sides, British and German, by exacting conditions that Germany was powerless or unwilling to fulfil.

Opinion was split in Berlin over how to draw Afghanistan into the Nazi camp. Two schools of thought prevailed in the Wilhelmstrasse, with the

Abwehr, or Military Intelligence Bureau, lobbying to push the Zahir Shah regime into rousing the Pashtun tribes to jihad, while the Auswärtiges Amt argued that it was time to consider the king a lost cause and find a more compliant replacement. It was the latter position that in the end prevailed, and this was when the 'Amanullah Plan' began to take shape under the direction of Werner Otto von Hentig. The untiring Hentig had not even remotely withdrawn from the scene after he returned from Afghanistan. His expertise made him a valuable asset in the Auswärtiges Amt in the 1920s, when he took up diplomatic jobs in Constantinople, then San Francisco between 1928 and 1932, and Bogotá for the next four years, a hazardous posting even in those days, for he became the victim of several assassination attempts. He was then sent to Amsterdam until 1937, returning thereafter to Berlin, where he remained attached to the Wilhelmstrasse for the duration of the war. From 1940 onwards, Hentig was sent on missions to the Middle East, where his movements were monitored by British intelligence every step of the way.

The artful Max von Oppenheim enters Hentig's life in late 1940. The Auswärtiges Amt decided to send a trusted staff officer to Syria to report on the political and military position in that Vichy-controlled territory, which was to fall into Allied hands the following year. That was the stated aim: Oppenheim had a different idea, in line with his lifelong jihadist designs. What he envisaged was a mission to create trouble for the Allies in the Arab world. The choice of candidates was narrowed to two, who also happened to be sworn enemies: Werner Otto von Hentig and Fritz Grobba, the man formerly in charge of German relations with the Arabs. Oppenheim was in his early eighties and in spite of his Jewish background, his brilliance still commanded Foreign Ministry respect in Hitler's Germany. 'There is in fact every reason to believe that Oppenheim was later quite actively involved in relations and negotiations between officials of the Third Reich and the leaders of the pro-Axis Arab independence and unity movements.'[23] This time, however, Oppenheim's objectives, as well as the person he proposed to carry them off, were spurned by the Auswärtiges Amt. Hentig, not Grobba, was selected as the Middle East agent. He was given specific instructions that his trip was to be purely of

an intelligence-gathering nature and was cautioned to avoid any provoca-
tive activities with Arab insurgents. With this brief under his arm, Hentig
left Berlin for Damascus in January 1941.

It is unlikely that Hentig's month-long visit to the Middle East paid strict
adherence to these guidelines. The British had been tracking his movements
since his return to Berlin in 1918 and they were by no means convinced that
this was a simple fact-finding mission. Dispatches to Whitehall from British
intelligence in Damascus sent warning signals that Hentig was attempting
to establish contact with Syrian nationalist leaders, while achieving strides
to launch an anti-British propaganda campaign. In the months preceding
America's entry into the war, the US also became aware of German seditionist activities in the Middle East and, of course, they were well acquainted
with Hentig from his travels and diplomatic posting in the US. According
to one secret dispatch relayed from Whitehall to various British legations
in the Middle East:

> Syrian circles in Cairo had heard that von Hentig was well provided with
> funds and that he was recruiting Arab agents for conducting propaganda in
> Syria, Palestine and Iraq. Travellers who arrived in Baghdad from Damascus
> at the end of January [1941] claimed to know that von Hentig was exploring
> the possibility of utilising tribesmen and special agents for carrying out
> sabotage of the railway line between Iraq and Turkey in the event of the
> Turks being drawn into the war.[24]

The story of Hentig's trip to Syria was picked up by the American press after
his return to Berlin. The *New York Times* featured a scathing attack on Hentig
and his colleagues, in which it held them responsible for Nazi agitation in
Syria, with supplementary plans to bring off a *coup d'état* in Iraq.

> They were Herr von Hoentig [sic], a specialist in agitation in the Orient, Dr
> Fritz Grobba, the German Minister to Iraq and Saudi Arabia, and Max von
> Oppenheim, a distinguished archaeologist and acute propagandist. Herr
> von Hoentig devoted himself exclusively to stirring up unrest.[25]

The paper also accused Hentig of organising sabotage and assassination gangs, introducing German agents into Syria and penetrating illegally into Iraq, where he set the stage for the government's overthrow.

Hentig served the Third Reich as a believer in the German cause, but he was not a Nazi. He was too much a humanist to feel anything but contempt for Hitler's persecution of the Jews. There is evidence that on more than one occasion Hentig put himself in jeopardy by denouncing the deportations to the Nazi hierarchy and that he literally risked his neck by helping Jewish families to escape Germany. There is no denying, however, that he was a strong believer in Germany's cause, which he did all he could to further in the Arab world. He had no qualms about acting as Hitler's personal representative at the Egyptian royal wedding in Cairo in 1939, an event that brought together the ruling dynasties of Egypt and Persia. According to British intelligence reports, Hentig, as head of the Foreign Ministry's Middle East section, authorised the publication of the Arabic version of Mein Kampf. During the war, British agents tracked Hentig to Beirut where, assisted by the indefatigable Max von Oppenheim, he was reported to be 'exploring the possibility of utilising tribesmen and special agents for carrying out sabotage of the railway line between Iraq and Turkey in the event of the Turks being drawn into the war'.[26]

Hentig was a strong advocate of the ill-fated Amanullah Plan. This was a scheme drawn up in tandem with the ex-king's brother-in-law, Ghulam Siddiq Khan, who, in spite of his former Amanullah connection, was serving as Zahir Shah's minister to Berlin. The highest-ranking Nazi official (and almost the only one) who gave Hentig's proposal an enthusiastic reception was Foreign Minister Joachim von Ribbentrop. As the co-architect with his Russian counterpart, Vyacheslav Molotov, of the 1939 Soviet–German Non-Aggression Pact, Ribbentrop believed the scheme could count on Soviet backing. But he envisaged something different, an idea that was not to Hentig's liking, which was a guerrilla incursion into British India to be launched from Afghanistan with Russian connivance. The scheme appealed to Ghulam Siddiq, who

> wanted to assemble a group of one to two thousand armed tribesmen [...] equipped and advised by German military personnel. They would later

cross into northern Afghanistan [...] and help to instigate tribal uprisings against the Kabul government among the Frontier tribes.[27]

The British were informed by agents in Afghanistan of the German-inspired threat to depose Zahir Shah. 'There are indications that such a conspiracy is in the process of being hatched in Berlin, where a very well-known ex-official, Ghulam Siddiq Khan, is making the preliminary overtures to Nazi officials.'[28] The ground for fomenting disorder, according to this report classified as top secret, was to be prepared by German technicians resident in Kabul, of whom there were plenty. At the outset of war, Berlin could count on a network of 112 German nationals based in Afghanistan, compared with a British contingent of six. Not a few of these 'technicians' were employed as espionage agents for various Nazi departments. One of the strangest covers employed by an operative of this spy network had been dreamt up by Himmler, who sent SS officer Kurt Brinkmann to Kabul to run a dental surgery.

Amanullah had been sounded out on the plot to restore him to power. Although he paid lip service to the scheme, the ex-king was comfortably ensconced in his Roman villa, with the benefit of an Italian government allowance, and thus did little more than authorise Ghulam Siddiq Khan to carry through negotiations with the Nazis. The Germans soon cooled to the idea of providing support for someone they considered a man of straw, lacking the strength of character to lead a coup. As an alternative, Ghulam Siddiq Khan might be the man to grab power in Kabul, but as he was not a member of the royal family his role would have to be that of the power behind the throne. Nazi top brass Ribbentrop and Rudolf Hess held meetings with Ghulam Siddiq Khan to discuss possible candidates to replace Zahir Shah. There was Amanullah's younger brother Obeidullah, who was living in Rome with his German mistress. Mohammed Hussain Jan, one of Amanullah's cousins, was actively working for Zahir Shah's ouster. Amanullah's eldest son, Crown Prince Rahmatullah Jan, was also living in Rome. Any one of these Afghan exiles might serve Germany's purposes, but at that moment other factors intervened to scotch the Amanullah Plan.

The scheme lost its key supporter in October 1939, when Hentig left the Auswärtiges Amt in a dispute over the Nazi government's foreign policy.

Alfred Rosenberg, leader of the political office and a leading Nazi ideologue, disliked the Amanullah Plan from the outset. 'He even found a supporter within the Oriental Department in Dr [Fritz] Grobba, Hentig's chief rival among the Foreign office's orientalists.'[29] It was Hitler who had the last word on this, as well as all other foreign-policy decisions. After the failure of the Führer's peace feelers to Britain and France in October 1939, his mind turned to a strategy for conducting the inevitable wider European conflict. Afghanistan was far from Hitler's thoughts at this time and he found little appeal in the proposal for an attack on British India. Britain had to be defeated at home, and the Raj could be dealt with at a later date. It was a simple matter for Rosenberg to convince Hitler to call off the Amanullah Plan, which was officially cancelled in the final days of 1939. Unofficially, the Foreign Ministry held out hope that the Soviets would cooperate with Germany to move on Afghanistan and instigate unrest among the tribes. These hopes were dashed in the pre-dawn hours of 22 June 1941, when Hitler launched his invasion of Russia.

Amanullah was not unduly distressed by his failure to be reinstated as king of Afghanistan. He had resigned himself to living out his days as another Afghan exile in Rome. From time to time he would issue statements expressing delight that his native land remained at peace, without mentioning any hopes of recovering the throne. He never saw Afghanistan again, and after his death in 1960 his body was removed for burial in a marble mausoleum in Jalalabad, where he now rests alongside his remarkable wife Soraya, a passionate fighter for Afghan women's rights, who survived her husband by eight years.

For the time being, Zahir Shah sat securely on the throne of Kabul. This did not mean the Nazis had given up using Afghanistan as a base for undermining British India. A letter from the India Office in London to Fraser-Tytler in Kabul speaks of suspicions that 'the large number of Germans employed in Afghanistan, apparently in somewhat un-remunerative posts might not all be there for purely personal or altruistic motives'. [30] Another report provided intelligence on a strange letter found circulating in Peshawar, sent at the instigation of a German in Kabul. The author of this letter quaintly requested that a complete poem be written to complete the couplet in Pashtu, 'Why

should I fight the Germans for another [merely] because I am a Pashtun?'[31]
This was one of the Abwehr's clumsier attempts to provoke trouble on India's
North-West Frontier.

In April 1941 the Germans sent undercover agents into Afghanistan to
arrange for the transport of weapons to Indian revolutionaries in India,
in what became one of the more quixotic adventures of the war. Manfred
Oberdöffer, a physician, had persuaded an Afghan minister attending a
dinner in Berlin that it would be to Afghanistan's advantage to rid his country
of leprosy, which was Oberdöffer's area of specialisation. The Afghan government heartily agreed and Oberdöffer chose as his assistant Fred Hermann
Brandt, an entomologist whose passion for butterflies was boundless. He
was acquainted with the Middle East and had travelled to Iran between
1937 and 1939 to study and collect butterflies and moths. Brandt was also
a member of the Wehrmacht and had headed a Brandenburg Battalion in
1939. Most useful of all was his wartime training as a counter-espionage
officer. Oberdöffer and Brandt were granted permits to travel to Kabul. They
forwarded to Afghanistan, under diplomatic cover, two tonnes of small
arms and an anti-aircraft gun, along with ammunition, to be distributed
among the North-West Frontier tribes. For the real objects of their mission
were to persuade the ferocious Waziri frontier tribe to rise up against the
British, to distribute what was required in the way of money and munitions,
and to place agents in India. On 20 April 1941, Hitler's 52nd birthday, the
Abwehr instructed the German legation in Kabul to commence sabotage
operations on the frontier. After attending a two-week sabotage course, on
22 May the two men departed Berlin for Afghanistan. At the border, they
made themselves out to be famous physicians. As the customs officials lined
up for treatment of various ailments, Oberdöffer gave them all laxatives and
there was subsequently no examination of their luggage. On their arrival in
Kabul, Brandt spent much of his time in the surrounding hills, alone with
his butterflies, having no stomach for Oberdöffer's drunken debaucheries
at the German legation. Brandt, suffering from toothache, made use of the
services of Brinkmann, Himmler's dentist-spy.

On 15 July 1941, Oberdöffer and Brandt set out for Waziristan, eventually
managing to penetrate 20 miles inside British territory, where they carried

out a few relatively inconsequential acts of sabotage, including an attack on a British radio station. On their return to the border the two Germans bedded down for the night behind an earthwork parapet that Oberdöffer had put up in a hollow. An hour later they awoke to the sound of gunfire. Oberdöffer sat up, ordered Brandt to return the fire and immediately took bullets to his lung and stomach. Brandt was wounded in the face by rock splinters. It was a trap: they had been betrayed by an Afghan in Kabul who had told the government of the real intention of their mission. The attackers were Afghan troops, who captured the two Germans and stripped them of their watches, money, cameras and clothes. Brandt was left wearing only his shorts, which were in shreds. Oberdöffer died in the lorry that took them back to Kabul and Brandt spent more than three months in hospital before being repatriated with the rest of the Germans expelled from Afghanistan in November 1941.

Their expedition had accomplished almost nothing and it also failed in one of its primary objectives, which was to recruit the 'Fakir of Ipi', Mirza Ali Khan, a guerrilla fighter from Waziristan, to the Nazi cause. The fakir was prepared to lend his services to the Germans who, along with the Italians, supplied him with enough money and weapons to carry out an average of two attacks a week against British targets. The fakir was potentially an asset of enormous value to the Germans, for by stirring up turmoil on the frontier Britain would be prevented from sending reinforcements to Iraq. It could be argued that the Germans achieved an indirect success in dealing with the fakir, in so far as Indian army units that were technically free to serve in the Middle East were deployed to hold down Waziristan, the fakir's main base of operations. Apart from that, the Nazis' relationship with the fakir was a relatively harmless episode. It came to an end in October 1941 when the firebrand insurgent got fed up dealing with foreigners of any persuasion and declared himself anti-German as well as anti-British. The fakir continued to elude capture and he led the British a merry chase right up to the partition in 1947.

The Oberdöffer–Brandt mission was not the last German attempt to strike at their enemies through Afghanistan. In September 1941 the Abwehr's Dietrich Witzel-Kim was dispatched to Kabul with a party of Afghan and

Indian agents specially trained for an espionage mission. His orders were to make his way by footpath and road to the Indian border to set a transmitter base and secure the goodwill of the frontier tribes. Their task was to carry out sabotage operations against Russian as well as British targets, and they carried off their objective with greater success than their predecessors, Brandt and the ill-starred Oberdöffer:

> On a single night, 19 October 1941, three Russian border posts and a railway terminus were attacked and blown up. Before the Russians could react, the next night a railway repair facility and a small power plant that also supplied power to the Russian border garrisons were destroyed.[32]

The attacks continued into March 1942, now against British targets, with raids on patrols and outposts, supply routes and communications services. In May, Witzel-Kim was instructed to carry out a reconnaissance mission on a north–south axis between Kabul and Ghazni, seeking out potential sites for sabotaging this strategic supply-and-communications road. He and his Afghan agent set out on 3 June, dressed as mountain tribesmen. Witzel-Kim darkened his face and body with walnut juice, which enabled them boldly to link up at one point with a small caravan travelling under British escort. They returned to Kabul a week later with valuable intelligence reports that detailed potential invasion routes into the Caucasus. The British were by now aware of Witzel-Kim's activities and brought pressure to bear on Zahir Shah to have him and all other German agents arrested. A number of spies were picked up, but Witzel-Kim went into hiding and later escaped to Germany to carry on with his daredevil exploits. In 1944 he was parachuted into Ukraine to coordinate German–Ukrainian joint resistance to the Red Army onslaught.

In late 1941 Britain decided to put an end to Nazi intrigues in Afghanistan. In August of that year Fraser-Tytler was replaced by the long-serving Indian Civil Service diplomat Sir Francis Verner Wylie, whose first act was to request the expulsion of all Axis personnel in Kabul within one month. Wylie's proposal was seconded by his Soviet colleague. It was time for Zahir Shah to show his true colours. The king's decision to grant the Allied request was facilitated by British victories in Persia, campaigns that severed Afghanistan's last land links with Germany. That same month more than 200 Axis nationals were sent home to Europe via still-neutral Turkey. Although this enabled the Allies to bring to a halt large-scale German conspiracies and espionage activities in Afghanistan, small diplomatic staffs were allowed to remain. These agents continued to spread pro-Nazi propaganda, which played up the battle to defeat the godless Soviet Union. As late as 1944, the German chargé d'affaires in Kabul was assuring Berlin that the 'diminution of Britain's position as a world power' was welcomed by the Afghans who, on the other hand, greatly feared the consequences of a possible Soviet victory. 'The solution is seen in a German victory over Bolshevism, and our continually emphasised confidence in victory, as expressed in the Führer's speech of the 30th January [1944], represents the main credit in our propaganda account.'[33] The Nazis also succeeded in setting up a relay station in the Caucasus to secure the radio link between Kabul and Berlin. This set-up lasted almost to the end of the war, even after the Caucasus had been evacuated by German forces, enabling Nazi agents to carry out minor acts of sabotage in Afghanistan as well as India. A further sign that the king was leaning towards the Allied camp was his submission pressure from Delhi to veto the appointment of Hentig as Germany's envoy to Kabul, an idea that had originated with Ribbentrop. Britain did not wish to have Hentig carrying on the activities that had taken him to Kabul 25 years previously.

Hentig had the proverbial last word in the tension that plagued his relationship with Niedermayer, for he outlived his rival by 36 years. Both men served their country during the Second World War, although it cannot be asserted that either was adherent to Nazi ideology. Niedermayer had the greatest contempt for Hitler, whom he considered a vulgarian and a demagogue, and in several instances he found himself landed in hot water with the Gestapo. His narrowest escape came when he was arrested in 1944 on suspicion of having had a hand in the failed assassination attempt on Hitler. It was only his impeccable service record and testimonials from fellow army officers that saved him from an unpleasant fate. Niedermayer's Middle East expertise made him the ideal officer, now with the rank of major-general, to lead one of the Wehrmacht's Muslim battle groups. He took charge of the 162nd Turkmen Division, whose troops were recruited from Central Asian and Azerbaijani prisoners of war. He was later appointed the commander of Volunteer Units East. Niedermayer was arrested by the Russians after the war and died three years later, aged 63, in a Soviet prisoner-of-war camp hospital.

Hentig risked his neck to save German Jews from persecution and deportation. After the *Kristallnacht* riots of November 1938, when rampaging mobs were exhorted by Gestapo storm-troopers to attack and destroy Jewish shops and homes, the Nazis shut down the Reichsvertretung der Deutschen Juden (Representative Council of Jews in Germany), whose terrified officials attempted to contact government offices to plead for a halt to the vandalism. Himmler's SS had cut almost all their lines of communication, except with the Foreign Ministry. Ernst Marcus, director of the Jewish-run Paltreu Company, called Hentig, the head of the Oriental Department, and was immediately granted an interview. Hentig expressed his shame at the barbaric behaviour of the Nazis and used his influence, at great personal risk, to prevent a fresh outbreak of violence. Marcus had heard that Propaganda Minister Joseph Goebbels planned to organise a procession of Jewish men through the streets of Berlin under SA escort, and other degrading actions. Hentig got on the telephone to Under-Secretary of State Ernst von Weizsäcker, pointing out the detrimental impact this would have on German foreign policy. Hentig also secured the release of the arrested members of the Reichsvertretung and other prominent Jews from concentration camps. He was playing a dangerous game, in the hope that his brilliant service record would safeguard him from Nazi persecution. Hentig instructed Marcus to draw up a document detailing how the German contribution to the creation of a Jewish state in Palestine was insignificant compared with the work being carried out by Polish and American Jews. 'This memorandum served as a basis for the *Report to Hitler by the Foreign Office*, to which Hentig attached a brief arguing that there were certain advantages to Germany in the establishment of a Jewish state.'[34]

When Hentig entered Hitler's office to explain his plan, the Führer laid his hand limply in Hentig's as a form of greeting – a soft hand, Hentig noted, with chewed nails. Hitler knew that Hentig had served in Bogotá and he launched into a discourse about South America, then suddenly stopped to gaze out of the window. Hentig attempted to fill the awkward silence with some more comments about South America and when it came time to expound the rationale for allowing Jewish emigration, he played to Hitler's crafty but twisted mind: by concentrating the Jewish population in a single foreign entity, he explained, Germany's diplomatic policy and containment of the Jews would become easier. Waiting outside Hitler's office was the government official Fritz-Dietlof von der Schulenburg, hanged in August 1944 as a co-conspirator in the plot to assassinate Hitler. Hentig's contempt for the Nazi leader was reflected in his comment, 'Hitler's cruelty to civil servants who were superior to him in knowledge and character showed itself [...] when he had Schulenburg hanged some time later.'[35] A short while later, Hentig was able to give Marcus cause for celebration with the news that Hitler, after much prevarication, had at last made a favourable decision and that all obstacles in the way of emigration to Palestine were now removed.

Hentig died in Norway in 1984 at the advanced age of 98. To the end, he was always happy to share his version of events with journalists and historians. There is even a posthumous article by Hentig in a German magazine accusing Niedermayer of having usurped the mission and gathered all the accolades for himself, while Hentig was still struggling across China on his perilous homeward journey. Niedermayer, the son of a Bavarian civil servant, and Hentig, the Prussian aristocrat, shared a number of traits which almost necessarily were to result in a fractious relationship between the two men: both were highly intelligent, ambitious and strong-willed adventurers, cast together in alien and hostile surroundings. Niedermayer could be infuriatingly secretive about his doings in a situation that demanded open collaboration, while Hentig's arrogance often undermined what should have been a team effort. This conflict of personalities compromised the mission from the outset, leaving aside the greater political issues that doomed it to an unsatisfactory conclusion, if not outright failure. However, the legacy Germany left in Afghanistan over the years ensured its esteem in the eyes of future Afghan leaders. After the 2001 terrorist attacks on the US and the toppling of the Taliban regime, it was decided to call an international conference to devise a plan for governing Afghanistan and to elect a new leadership. The Afghans' long collective memory perceived Germany as a friend in time of conflict, so the idea was put forward and eagerly embraced by Afghanistan that the venue for this gathering should be Bonn.

Germany still sees itself as tightly connected to Afghanistan, culturally and, since 2001, militarily. German troops represent the third-largest foreign contingent serving in that country, after the United States and Britain, and Berlin has said it will keep at least 800 deployed in the country after the withdrawal of ISAF combat troops. There are almost 90,000 people of Afghan extraction living in Germany and 'to this day, many Afghans see Germans as fellow Aryans, creating the occasional awkward moment for German officers deployed there'.[36] Such fanciful racial bonds aside, Germans have always enjoyed a good reputation in Kabul, and it is likely they will take a significant part in many of the country's postwar development programmes.

Epilogue

It could be argued that the story of the German mission to Afghanistan is that of a failed military-diplomatic operation. Despite months of persistent efforts, Amir Habibullah was never drawn from his policy of neutrality throughout the years of the Great War. The Afghan ruler's steadfast friendship was of immense benefit to Britain, a nation engaged in a desperate struggle on the Western Front and the Middle East against a superbly organised and powerful German war machine. It must also be said that upon close analysis at no time did the German presence in Kabul represent a threat to British dominion of its Indian Empire. Never did any German or Turkish fighting units cross the Afghan border. Every attempt to set the North-West Frontier ablaze failed to escalate what had always been sporadic outbreaks of tribal raiding, and the British had been grappling skilfully with these incidents for nearly half a century.

Hentig and Niedermayer did not succeed in persuading Habibullah to take up arms against India. Yet it can equally be argued that the German mission was successful in so far as it achieved a number of its objectives. It disturbed Russia and Britain greatly with its activities, and it carried hostile propaganda into an area hitherto the exclusive concern of these two European powers. The expedition came with a message and it nearly succeeded in involving Afghanistan in the war.[1] The Germans in fact arrived with multiple messages – jihad, Indian liberation and Afghan sovereignty, to name but three of the most powerful. The message of anti-colonialism was one that appealed greatly to the Afghans, as well as to the Persians, and in this regard Niedermayer and Hentig, not to omit the intrepid Wassmuss, were ahead of their time. It can also be argued that Britain had the Germans to thank for the outbreak of the Third Anglo-Afghan War. Habibullah stuck to his unpopular policy of neutrality, which resulted in his assassination and the proclamation of Amanullah, his hardliner successor. Perhaps the most important consequence of the mission was totally unintended: the arrival of the Germans marked the end of Afghanistan's policy of isolationism. After the Great War, the development of a more or less permanent German presence in Afghanistan enhanced the country's profile in the international political arena. In Kabul the presence of foreigners hostile to Britain and Russia contributed to the Afghan nationalist fervour. It also accustomed the Afghan people to seeing large numbers of foreigners in their country.[2]

Niedermayer himself proudly lays claim to their success, while expressing the paternalistic yet genuine benevolence that he and Hentig felt towards Afghanistan:

> The Mission introduced new ideas, and it aroused and strengthened forces and indicated methods in countries which had hitherto been affected solely by British and Russian interests. The internal development in Persia and Afghanistan since the War and the efforts of these countries in the direction of independence, were the logical sequence of the work begun by us.[3]

He also says, rather astonishingly given that this took place a century ago, that they made it a matter of principle not to offend the Afghans by purchasing any foreign-made goods during the months spent in Kabul.

> We were able to give the businessmen many a stimulating idea for turning the excellent handmade cotton and other dress materials to account. Above all, the people listened eagerly when we told them about the state of affairs in the great world outside.[4]

One wonders what the tribesmen, greybeards for the most part who had never laid eyes on the sea or whose only notion of a man-made flying object was a musket ball, made of Niedermayer's fantastic tales of submarines and Zeppelins. There was never any doubt about Niedermayer's professionalism as a soldier. This was even acknowledged by his adversaries. Brigadier General Sir Percy Sykes, who with the agreement of Tehran raised a Persian force to counter the German influence in that country, considered the mission 'a complete failure'. Nevertheless, he held a great admiration for Niedermayer, praising 'his courage and initiative' which 'under most difficult conditions, were remarkable'.[5]

Hentig was another of the few Europeans of his day to show genuine concern for Afghanistan's welfare beyond its strategic usefulness as a buffer between great empires. He took great personal satisfaction in what had been achieved during the many months spent in Kabul during the Great War, including, in his estimate, having kept at least 100,000 troops tied up in India.

> The German diplomatic Mission resulted unexpectedly [...] in awakening an unknown national pride in Afghanistan, supported by youth eager to learn, and in making it possible for the minorities to play a role in the state. Our politics were absolutely clear and open and therefore we did not disappoint anyone.[6]

There is the debatable question of which of the two leaders could legitimately take credit for whatever the mission accomplished. I have chosen to call this the Hentig–Niedermayer mission, though in the years that followed, at times marred by acrimony, nobody could decide which was the senior leader of the mission. This remained a bone of contention between the two men for a long time and led to some bitter words from Hentig, well into old age. But they appeared to be on the best of terms after their return to Germany. Hentig in fact recommended Niedermayer for the title of Ritter, the German equivalent of a knighthood, with the military Order of Max Joseph. Not to be left unrewarded for his own services, the kaiser bestowed on Hentig the chivalrous Hausorden von Hohenzollern. The relationship turned sour later on, when Hentig blamed Niedermayer for the breakdown of his marriage, due to the fact that Hentig's wife had allegedly ridiculed Niedermayer for having portrayed Hentig as a peripheral character in Kabul. Hentig, on the contrary, categorically states in his published account of the mission that he was always the man in charge. Hentig wrote to Niedermayer, demanding a formal apology and a public explanation, stating that these were always to be considered separate diplomatic and military missions, with Hentig indisputably in charge of the former. He insisted that Niedermayer, who was serving in Moscow at the time, return to Berlin to clear Hentig's name. When Niedermayer's lawyer replied in the negative, Hentig's Prussian blood rose in fury: there were only two choices left, a duel or a military 'court of honour'. Given the physical distance between the two men and the fact that Niedermayer refused to travel to Berlin, the duel option was dismissed as impractical. Hentig approached the commanding officer of Niedermayer's old regiment to lodge a formal judicial complaint. No action was ever forthcoming and there the matter was left to die a natural death.

There was always going to be a conflict between two groups with different objectives travelling as one, the first sent by the General Staff and the other under Foreign Ministry auspices. When in June 1915 Hentig and Niedermayer met in Tehran, they failed to reach an agreement on who was to assume the leadership. Historians are divided over this touchy issue. The British High Command, in a number of official dispatches, refers to Hentig as the senior figure in Kabul. But there are those who contend that the mission's aim was primarily military, albeit under nominal political jurisdiction, which would therefore argue in favour of Niedermayer being effectively in charge. Ultimately, the issue became that of the subordination of the military to political control. But even on ostensibly neutral territory, practicality gave the weight to the former, not the latter. Whatever were the achievements of the mission to Afghanistan, the credit is Niedermayer's, argues one historian.[7] Perhaps. However, it is beyond dispute that the mission would not have accomplished what it did without the presence of both men in Kabul.

Writing a decade after he and Hentig had returned to Germany, with Hitler giving his first public speech since his release from jail and darkness

descending on the country, Niedermayer looked back and reflected on the
two years that had marked the most momentous events of his life:

> Even though the visible traces of the German Mission may, by this time,
> have almost disappeared and though the graves we left may have been
> levelled with the soil by sun, wind and rain, yet our efforts and sacrifices
> have not been in vain. These graves were scattered over the whole length of
> the route, nearly fourteen thousand miles across hot deserts and steppes,
> a route which will probably not again be followed by any European.[8]

Appendix 1

THE ANGLO-RUSSIAN CONVENTION
CONCERNING PERSIA AND AFGHANISTAN
ST PETERSBURG, 31 AUGUST 1907
PERSIA

The Governments of Great Britain and Russia having mutually engaged to respect the integrity and independence of Persia, and sincerely desiring the preservation of order throughout that country and its peaceful development, as well as the permanent establishment of equal advantages for the trade and industry of all other nations;

Considering that each of them has, for geographical and economic reasons, a special interest in the maintenance of peace and order in certain Provinces of Persia adjoining, or in the neighbourhood of, Russian frontiers on the one hand, and the frontiers of Afghanistan and Baluchistan on the other hand; and being desirous of avoiding all cause of conflict between their respective interests in the above-mentioned provinces of Persia;

Have agreed on the following terms:

I.

Great Britain engages not to seek for herself, and not to support in favour of British subjects, or in favour of the subjects of third Powers, any Concessions of a political or commercial nature – such as Concessions for railways, banks, telegraphs, roads, transport, insurance, etc. – beyond a line starting from Kas'r-i-Shirin, passing through Isfahan, Yezd, Kakhk, and ending at a point on the Persian frontier at the intersection of the Russian and Afghan frontiers, and not to oppose, directly or indirectly, demands for similar Concessions in this region which are supported by the Russian Government. It is understood that the above-mentioned places are included in the region in which Great Britain engages not to seek the Concessions referred to.

II.

Russia, on her part, engages not to seek for herself and not to support, in favour of Russian subjects, or in favour of the subjects of third Powers, any Concessions of a political nature – such as Concessions for railways, banks, telegraphs, roads, transport, insurance, etc. – beyond a line going from the Afghan frontier by way of Gazik, Birjand, Kerman, and ending at Bunder Abbas, and not to oppose, directly or indirectly, demands for similar Concessions in this region which are supported by the British Government. It is understood that the above-mentioned places are included in the region in which Russia engages not to seek the Concessions referred to.

III.

Russia, on her part, engages not to oppose, without previous arrangement with Great Britain, the grant of any Concessions whatever to British subjects in the regions of Persia situated between the lines mentioned in Articles I and II.

Great Britain undertakes a similar engagement as regards the grant of Concessions to Russian subjects in the same regions of Persia.

All Concessions existing at present in the regions indicated in Articles I and II are maintained.

CONVENTION RESPECTING AFGHANISTAN

The High Contracting Parties, in order to ensure perfect security on their respective frontiers in Central Asia and to maintain in these regions a solid and lasting peace, have concluded the following Convention:

ARTICLE I

His Britannic Majesty's Government declare that they have no intention of changing the political status of Afghanistan.

His Britannic Majesty's Government further engage to exercise their influence in Afghanistan only in the pacific sense, and they will not themselves take, nor encourage Afghanistan to take, any measures threatening Russia.

The Russian Government, on their part, declare that they recognise Afghanistan as outside the sphere of Russian influence, and they engage that all their political relations with Afghanistan shall be conducted through the intermediary of His Britannic Majesty's Government; they further engage not to send any Agents into Afghanistan.

ARTICLE II

The Government of His Britannic Majesty having declared in the Treaty signed at Kabul on the 21st March, 1905, that they recognise the Agreement and the engagements concluded with the late Amir Abdur Rahman, and that they have no intention of interfering in the internal government of Afghan territory, Great Britain engages neither to annex nor to occupy in contravention of that Treaty any portion of Afghanistan or to interfere in the internal administration of the country, provided that the Amir fulfils the engagements already contracted by him towards His Britannic Majesty's Government under the above-mentioned Treaty.

ARTICLE III

The Russian and Afghan authorities specially designated for the purpose on the frontier or in the frontier provinces, may establish direct relations with each other for the settlement of local questions of a non-political character.

ARTICLE IV

His Britannic Majesty's Government and the Russian Government affirm their adherence to the principle of equality of commercial opportunity in Afghanistan, and they agree that any facilities which may have been, or shall be hereafter obtained for British and British Indian trade and traders, shall be equally enjoyed by Russian trade and traders. Should the progress of trade establish the necessity for Commercial Agents, the two Governments will agree as to what measures shall be taken, due regard, of course, being had to the Amir's sovereign rights.

ARTICLE V

The present arrangements will only come into force when His Britannic Majesty's Government shall have notified to the Russian Government the consent of the Amir to the terms stipulated above.

Appendix 2

PROPOSED TREATY BETWEEN THE AMIR
OF AFGHANISTAN AND THE GERMAN MISSION
KABUL, 24 JANUARY 1916

The following Friendship Treaty shall exist for the present and future between the All-highest God-given Afghan Government and the Highest German Government.

(1)   The Afghan Government affirms her complete independence and political freedom.

(2)   The German Government takes it upon herself to help the Afghan Government so far as she can do so. Germany recognises the independence of Afghanistan, and will cause the Austrian and Bulgarian Governments to recognise it on their part.

(3)   The Afghan Government begins forthwith with the perfecting of her military resources and administration, and also with political relations with the peoples of Persia, India and Russian Turkestan.

(4)   The German Government is pledged to furnish the Afghan Government as assistance, as quickly as possible, gratis and without return, 100,000 rifles of the newest pattern, and 300 guns, big and small, with complete new pattern equipment of the appropriate munitions, and other necessary war materiel, and a crore fund, i.e. 10 mil. sterling. She takes it upon herself, moreover, to open the way through Persia in order that the German Empire may give the Afghan Kingdom officers, engineers, and

other officials, of whom Afghanistan stands in need and that these may remain officials of the Afghan Kingdom and be honoured as such.

(5)   The Afghan Kingdom lays down categorically that these measures are for this purpose, that when they are taken she may strengthen herself and will draw benefit from them in time of necessity.

(6)   The German Government is pledged in the event of Afghanistan having entered into the war or making expeditious preparations of a military or external political character, to enter the lists for the possession of lost and conquered territories and always to defend the Afghan Kingdom with all measures against foreign conquest to the rear of the Afghan Kingdom.

(7)   The Afghan Government recognises the Embassy Secretary of the German Empire, Herr von Hentig, and sends forthwith her own envoy with limited powers to the Persian capital, in order to negotiate there in secrecy with the German, Turkish and Austrian envoys. As soon as the time is come and he can show openly that he is the deputy of the Afghan Government, he will openly declare himself Minister of Afghanistan: and at the time of the general conclusion of peace a plenipotentiary, qualified for the Conference, will be appointed with plenary powers as Afghanistan's plenipotentiary on behalf of the rights of the Afghan Government.

(8)   Relating to the Embassy are:

   a) The escort of the Embassy shall not be more than 20 to 30 strong.

   b) It will be permitted to buy up to 20 jaribs [approximately 10 acres] of land for the Ambassador's residence and to build the Embassy on it.

   c) If a subject of Afghanistan or some other Power seeks refuge in the Embassy after the commission of a crime, it is essential that the Embassy should give him no protection.

   d) If a subject of the Kingdoms possessing an Embassy in Afghanistan has a lawsuit, the decision shall be pleaded according to Afghan laws, and his Ambassador shall have no concern with it. For various commercial suits and others which have not yet arisen in any form in Afghanistan, the Afghan Government will make new laws.

(10)   After the general peace a Commercial Treaty will be concluded between the Afghan and German Governments with mutually binding conditions.[1]

(11)   Both parties shall regard themselves bound when the Afghan envoy in the Persian capital receives news from the German Government that this Treaty has been ratified by the German Government.

True copy of His Majesty's endorsement.

I, on behalf of the Highest Afghan Government, in accordance with the conditions of the above Treaty with the German Government, desire that an alliance shall be concluded.

Signed. Lamp of the Nation and Religion, Kabul, the 18th Rabi-ul-Awal 1916.

True copy of the endorsement by Captains Niedermayer and Hentig.

The Afghan Government desires the friendship of the German Government and to conclude a Treaty in accordance with this draft. I send this copy of the Afghan Treaty to the German Government. Now that I have seen Afghanistan I recommend one to the German Government, and I hope that she will accept this Friendship Treaty.

Signed. Niedermayer. Hentig. 24 January 1916.

Glossary

Abwehr – Germany's Military Intelligence Bureau.

amban and *taotai* are titles for Chinese district officials in charge of civil and military affairs.

Auswärtiges Amt – German Foreign Ministry.

Bala Hissar – Historic hilltop fortress and former royal residence overlooking Kabul.

caravanserai – A caravan rest stop, generally a walled enclosure serving as a guest house for travellers on commercial routes from south-eastern Europe to Asia.

lashkar – A tribal fighting force of North-West Frontier tribesmen, raised like a militia.

loya jirga – A grand council of Afghan elders and religious leaders, usually convened to decide on issues of State.

Petrograd – St Petersburg's name was changed to Petrograd in 1914. Ten years later it became Leningrad, and then readopted its original name when the Soviet Union collapsed in 1991.

Wilhelmstrasse – Until 1945 the German centre of government in Berlin, housing the Reich Chancellery and the Foreign Ministry.

Notes

NA = National Archives
FO = Foreign Office
IOR = British Library India Office Records
MSS Eur = British Library European Manuscripts

ACKNOWLEDGEMENTS

1   Peter Hopkirk, *On Secret Service East of Constantinople* (London: John Murray, 1994), p. 217.

CHAPTER 1 • THE KAISER, THE AMIR AND THE VICEROY

1   *The Daily Telegraph*, 1 March 1928, p. 3.
2   Rhea Talley Stewart, *Fire in Afghanistan: 1914–1929* (New York, NY: Doubleday & Co., 1973), p. 38.
3   *The Times*, 28 October 1898, p. 7.
4   Evans Lewin, *The German Road to the East* (London: Heinemann, 1916), p. 99.
5   William Treloar, *With the Kaiser in the East* (London: Horace Marshall & Sons, 1898), pp. 27–8.
6   Lewin, *The German Road*, p. 106.
7   Wolfram W. Gottlieb, *Studies in Secret Diplomacy during the First World War* (London: George Allen & Unwin Ltd., 1957).
8   Max Hastings, 'The Turkish-German jihad', *The New York Review of Books*, 9 December 2010, p. 10.
9   Frank G. Weber, *Eagles on the Crescent* (Ithaca, NY: Cornell University Press, 1970), p. 137.
10 Martin Ewans (ed.), 'Is a campaign by Russia to India possible?', in *Britain and Russia in Central Asia* (London: Routledge, 2004), vol. 1, p. 219.
11 Ravinder Kumar, 'The records of the government of India on the Berlin–Baghdad railway question', *The Historical Journal* v/1 (1962), p. 72.
12 The capital of British India was moved from Calcutta to Delhi in 1912.
13 Christopher M. Wyatt, *Afghanistan and the Defence of Empire* (London: I.B.Tauris, 2011), p. 182.
14 Mikhail Grulev, *The Rivalry of Russia and England in Central Asia*, IOR, L/PS/20/161, 1909, pp. 67–8.

15 IOR, L/MIL/17/14/15/2, pp. 12–13.
16 Amin Saikal, *Modern Afghanistan* (London: I.B.Tauris, 2004), p. 52.
17 Martin Ewans, *Afghanistan* (London: HarperCollins, 2002), p. 82.
18 Arthur Cecil Edwards, 'German intrigues in Persia', *The Yale Review* vii (1918), p. 34.
19 Lieutenant General Henry McMahon, *An Account of the Entry of H.M. Habibullah Khan Amir of Afghanistan into Freemasonry* (West Sussex: Favil Press, 1940), p. 3.
20 Brigadier General Percy Sykes, *A History of Afghanistan* (London: Macmillan & Co., 1940), vol. 2, pp. 226–7.
21 The first Grand Lodge was formed in London in 1717.
22 McMahon, *Account of the Entry*, pp. 10–11.
23 Bijan Omrani, *Afghanistan: A Companion and Guide* (Hong Kong: Odyssey Books, 2005), p. 81.
24 The system of postal dak runners was introduced in the Indus Valley in the days of the Mughal emperors. The runners were paid according to their distance of travel and the weight of their letters. In the early twentieth century, letters from Afghanistan took on average three days to reach India.
25 Saikal, *Modern Afghanistan*, p. 45.
26 There is a long history of US involvement in Afghan civil engineering projects. From the end of the Second World War until the Soviet invasion in 1979, numerous American engineers worked to develop Afghanistan's infrastructure through the construction of dams and highways. The Morrison-Knudsen Company, a private US firm, completed the monumental Arghandab and Kajaki dams in Helmand Province in 1953. Two of the major roads, the Kabul–Kandahar and Herat–Islam Qala highways, were completed in the 1960s by the US Army Corps of Engineers. The Helmand Valley Authority (HVA) was one of the most ambitious and complex undertakings in the history of US–Afghan collaboration. In addition to building a network of irrigation canals to promote agricultural production, the HVA constructed thousands of houses and even entire towns, such as the modern provincial capital of Lashkar Gah, as well as two new airports.
27 Ikbal Ali Shah, *Afghanistan and the German Threat* (Edinburgh: *Edinburgh Review*, 1918), p. 60.
28 Peter Levi, *The Light Garden of the Angel King* (London: Pallas Athene, 2000), p. xvii.

CHAPTER 2 • WE'RE OFF TO JOIN THE CIRCUS

1 Ludwig Adamec, *Afghanistan: 1900–1923* (Berkeley, CA: University of California Press, 1967), p. 5.
2 In all, 1.6 million Indians volunteered to fight for Britain in the Great War. Of these, 138,000 fought on the Western Front, and they took part in every major battle. Seven were given the coveted Victoria Cross, Britain's highest military decoration awarded for valour.
3 Quoted in Philip Mason, *A Matter of Honour* (London: Jonathan Cape, 1974), p. 413.
4 Quoted in Fritz Fischer, *Germany's Aims in the First World War* (New York, NY: W.W. Norton & Co., 1967), p. 126.
5 Tilman Lüdke, *Jihad Made in Germany* (Berlin: LIT Verlag, 2005), p. 115.
6 Ibid., p. 117.
7 Montagu R. Lawrence (ed.), *The Home Letters of T.E. Lawrence and His Brothers* (Oxford:

Basil Blackwell, 1954), p. 225.

8   Franz von Papen, *Memoirs* (London: André Deutsch, 1952), p. 40.

9   Thomas Grant Fraser, 'Germany and Indian revolution, 1914–1918', *Journal of Contemporary History* xii/2 (1977), p. 261.

10 Papen, *Memoirs*, p. 40.

11 Charles Hardinge, MSS Eur, Microfilm D613, p. 280.

12 Charles Hardinge, *My Indian Years: 1910–1916* (London: John Murray, 1948), pp. 131–2.

13 Oliver Stone, *World War One* (London: Penguin, 2008), p. 74.

14 George Roos-Keppel, MSS Eur, Microfilm D613.

15 Christopher Sykes, *Wassmuss: The German Lawrence* (London: Longmans, 1936), p. 44.

16 Oskar Ritter von Niedermayer, *Under the Burning Sun of Iran*, unattributed translation of *Unter der Gut Sonne Irans* (Dachau: Einhorn-verlag, 1925), held in the archives of the Imperial War Museum, London, p. 4.

17 Ibid., p. 5.

18 Brigadier General William Dickson, *East Persia: A Backwater of the Great War* (London: Edward Arnold & Co., 1924), pp. 29–30.

19 Werner Otto von Hentig, *Into the Closed Land*, unattributed translation of *Ins Verschlossene Land* (Berlin: Ullstein, 1918), held in the archives of the Afghanistan-Institut, Basel, p. 3.

20 Thomas L. Hughes, 'The German mission to Afghanistan, 1915–1916', *German Studies Review* xxv/3 (2002), p. 450.

21 Ibid.

22 Ibid., p. 456.

23 Hentig, *Into the Closed Land*, p. 5.

24 Hew Strachan, *The First World War* (London: Oxford University Press, 2001), vol. 1, p. 771.

25 Niedermayer, *Under the Burning Sun*, p. 10.

26 IOR, L/MIL/17/15/28, p. 76.

27 Freya Stark, *Baghdad Sketches* (London: John Murray, 1937), p. 49.

28 Ibid., pp. 42–3.

29 Robert Byron, *The Road to Oxiana* (London: Macmillan & Co. 1937), pp. 46–7.

30 Frank G. Weber, *Eagles on the Crescent* (Ithaca, NY: Cornell University Press, 1970), p. 171.

31 Sykes, *Wassmuss*, p. 55.

32 Walter Griesinger, *German Intrigues in Persia* (New York, NY: Hodder and Stoughton, 1918), p. 17.

33 Hughes, 'The German mission to Afghanistan', p. 451.

34 Niedermayer, *Under the Burning Sun*, p. 25.

35 Strachan, *The First World War*, vol. 1, p. 781.

36 In the rush to escape his captors in Behbehan, Wassmuss left behind a copy of the German code book, which fell into British hands and later assisted Britain in deciphering the infamous Zimmermann telegram. This was a message by Arthur Zimmermann, Secretary of State at the German Foreign Ministry, sent via the German Embassy in Washington to the government of Mexico, urging the Mexicans to invade the United States. The public outrage caused by this decoded telegram is credited as one of the chief factors behind President Woodrow Wilson's decision to declare war on Germany.

37 Hentig, *Into the Closed Land*, p. 10.

38 Ibid.

39 NA, FO 371/2444, p. 2.

40 Mahendra Pratap, 'My German mission to High Asia', *Asia Magazine* xxv/5 (1925), p. 382.
41 Ibid., p. 383.
42 Hughes, 'The German mission to Afghanistan', p. 460.
43 Hentig, *Into the Closed Land*, p. 14.
44 In 1916 the American diplomat Arthur Cecil Edwards, by unknown means, came by one of these presents. 'It was my fortune to carry across Persia and deliver to the British Minister in Tehran an interesting memento of German intrigue in Afghanistan. This was a present from the Kaiser intended for the amir, which had fallen into the hands of the British. It consisted of an eagle, about six inches high, in gold studded with rubies and emeralds. On the whole, not much of a present for an Eastern potentate. But then, the Germans have yet to learn how these things are done.' Arthur Cecil Edwards, 'German intrigues in Persia', *The Yale Review* vii (1918), p. 34.
45 Hentig, *Into the Closed Land*, p. 15.
46 NA, FO 371/2444, p. 1.
47 Ibid.
48 IOR, L/PS/10/473, p. 99.
49 Antony Wynn, *Three Camels to Smyrna* (London: Estate of Bryan Meredith Huffner, 2008), p. 141.
50 Griesinger, *German Intrigues in Persia*, p. 17.
51 Hentig, *Into the Closed Land*, p. 20.
52 Ibid., p. 21.

CHAPTER 3 • INTO THE FEARFUL WASTELAND

1   Werner Otto von Hentig, *Into the Closed Land*, unattributed translation of *Ins Verschlossene Land* (Berlin: Ullstein, 1918), held in the archives of the Afghanistan-Institut, Basel, p. 22.
2   Mahendra Pratap, 'My German mission to High Asia', *Asia Magazine* xxv/5 (1925), p. 451.
3   Oskar Ritter von Niedermayer, *Under the Burning Sun of Iran*, unattributed translation of *Unter der Gut Sonne Irans* (Dachau: Einhornverlag, 1925), held in the archives of the Imperial War Museum, London, p. 78.
4   Ibid.
5   Hentig, *Into the Closed Land*, p. 25.
6   Niedermayer, *Under the Burning Sun*, p. 85.
7   Antony Wynn, *Persia in the Great Game* (London: John Murray, 2003), p. 259. In 1916 the East Persian Cordon became the Seistan Force, composed of British Indian Army troops.
8   George Roos-Keppel, MSS Eur, Microfilm D613, p. 188.
9   Niedermayer, *Under the Burning Sun*, p. 127.
10 Ibid., p. 131.
11 Abdul Ali Arghandawi, *British Imperialism and Afghanistan's Struggle for Independence* (New Delhi: Munshriram Manoharlal Publishers, 1989), p. 93.
12 Niedermayer, *Under the Burning Sun*, p. 145.
13 Mahendra Pratap, *My Life Story* (Dehra Dun: World Federation, 1947), p. 48.
14 Niedermayer, *Under the Burning Sun*, p. 167.
15 Ibid., p. 172.
16 IOR, 'Diary of the British Agent at Kabul for the week ending 15th October 1915', p. 1.

17 Rhea Talley Stewart, *Fire in Afghanistan: 1914–1929* (New York, NY: Doubleday & Co., 1973), p. 13.
18 Ibid., p. 14.
19 Charles Hardinge, *My Indian Years: 1910–1916* (London: John Murray, 1948), p. 107.
20 Roos-Keppel, MSS Eur, Microfilm D613, p. 199.
21 Quoted in Peter Hopkirk, *On Secret Service East of Constantinople* (London: John Murray, 1994), p. 159.
22 MSS Eur, Microfilm 8825, p. 174.
23 Quoted in Stewart, *Fire in Afghanistan*, p. 15.
24 Hentig, *Into the Closed Land*, p. 70.
25 Niedermayer, *Under the Burning Sun*, p. 179.
26 Hentig, *Into the Closed Land*, p. 72.
27 Ibid., p. 73.
28 Ibid.
29 Thomas L. Hughes, 'The German mission to Afghanistan, 1915–1916', *German Studies Review* xxv/3 (2002), p. 466.
30 Niedermayer, *Under the Burning Sun*, p. 180.
31 Ibid.
32 Ibid., p. 181.

CHAPTER 4 • THE WAITING GAME

1   NA, FO 371/2444, p. 3.
2   Abdul Ali Arghandawi, *British Imperialism and Afghanistan's Struggle for Independence* (New Delhi: Munshriram Manoharlal Publishers, 1989), p. 95.
3   George Roos-Keppel, MSS Eur, Microfilm D613, pp. 226–7.
4   Lal Baha, *NWFP Administration under British Rule* (Islamabad: National Commission on Historical and Cultural Research, 1978), p. 84.
5   Werner Otto von Hentig, *Into the Closed Land*, unattributed translation of *Ins Verschlossene Land* (Berlin: Ullstein, 1918), held in the archives of the Afghanistan-Institut, Basel, p. 77.
6   *Chelmsford Papers*, MSS Eur, E.264.7, p. 28.
7   Oskar Ritter von Niedermayer, *Under the Burning Sun of Iran*, unattributed translation of *Unter der Gut Sonne Irans* (Dachau: Einhornverlag, 1925), held in the archives of the Imperial War Museum, London, p. 193.
8   Ibid., p. 191.
9   The Ottoman army's five-month siege of Kut-al-Amara, 100 miles south of Baghdad, ended with the surrender to the Turks of an 8,000-strong British garrison with its colours in April 1916, the first time a British army had done this since the battle of Yorktown in 1781. This went down as Britain's most humiliating defeat of the First World War.
10 NA, FO 371/2436, p. 1.
11 Ibid., p. 2.
12 Walter Griesinger, *German Intrigues in Persia* (New York, NY: Hodder and Stoughton, 1918), p. 12.
13 NA, FO 371/2436, p. 4
14 Hentig, *Into the Closed Land*, p. 80.
15 Ibid., p. 81.

16 IOR, L/PS/10/200, p. 48.

17 Ursula Sims-Williams, 'The Afghan newspaper *Siraj ul Akhbar*', *British Journal for Middle Eastern Studies* vii/2 (1980), p. 120.

18 Niedermayer, *Under the Burning Sun*, p. 191.

19 Oliver Stone, *World War One* (London: Penguin, 2008), p. 93.

20 *Hardinge Letters*, IOR, Neg. 8825, 29 October 1915, p. 174.

21 Brigadier General Percy Sykes, *A History of Afghanistan* (London: Macmillan & Co., 1940), vol. 2, p. 256.

22 *Hardinge Letters*, p. 133.

23 Thomas L. Hughes, 'The German mission to Afghanistan, 1915–1916', *German Studies Review* xxv/3 (2002), p. 468.

24 Ibid.

25 Ibid., p. 469.

26 Mahendra Pratap, *My Life Story* (Dehra Dun: World Federation, 1947), p. 54.

27 Thomas Grant Fraser, 'The intrigues of the German government and the Ghadr Party', PhD thesis (University of London, 1974), p. 281.

28 *Chelmsford Papers*, MSS Eur, E.264.7, p. 25.

29 General Sir Michael O'Dwyer, *India as I Knew It* (London: Constable & Co., 1925), p. 188.

30 Sir George Macmunn, *The Romance of Indian Frontiers* (Lahore: Vanguard Books Pvt. Ltd., 1998 reprint), p. 256.

31 Hentig, *Into the Closed Land*, p. 90.

32 IOR, L/PS/10/460, Part 920.

33 Ibid.

34 In a belligerent speech delivered in Liverpool in 1896, Gladstone stated, 'The Sultan is responsible for the atrocities which have been committed, despite his denials. England has the right to act alone in putting an end to them.' *New York Times*, 29 September 1896, p. 12.

35 IOR, L/PS/10/460, Part 920.

36 Baha, *NWFP Administration*, p. 84.

37 India Office Private Papers, George Roos-Keppel, File D613, p. 290.

38 George Roos-Keppel, MSS Eur, Microfilm D613, p. 188.

39 In October 1915 a combined Franco-British force of some two large brigades was landed at Salonika to help the Serbs in their fight against Bulgarian aggression. It was decided to keep the force in place for future operations, even against Greek opposition.

40 Hughes, 'The German mission to Afghanistan', p. 471.

41 Ludwig Adamec, *Afghanistan: 1900–1923* (Berkeley, CA: University of California Press, 1967), p. 94.

42 IOR L/PS/14/7, Document 1164.

43 Ibid.

44 MSS Eur, E.261.1, p. 31.

45 L/PS/10/400, Part 4378.

46 Ibid.

CHAPTER 5 • TO BERLIN THE HARD WAY

1   Thomas L. Hughes, 'The German mission to Afghanistan, 1915–1916', *German Studies Review* xxv/3 (2002), p. 472.

2   Brigadier General Percy Sykes, *A History of Afghanistan* (London: Macmillan & Co., 1940), p. 254.

3   John M. Ewart, *Story of the North-West Frontier* (Peshawar: Government Printing and Stationery Office, 1930), p. 44.

4   Oskar Ritter von Niedermayer, *Under the Burning Sun of Iran*, unattributed translation of *Unter der Gut Sonne Irans* (Dachau: Einhornverlag, 1925), held in the archives of the Imperial War Museum, London, p. 198.

5   Ibid., p. 199.

6   Pashtun tribal life is governed by Pashtunwali, under which each man is bound to abide by a number of precepts. The most important of these is that the Pashtun is obliged to grant hospitality to all who seek it, friend or foe. There is also the law of retaliation, or *badal*, the most sacred rule of the Pashtun code. This normally takes the form of blood feuds, often inherited from past generations, arising from murders, violations of safe conduct or disputes about debts, or inheritance, or tribal quarrels over land or water. Rivalry over women is another common cause of feuding.

7   IOR, L/PS/10/461, Part 252, p. 9.

8   Ibid.

9   Christopher Sykes, *Wassmuss: The German Lawrence* (London: Longmans, 1936), p. 160.

10   Niedermayer, *Under the Burning Sun*, p. 200.

11   Sykes, *Wassmuss*, p. 160.

12   Werner Otto von Hentig, *Into the Closed Land*, unattributed translation of *Ins Verschlossene Land* (Berlin: Ullstein, 1918), held in the archives of the Afghanistan-Institut, Basel, p. 110.

13   The historian of the Bala Hissar, Brigadier Bill Woodburn, points out that, contrary to most accounts, the British did not destroy the Bala Hissar. They strengthened the outer walls in places but dismantled, or damaged, a lot of the structures within it. When Abdur Rahman ascended the throne in 1880 he decided to build his fortress-palace elsewhere.

14   The transfer of power in India from the East India Company to the British Crown took place in 1858, a year after the outbreak of the Indian Mutiny. From that date the governor general, as the direct appointee of the Crown, was given the added title of viceroy.

15   Niedermayer, *Under the Burning Sun*, p. 200.

16   MSS Eur, E.264.7, p. 55.

17   There is an intriguing story about Niedermayer's supposed conversion to Islam, almost certainly without foundation. What seems more likely is that in his earlier expedition with the Austrian Diez, Niedermayer entered the Baha'i faith, which has affinities with Sufism and holds that God can be made known to Man through manifestations, which have come at various stages of human progress. Niedermayer himself spoke enigmatically of being approached by some men during his 1915 journey through the Persian djesert. He said they made themselves known to him through secret hand signals and provided him with help in the crossing.

18   Ikbal Ali Shah, *Afghanistan and the German Threat* (Edinburgh: *Edinburgh Review*, 1918), p. 68.

19   NA, CAB/24/247, February 1934, p. 345.

20   Mahendra Pratap, 'My German mission to High Asia', *Asia Magazine* xxv/5 (1925), p. 455.

21 IOR, L/PS/10/593, p. 223. The Wakhan Corridor was a political creation of the Great
    Game. It is a 140-mile-long valley that snakes its way in a north-easterly direction
    between the Hindu Kush and the Pamirs. This appendix to Afghan territory was carved
    out in 1893 as a buffer to prevent Britain and Russia's empires meeting head on.

22 Ibid.

23 IOR, L/PS/10/593, File 1633.

24 IOR, L/PS/10/898, p. 161.

25 General Sir Michael O'Dwyer, *India as I Knew It* (London: Constable & Co., 1925), p. 178.

26 Ibid., p. 179.

27 Sykes, *Wassmuss*, p. 186.

28 Ibid., p. 219.

29 *Daily Mail*, 27 June 1919, p. 17. The SMS *Goeben* was a German battleship that evaded
    British naval forces in the Mediterranean and reached Constantinople.

CHAPTER 6 • WEST TO BERLIN

1   Oskar Ritter von Niedermayer, *Under the Burning Sun of Iran*, unattributed translation
    of *Unter der Gut Sonne Irans* (Dachau: Einhornverlag, 1925), held in the archives of the
    Imperial War Museum, London, p. 204.

2   Ibid., p. 205.

3   Ibid., p. 214.

4   Ibid., p. 227.

5   Ibid., p. 240.

6   Ibid., p. 257.

7   Ibid., p. 263.

8   Ibid., p. 371.

9   Ibid.

CHAPTER 7 • EAST TO BERLIN

1   Peter Hopkirk, *On Secret Service East of Constantinople* (London: John Murray, 1994), p. 217.

2   Ibid.

3   Werner Otto von Hentig, *Into the Closed Land*, unattributed translation of *Ins Verschlossene
    Land* (Berlin: Ullstein, 1918), held in the archives of the Afghanistan-Institut, Basel,
    p. 150.

4   *Taotai* and *amban* are the names of Chinese district officials in charge of civil and
    military affairs.

5   On his own secret military missions in Central Asia, the British army captain L.V.S.
    Blacker had occasion to come across this same family of Swedish missionaries in
    Yarkand, who told him about their encounter with the elusive Hentig. 'The kindly Swedes
    made me feel at home again, though it was rather a shock when they described Hentig's
    dash through Yarkand in 1916, on his way from North Afghanistan to Shanghai. This
    was before China came into the War, and he spent the night with them, resting from
    his hurried ride from Kashgar, where the Orenburg Cossacks were hunting for him.
    He covered the 155 miles in two days, on a fine, raking Badakshi horse that he said
    the amir of Kabul had given him.' L.V.S. Blacker, *On Secret Patrol in High Asia* (London:
    John Murray, 1922), p. 34.

6   Hentig, *Into the Closed Land*, p. 199.
7   NA, KV 2/394.
8   Hentig, *Into the Closed Land*, p. 210.
9   Ibid., p. 220.
10 NA, KV 2/393, 8381338, p. 3.
11 Ibid., p. 2.
12 Hentig, *Into the Closed Land*, p. 236.
13 Ibid., p. 237.

CHAPTER 8 • MY ENEMIES' ENEMY IS GERMANY

1   William Kerr Fraser-Tytler, *Afghanistan* (London: Oxford University Press, 1950), pp. 194–5.
2   *The Times*, 20 August 1919, p. 9.
3   Brigadier General Percy Sykes, *A History of Afghanistan* (London: Macmillan & Co., 1940), vol. 2, p. 268.
4   Ludwig Adamec and George Grassmuck, *Afghanistan: Some New Approaches* (Ann Arbor: The University of Michigan, 1969), p. 213.
5   Ibid., p. 217.
6   Amanullah settled in Italy after his overthrow in 1929 and Rome is where the remnants of the Afghan royal family currently reside.
7   NA, CAB/24/247, p. 218.
8   Ibid., Appendix I, p. 4.
9   Ludwig Adamec, *Afghanistan's Foreign Affairs to the Mid-Twentieth Century* (Tucson, AZ: University of Arizona Press, 1974), p. 101.
10 NA, FO/371 3296, p. 116.
11 Shahram Chubin (ed.), *Germany and the Middle East* (London: Pinter Publishers, 1992), p. 79.
12 Ibid.
13 Ibid., p. 80.
14 Adamec and Grassmuck, *Afghanistan*, p. 230.
15 Stephen Tanner, *Afghanistan: A Military History from Alexander the Great to the Fall of the Taliban* (Oxford: Oxford University Press, 2002), p. 222.
16 Adamec and Grassmuck, *Afghanistan*, p. 246.
17 Ibid., p. 247.
18 Fraser-Tytler, *Afghanistan*, p. 253.
19 NA, FO 371/22257, p. 3.
20 Hugh Toye, *The Springing Tiger* (London: Cassell, 1959), p. v.
21 Ibid., p. 39.
22 Milan Hauner, 'Afghanistan between the Great Powers, 1938–1945', *International Journal of Middle East Studies* xiv/4 (1982), p. 494.
23 Lionel Gossman, *The Passion of Max von Oppenheim* (Cambridge: Open Book Publishers, 2013), p. 232.
24 NA, KV2/394, p. 30.
25 *New York Times*, 7 April 1941, p. 8.
26 NA, KV2/394, p. 1.
27 Milan Hauner, *India in Axis Strategy* (Stuttgart: Klett-Cotta, 1981), pp. 161–2.

28 IOR, L/PJ/12/123, p. 4.
29 Hauner, *India in Axis Strategy*, p. 164.
30 NA, FO 371/23631, p. 119.
31 Ibid., p. 116.
32 Franz Kurowski, *The Brandenburger Commandos* (Mechanicsburg, PA: Stackpole Books, 2005), p. 168.
33 NA, HW 12/297, File 127945.
34 Nora Levin, *The Holocaust: The Destruction of European Jewry 1933–1945* (New York, NY: Thomas Y. Crowell Co., 1968), p.132.
35 Werner Otto von Hentig, *Mein Leben, eine Dienstreise* (Göttingen: Vandenhoeck & Ruprecht, 1962), p. 345.
36 Timo Noetzel and Thomas Rid, 'Germany's options in Afghanistan', *Survival: Global Politics and Strategy* li/5 (2009), p. 3.

EPILOGUE

1 Ludwig Adamec, *Afghanistan: 1900–1923* (Berkeley, CA: University of California Press, 1967), p. 96.
2 Ludwig Adamec, *Afghanistan's Foreign Affairs to the Mid-Twentieth Century* (Tucson, AZ: University of Arizona Press, 1974), p. 41.
3 Oskar Ritter von Niedermayer, *Under the Burning Sun of Iran*, unattributed translation of *Unter der Gut Sonne Irans* (Dachau: Einhornverlag, 1925), held in the archives of the Imperial War Museum, London, p. 379.
4 NA, FO 2952, p. 15
5 Brigadier General Percy Sykes, *A History of Afghanistan* (London: Macmillan & Co., 1940), p. 258.
6 Hans-Ulrich Seidt, *Berlin, Kabul, Moskau: Oskar Ritter von Niedermayer und Deutschlands Geopolitik* (Munich: Universitas, 2002), p. 89.
7 Hew Strachan, *The First World War* (London: Oxford University Press, 2001), vol. 1, p. 772.
8 Niedermayer, *Under the Burning Sun*, p. 379.

APPENDIX 2

1 After the Second World War both German states kept up their commercial relations with Afghanistan. In 1958 the Federal Republic of Germany signed a treaty of economic and technical cooperation, by which Bonn pledged to make available free technical aid, machinery, tools, textbooks and teachers. Afghan students were offered scholarships to study in West Germany, whose government also set up an Afghan geological service and hydrological authority. Not to be upstaged, in 1965 the Russians persuaded Kabul to accept East German commercial aid in the form of synthetic fibre and fertiliser plants, both to be supplied on favourable credit terms.

Bibliography

BOOKS

Adamec, Ludwig, *Afghanistan: 1900–1923* (Berkeley, CA: University of California Press, 1967)
——— *Afghanistan's Foreign Affairs to the Mid-Twentieth Century* (Tucson, AZ: University of Arizona Press, 1974)
——— and Clements, Frank, *Conflict in Afghanistan* (Santa Barbara, CA: ABC-CLIO, 2003)
——— and Grassmuck, George, *Afghanistan: Some New Approaches* (Ann Arbor, MI: The University of Michigan, 1969)
Ansary, Tamim, *Games without Rules* (New York, NY: Public Affairs, 2012)
Arghandawi, Abdul Ali, *British Imperialism and Afghanistan's Struggle for Independence* (New Delhi: Munshriram Manoharlal Publishers, 1989)
Baha, Lal, *NWFP Administration under British Rule* (Islamabad: National Commission on Historical and Cultural Research, 1978)
Balfour, Michael, *The Kaiser and His Times* (London: The Cresset Press, 1964)
Blacker, Latham V.S., *On Secret Patrol in High Asia* (London: John Murray, 1922)
Buchan, John, *Greenmantle* (London: Hodder and Stoughton, 1916)
Byron, Robert, *The Road to Oxiana* (London: Macmillan & Co., 1937)
Chubin, Shahram (ed.), *Germany and the Middle East* (London: Pinter Publishers, 1992)
Collingham, Elizabeth M., *Imperial Bodies* (Cambridge: Polity Press, 2001)
Dickson, William, Brigadier General, *East Persia: A Backwater of the Great War* (London: Edward Arnold & Co., 1924)
Dunsterville, Lionel Charles, Major-General, *The Adventures of Dunsterforce* (Eastbourne: The Naval & Military Press Ltd., 2007; originally published by Edward Arnold, London, 1920)
Dupree, Louis, *Afghanistan* (Princeton, MA: Princeton University Press, 1973)
Ewans, Martin, *Afghanistan* (London: HarperCollins, 2002)
——— (ed.), *Britain and Russia in Central Asia* (London: Routledge, 2004)
Ewart, John M., *Story of the North-West Frontier* (Peshawar: Government Printing and Stationery Office, 1930)
Fischer, Fritz, *Germany's Aims in the First World War* (New York, NY: W.W. Norton & Co., 1967)
Ford, Roger, *Eden to Armageddon* (London: Weidenfeld & Nicolson, 2009)

Fraser-Tytler, William Kerr, *Afghanistan* (London: Oxford University Press, 1950)

Gossman, Lionel, *The Passion of Max von Oppenheim* (Cambridge: Open Book Publishers, 2013)

Gottlieb, W.W., *Studies in Secret Diplomacy during the First World War* (London: George Allen & Unwin, Ltd., 1957)

Griesinger, Wilhelm, *German Intrigues in Persia* (New York, NY: Hodder and Stoughton, 1918)

Hale, Christopher, *Himmler's Crusade* (New York, NY: Bantam Press, 2003)

Hardinge, Charles, *My Indian Years: 1910–1916* (London: John Murray, 1948)

Hauner, Milan, *India in Axis Strategy* (Stuttgart: Klett-Cotta, 1981)

Hentig, Werner Otto von, *Into the Closed Land*, unattributed translation of *Ins Verschlossene Land* (Berlin: Ullstein, 1918), held in the archives of the Afghanistan-Institut, Basel

—— *Mein Leben, eine Dienstreise* (Göttingen: Vandenhoeck & Ruprecht, 1962)

Hopkirk, Peter, *On Secret Service East of Constantinople* (London: John Murray, 1994)

Ingle, Harold, *Nesselrode and the Russian Rapprochement with Britain* (Berkeley, MA: University of California Press, 1976)

Jalazai, Musa Khan, *The Foreign Policy of Afghanistan* (Lahore: Sang-e-Meel Publications, 2003)

Jewett, A.C., *An American Engineer in Afghanistan* (Minnesota, MN: University of Minnesota Press, 1948)

Johnson, Robert, *Spying for Empire: The Great Game in Central and South-East Asia, 1757–1947* (London: Greenhill Books, 2006)

Keppel, Arnold, *Gun-Running and the Indian North-West Frontier* (London: John Murray, 1911)

Ker, James Campbell, *Political Trouble in India: 1907–1917* (Delhi: Oriental Publishers, 1973)

Krist, Gustav, *Alone through the Forbidden Land* (London: Faber and Faber, 1939)

Kurowski, Franz, *The Brandenburger Commandos* (Mechanicsburg, PA: Stackpole Books, 2005)

Leeson, Frank, *Frontier Legion* (West Sussex: The Leeson Archive, 2003)

Levi, Peter, *The Light Garden of the Angel King* (London: Pallas Athene, 2000)

Levin, Nora, *The Holocaust: The Destruction of European Jewry 1933–1945* (New York, NY: Thomas Y. Crowell Co., 1968)

Lewin, Evans, *The German Road to the East* (London: Heinemann, 1916)

Lüdke, Tilman, *Jihad Made in Germany* (Berlin: LIT Verlag, 2005)

McMahon, Henry, Lieutenant General, *An Account of the Entry of H.M. Habibullah Khan, Amir of Afghanistan, into Freemasonry* (West Sussex, Favil Press, 1940)

McMeekin, Sean, *The Berlin–Baghdad Express* (London: Penguin Books, 2010)

Macmunn, George, Sir, *Afghanistan from Darius to Amanullah* (London: G. Bell & Sons, 1929)

—— *The Romance of Indian Frontiers* (Lahore: Vanguard Books Pvt. Ltd., 1998 reprint)

Mason, Philip, *A Matter of Honour* (London: Jonathan Cape, 1974)

Meyer, Karl and Brysac, Shareen, *Tournament of Shadows* (London: Abacus, 1999)

Moberly, Frank J., *Mesopotamia Campaign: 1914–1918* (London: His Majesty's Stationery Office, 1923)

Moon, Penderel, Sir, *The British Conquest and Dominion of India* (London: Duckworth, 1989)

Niedermayer, Oskar Ritter von, *Under the Burning Sun of Iran*, unattributed translation of *Unter der Gut Sonne Irans* (Dachau: Einhornverlag, 1925), held in the archives of the Imperial War Museum, London

O'Dwyer, Michael, General Sir, *India as I Knew It* (London: Constable & Co., 1925)

Omrani, Bijan, *Afghanistan: A Companion and Guide* (Hong Kong: Odyssey Books, 2005)

Papen, Franz von, *Memoirs* (London: André Deutsch, 1952)

Popplewell, Richard J., *Intelligence and Imperial Defence* (London: Frank Cass, 1995)

Pratap, Mahendra, *My Life Story* (Dehra Dun: World Federation, 1947)

Richards, David, *The Savage Frontier* (London: Macmillan, 1990)

Robson, Brian, *Crisis on the Frontier* (Staplehurst: Spellmount, 2004)

Rumbold, Algernon, Sir, *Watershed in India: 1914–1918* (London: The Athlone Press, 1979)

Saikal, Amin, *Modern Afghanistan* (London: I.B.Tauris, 2004)

Seidt, Hans-Ulrich, *Berlin, Kabul, Moskau: Oskar Ritter von Niedermayer und Deutschlands Geopolitik* (Munich: Universitas, 2002)

Snouck Hurgronje, Christiaan, *The Holy War Made in Germany* (New York, NY: G.P. Putnam's Sons, 1915)

Stark, Freya, *Baghdad Sketches* (London: John Murray, 1937)

Stewart, Rhea Talley, *Fire in Afghanistan: 1914–1918* (New York, NY: Doubleday & Co., 1973)

Stone, Oliver, *World War One* (London: Penguin, 2008)

Strachan, Hew, *The First World War* (London: Oxford University Press, 2001)

Swinson, Arthur, *North-West Frontier* (London: Hutchinson, 1967)

Sykes, Christopher, *Wassmuss: The German Lawrence* (London: Longmans, 1936)

——— *Troubled Loyalty* (London: Collins, 1968)

Sykes, Percy, Brigadier General Sir, *A History of Afghanistan* (London: Macmillan & Co., 2 vols., 1940)

Tanner, Stephen, *Afghanistan: A Military History from Alexander the Great to the Fall of the Taliban* (Oxford: Oxford University Press, 2002)

Thornton, Ernest and Annie, *Leaves from an Afghan Scrapbook* (London: John Murray, 1910)

Toye, Hugh, *The Springing Tiger* (London: Cassell, 1959)

Treloar, William, *With the Kaiser in the East* (London: Horace Marshall & Sons, 1898)

Trigg, Jonathan, *Hitler's Jihadis* (Stroud: The History Press, 2008)

Weber, Frank G., *Eagles on the Crescent* (Ithaca, NY: Cornell University Press, 1970)

Winstone, Harry Victor Frederick, *The Illicit Adventure* (London: Jonathan Cape, 1982)

Woodward, David R., *Hell in the Holy Land* (Lexington, KY: University of Kentucky Press, 2006)

Wynn, Antony, *Persia in the Great Game* (London: John Murray, 2003)

——— *Three Camels to Smyrna* (London: Estate of Bryan Meredith Huffner, 2008)

PRIMARY SOURCES AND JOURNALS

IOR = British Library India Office Records

NA = National Archives

MSS Eur = British Library European Manuscripts

The Chelmsford Papers, MSS Eur, E.264.7

Daily Telegraph, 1 March 1928

Edwards, Arthur Cecil, 'German intrigues in Persia', *The Yale Review* vii (1918)

Fraser, Thomas Grant, 'The intrigues of the German government and the Ghadr Party', PhD thesis (University of London, 1974)

——— 'Germany and Indian revolution, 1914–1918', *Journal of Contemporary History* xii/2 (1977)

Grulev, Mikhail, *The Rivalry of Russia and England in Central Asia*, IOR L/PS/20/161, 1909

Hastings, Max, 'The Turkish–German jihad', *The New York Review of Books*, 9 December 2010, p. 10

Hauner, Milan, 'Afghanistan between the Great Powers, 1938–1945', *International Journal of Middle East Studies* xiv/4 (1982)

Hughes, Thomas L., 'The German mission to Afghanistan, 1915–1916', *German Studies Review* xxv/3 (2002)

Hussein, Haji Mirza [pseud. of Oskar Ritter von Niedermayer], 'Everyday life in Afghanistan', *National Geographic Magazine* xxxix/1 (1921)

Kumar, Ravinder, 'The records of the government of India on the Berlin–Baghdad railway question', *The Historical Journal* v/1 (1962)

Lawrence, Montagu R. (ed.), *The Home Letters of T.E. Lawrence and His Brothers* (Oxford: Basil Blackwell, 1954)

Marcus, Ernst, 'The German Foreign Office and the Palestine question', *Yad Vashan Studies* ii (1956)

National Archives, Foreign Office Files Series FO 371

New York Times, 7 April 1941

Nicosia, Francis R., 'Drang nach Osten continued?', *Journal of Contemporary History* xxxii/2 (1997)

Noetzel, Timo and Rid, Thomas, 'Germany's options in Afghanistan', *Survival: Global Politics and Strategy* li/5 (2009)

Pratap, Mahendra, 'My German mission to High Asia', *Asia Magazine* xxv/5 (1925)

Roos-Keppel, George, MSS Eur, Microfilm D613

Schwanitz, Wolfgang G., 'Germany's Middle Eastern Policy', *The Middle East Review of International Affairs* xi/3 (2007)

Seidt, Hans-Ulrich, 'From Palestine to the Caucasus – Oskar Niedermayer and Germany's Middle Eastern Strategy in 1918', *German Studies Review* xxiv/1 (2001)

Shah, Ikbal Ali, *Afghanistan and the German Threat* (Edinburgh: Edinburgh Review, July, 1918)

Shah, Syed Wikar Ali, 'German interest in the NWFP during the war years', paper delivered to the Pakistan–German Friendship Forum, Islamabad, 7 December 2000

Sims-Williams, Ursula, 'The Afghan newspaper *Siraj ul Akhbar*', *British Journal for Middle Eastern Studies* vii/2 (1980)

The Third Afghan War, Official Account (Calcutta: Government of India Central Publication Branch, 1925)

The Times, 28 October 1898

'Where is Wassmuss?', *The Auckland Star*, 28 June 1919

Index

5th Royal Bavarian Infantry Division 38
10th Bavarian Field Artillery Regiment 37
162nd Turkmen Division 120, 192

Abadan oil refinery 45
Abdul Hamid II, Ottoman sultan 6, 8,
    10–11
Abdul Karim 173
Abdul Majid 179
Abdul Wahab 136–7
Abdur Rahman 51
Abdur Rahman, King of Afghanistan
    14, 16, 18, 20, 35, 75, 97, 117, 203
Abteilung III 164, 172
Abwehr 183, 188–9
AEG (General Electric Company) 2
Afghan National Bank 179
Afghan–German draft treaty 101–2,
    105, 111, 114, 117, 122, 205–7
Afghanistan
    British invasion of (1838) 3–4
    British invasion of (1878) 3–4
    civil war 3, 35, 173
    Soviet invasion of (1979) ix, 132
Afridis 51, 53, 85, 88, 120
Ahmad Shah Massoud 132
Ahmad Shah Qajar 56, 90
Aleppo 46–7, 57
Alexander the Great 25, 57, 132–3, 145, 178
Alvand 139
Amanullah, King of Afghanistan xvii,
    1–3, 23, 29, 70, 78, 86, 100, 116, 124,
    159–68, 170–6, 186–7, 196

Amanullah Plan 183, 185–7
Amanus Mountains 12
Ampthill, Lord 18
Amsterdam 183
Anarak 60–1
Anatolische Eisenbahn Gesellschaft 10
Anglo-Afghan War
    First (1838–42) 85
    Second (1880) 13
    Third (1919) 161–2, 168
Anglo-Persian Oil Company 15, 127
Anglo-Russian Convention of 1907
    201–3
Anglo-Russian entente 13, 15, 19
Annie Larsen Affair 32–3
Arab Revolt 111
Armenia 8, 11, 47, 103, 128
arms shipping and gun running 32,
    44, 52, 85–7, 90, 162, 165, 188
Ashgabat 106
Asquith, Herbert 107
Auckland, Governor General Lord 4,
    117
Augusta Victoria of Schleswig-
    Holstein 7
Austria 56, 63, 86, 88, 90, 97, 103,
    116, 119, 121, 134, 143, 150, 154–5,
    164–5
Austria-Hungary 28
Auswärtiges Amt 9, 151, 156, 180, 183,
    186
Aydın 10
Azerbaijani prisoners of war 192

Babur 25, 35
Bacha-i Saqao 174–6
Badakhshan 123, 147
Badasia 71
Baghdad 7, 10, 34, 46–50, 56–7, 94,
    131, 143, 172, 184
Baghdad Railway Company 12, 57
Baghdad Eisenbahn Gesellschaft
    10
Bagh-e-Babur also Bagh-i-Babur 35,
    70–1, 73, 77, 93, 98, 100, 104, 106,
    112, 118
Bala Hissar xvi, 117
Balfour, Arthur 12
Balkh 25, 133–4
Baluchistan 1, 40, 72, 91, 114, 131,
    136, 201
Bamyan 133
Barakatullah, Maulavi 51–3, 66, 77–9,
    93, 98, 122
Barakatullah, Moulana see
    Barakatullah, Maulavi
Belgium 2–3, 34
Bell, Gertrude 46, 111
Berlin Committee 30
Berlin–Baghdad railway 7, 10, 12, 46
Berlin–Kabul air service 180
Bethmann-Hollweg, Chancellor
    Theobald von 30, 79, 117, 125
Bey, Kazim 54, 57–8, 65–6, 77–9, 93
Bey, Khairi 70
Bey, Dr Munir 72
Bey, Rauf 47–9
Birjand 63, 202
Bismarck, Otto von 4–5, 54, 103
Bogotá 183, 193
Bokhara 4, 168
Bolan Pass 14
Borg, Arthur see Grobba, Fritz
Boshruyeh 63–4
Brandenburg Battalion 188
Brandt, Fred Hermann 188–90
Brauchitsch, General Walter von 182
Brinkmann, Kurt 186, 188
Bulgaria 89, 205
Burma 14, 32
Burundi 5

'butcher and bolt' tactic 74, 104
Byron, Robert 47

camels 21, 54, 59, 61–2, 64, 69, 87,
    140–2, 151, 171
Cameroon 5
caravans 21, 29, 45–7, 50, 54, 61–4,
    67–9, 87, 133, 139–40, 142, 145–6,
    148, 151, 190
caravanserai 60, 62, 137, 139–40,
    150
Carchemish 31
Carpathian front 150
Casement, Sir Roger 53
Cavagnari, Sir Louis 17
Central Powers xxi, 7, 19, 29, 34,
    42, 48, 68, 72, 79, 89–90, 92,
    100, 104–5, 113, 139, 152, 154,
    159
Chaman 1
Chamberlain, Austen 119–20
Chelmsford, Lord 99, 107–9, 114, 119,
    160, 163
Christmas Day Plot 33, 124
Churchill, Winston 13, 74, 84
Cleveland, Sir Charles 126
Committee of Imperial Defence 167
Connaught, Duke of 20
Constantinople 7–8, 10–13, 36, 39,
    41–7, 50, 53–4, 69, 125, 128, 144,
    168, 183
Consten, Hermann 44
Cossacks 4, 36, 40, 136, 142, 148
Cunningham, Consul-General James
    153
Curzon, Lord 10, 13, 15–18, 28

Damascus 8–9, 184
Damghan 138
Dane, Sir Louis 18
Dardanelles 34
Daruloman 171
Dasht-i-Kavir salt desert 37, 59, 61–2,
    69, 143
Dasht-i-Rewat 133
Dayal, Har 30, 51
Deir ez-Zor 47

Deoband Theological School 124
Derband 139
Deutsch-Afghanische Compagnie
(DACOM) 165
Deutsche Bank 6, 10–11, 53–4
dhows 87
Diez, Ernst 37, 136–7
Disraeli, Benjamin (Lord Beaconsfield)
103
Dost Mohammed 117
Drang nach Osten 7, 19
Duff, General Sir Beauchamp 28, 77
Durand, Sir Henry Mortimer 97,
117
Durand line 14, 18, 23, 74, 112, 117
Durrani, Ahmad Shah xvii, 3, 25

East Persia Cordon 65
Edward VII 27
Egypt 5, 9, 30–1, 95, 114, 185
Erzingjan 11
Erzurum 111
Euphrates River 45, 47, 57
Ewart, John 112

Faisal I 46
Faizabad 147
Faradonbeh 141
Fashoda incident 9
Feigel, August 172–3
Ferdinand, Archduke Franz 7
Fiat fighters 2
Finland, Russian invasion of 182
First World War 7, 12, 34, 159
First World War Armistice see
November Armistice 1918
Fleischer, Gottlieb 98
France 2–3, 5–6, 9, 28, 31–2, 34, 37–8,
85, 89, 94, 114, 139, 152, 164, 166,
177, 187
Franco-Prussian Wars 6
Fraser-Tytler, Sir William 179, 187, 190
Frederick III 5

Gallipoli 34, 94
Gandamak, Treaty of 14, 17, 102
Garde-Jäger-Bataillon 50

Genghis Khan 25, 69
George V x, 27, 75, 122
Gestapo 191–2
Ghadr Party 51–2, 124
Ghazni 87, 118, 190
Ghilzai traders 87, 104, 112–13
Ghulam Nabi Charkhi 176–7
Ghulam Siddiq Khan 185–6
Gladstone, William 103
Gobi Desert 2
Goebbels, Joseph 192
Goethe-Institut of Afghanistan 167
Goltz, General Colmar von der 7,
111–12
Grant, Sir Hamilton 161
Great Pashtun Uprising (1897) 84, 87
Grey, Sir Edward 90
Griesinger, Lieutenant Walter 45, 48,
56, 90–1, 106, 120, 131
Grobba, Fritz 164–5, 171–2, 183–4, 187
Gulf of Suez 6
Gurkhas 87

Habibullah Kalakani
see Bacha-i Saqao
Habibullah Khan, Amir of Afghanistan
x, xvii, 2–3, 14–24, 28–9, 35,
41–2, 48, 53, 55, 68–81, 83–6, 89,
93–109, 111–17, 119, 122–3, 131–2,
143, 145, 159, 161, 169, 180, 182,
195–6
Hafiz Saifullah Khan 54, 72, 102, 108,
114
Haidar Pasha 45
Halifax, Viscount 179
Halmondlager prisoner-of-war camp
120
Hamadan 139, 141
Hamilton, Lord George 16
Hankow 151–2
Hanum, Bibi 97–8
Hardinge, Viceroy Lord Charles 27–9,
34–5, 51, 55, 63, 67, 69, 71–7, 83,
92–4, 96, 99, 101, 104–5, 107
Hazarajat Mountains 68
Hedin, Sven 42
Henschel und Sohn 171

Hentig, Werner Otto von   x–xi, xvi,
    36–8, 40, 42–3, 49–55, 96–8, 126,
    144, 162, 165, 195–8, 206
  departure from Afghanistan   109,
    III–22, 132–3, 145–58
  early career   36
  entry into Afghanistan   55, 57–61,
    64–5
  in Afghanistan   67–8, 71–2
  later career   2–3, 164, 169, 172,
    183–7, 191–3
  with the King of Afghanistan
    77–80, 86, 92–4, 96, 99–102, 104,
    106–7
Hentig–Niedermayer mission   x, xvi,
    43, 93, 165, 170
Herat   II, 25, 55, 59, 65–71, 74, 83, 16,
    118–19, 131, 134, 143, 165, 169
Hess, Rudolf   186
Himalaya   14
Himmler, Heinrich   178, 186, 188, 192
Hindenburg, Paul von   2
Hindu Kush   25, 119, 121, 132–3, 147,
    169, 175
Hindu–German Conspiracy   52
Hintze, Admiral Paul von   151–2
Hitler, Adolf   31, 42, 167, 179, 181, 183,
    185, 187–8, 191–3, 198
  Mein Kampf   185
Honolulu   155–6
Honvéd, József   149
Hughes, Thomas L.   96
Humphrys, Sir Francis   168
Hussein bin Ali, Sharif of Mecca   III

Ikbal Ali Shah   120
Inayatullah   78, 119, 160, 174
Indian Criminal Investigation
    Department   52, 126
Indus river   88, 102
Intelligence Bureau, Department of
    Information   169
International Security Assistance
    Force (ISAF)   ix, xi, 90, 194
Iran   xvii, 172, 188
Iraq   xvii, 46, 172, 181, 184–5, 189
  see also Mesopotamia

ISAF see International Security
    Assistance Force
Isfahan   49–50, 56–8, 61, 67–8, 106,
    141–2, 201
Isfahan legation   59
Ishaq Aqasi Mulki   103
Islamia College   74
Italy   58, 164, 166, 174, 177, 181–2, 186,
    189
Izmir   10

Jakob, Hans   38, 44, 47, 71, 121
Jalalabad   22, 160, 187
Jalalabad uprising   173
Janosch, Josef   119
Japan   14, 52, 124, 151, 153, 155, 177,
    180
Jaxartes River   4
Jerusalem   7–9
Jewett, A.C.   22–3
jihad   3, 24, 31, 35, 40–2, 56, 66, 69,
    73, 75, 84, 95, 100, 104–6, 119, 172,
    183, 195
Johnston, Alexander Keith   44
Junkers aircraft company   170, 172

Kabul   x–xi, xvi, 2–4, 13–18, 21–4,
    29–30, 34–7, 41, 43, 53–4, 58,
    66, 68–74, 76–7, 79–81, 84–6,
    88–9, 92–3, 96–102, 104–6, 108–9,
    III–13, 115–17, 119–26, 132–3, 136,
    138, 140, 145–6, 151, 157, 160–180,
    182, 186–91, 194–8, 203
Kabul garrison   161
Kabul River   35, 181
Kabul University   175
Karakum Desert   134
Kariz   141
Kashan   127
Kashmir   3
Kasr-i-Dilgusha   23, 102
Kasr-i-Dilkushah see Kasr-i-Dilgusha
Kazerun   127
Kazvin garrison   91–2
Kermanshah   49, 57, 106, 126, 141–3
Khalifa Abdul Majid   41
Khawak Pass   133

Khorasan 141, 143
Khost 84, 161, 173
Khulum 133
Khyber Pass 14, 19, 75, 162, 166, 168,
    174, 182
Khyber Rifles 75
Kirkuk 10
Kitchener, Herbert (Lord) x, 12–13,
    20, 77
Kohistan 22
Kokand 4
Konya 11–12, 57
Kristallnacht riots 192
Krupp 6, 32, 98
Kurdistan 10
Kurram Valley 162
Kut-al-Amara 34, 89, 94, 113, 116, 126
Kuwait 12
Kyrgyz guides 147–8

Landi Khana 75
Lansdowne, Lord 12, 117
Lawrence, T.E. 31, 111, 127, 174
League of Nations 166, 177
Lebanon 166
Libya 181
London
    India Office 108, 187
    War Office 90, 96, 106
Ludendorff, General Erich 164
Ludwig Loewe & Co. 6
Lytton, Viceroy Lord Robert 4

Macartney, Sir George 123
MacDonald, Ramsay 167
Mahmud Serwar Khan 66–9
Maimana 84
Majid, Abdul (President of Afghan
    National Bank) see Abdul Majid
Majid, Khalifa Abdul see Khalifa
    Abdul Majid
Malakand campaign 84
malaria 58, 71
Malik Talib Mehdi Khan 17
Maralbexi 150
Marco Polo 149
Marcus, Ernst 192–3

Marling, Charles 90–1
Martini-Henry rifle 87
Maruchak fort 13
Maugham, Somerset xxi, 30
Mazar-i-Sharif 119–20, 146
Mecca 111, 12–65
    hajj to 6, 9
Medina 70, 125
Mehmed V 11
Meshchersky, Prince Vladimir 123
Meshed 63, 96, 120, 136–7
Meshedcheri 62
Mesopotamia 46, 57, 77, 89, 113, 129,
    143
    see also Iraq
MI5 (Directorate of Military
    Intelligence Section 5) 156
Mianchi 151
Minto, John 27
Mirza Ali Khan 189
Mohammed Aziz 176
Mohammed Daoud 177
Mohammed Hussain Jan 186
Mohammed Wali Khan 163
Mohammed Yakub Khan, King of
    Afghanistan 14
Mohammed Zahir Shah, King of
    Afghanistan 163
Mohmands 85, 88, 104
Molotov, Vyacheslav 185
Moltke, Helmuth Johann Ludwig von
    30, 32
Mongolia 124
Mongols 149
Montenegro 34
Mosul 47
Mussolini, Benito 2, 166

Nadir Shah, King of Afghanistan
    160–2, 174–7
Namibia 5
Nasrullah 16, 24, 29, 35, 55, 70, 72–4,
    78, 80, 84–5, 88, 95, 100, 102, 104,
    106, 116, 118–19, 132, 160–1
NATO 3, 92
Nicholas II, Tsar of Russia 99
Nicolson, Sir Arthur 15

Niedermayer, Fritz 45
Niedermayer, Oskar Ritter von x–xi,
    xvi, 42–50, 104–7, 126, 145, 162,
    169–70, 195–9, 207
    departure from Afghanistan 109,
        111–22, 131–41, 143
    early career 37–40
    entry into Afghanistan 52–9, 61–5
    in Afghanistan 67–8, 70–2
    later career 191–3
    with the King of Afghanistan 77–8,
        80, 86–9, 93, 95, 99–102
Niedermayer, Richard 169
Niedermayer, Waldman 141
North-West Frontier of India x, 14, 18,
    27–8, 34, 42, 51, 73, 74, 84, 87–8,
    102, 104, 122, 128, 151, 161, 166,
    174, 182, 188, 195
November Armistice 1918 ix, 127, 160
Nuristan 178

oases 13, 60–3, 65, 106, 136, 150
Obeidullah, Maulavi 98, 124–6, 186
Oberdöffer, Manfred 188–90
Oberdöffer–Brandt mission 189
O'Dwyer, General Sir Michael 99,
    125–6
Olympic Games (Berlin, 1936) 180
Oppenheim, Max von xi, 9, 30–1, 42,
    183–5
Order of Max Joseph 197
Order of the Red Eagle 53, 116
Orenstein & Koppel 6
Orient Express 11, 39
Oriental Department 187
Ottoman Bank 11
Ottoman Empire 3, 6–7, 10, 12–13, 19,
    28, 30, 40, 47–9, 56–8, 111, 141,
    143, 166
Ottoman–German alliance 27, 30,
    33–4
Oxus River 14, 146

Paghman 73, 83, 93, 106
Palestine 6, 184, 192–3
Palmerston, Lord 66
Paltreu Company 192

Pamir Mountains xi, 2, 120, 123, 146
Panjdeh 13, 136
Panjshir Valley 132–3
Papen, Franz von 31–3
Papua New Guinea 5
Paschen, Wilhelm 44, 46, 59, 68, 118,
    131, 141
Pasha, Enver 54, 84, 95, 170
Pashtun tribes 3, 23, 28, 42, 55, 65, 69,
    74, 86, 119, 170, 183
Pashtunwali code of honour 114
Persia x, xvii, 14–15, 19, 25, 31, 37,
    39–40, 45, 48–50, 54–60, 62–3,
    65–7, 77, 84–5, 89–92, 95–6, 101,
    103–4, 106, 111–12, 116, 120, 125–8,
    131, 136–9, 142–3, 163, 168, 172,
    185, 190, 196, 201–2, 205–7
Persian Army 66
Peshawar University 74
Petrograd 4, 6, 11, 14–15, 96, 99, 106,
    123
Pilger, Hans 175
Plessen, Baron Leopold von 175
Poland 34, 36
Pratap, Mahendra xi, 51–3, 57–8, 60,
    77–9, 93, 98–9, 122–4

Qasvin 128

Rahmatullah Jan 186
Rashid Ali 181
Rawalpindi, Treaty of (1919) 162, 164
Reichsvertretung der Deutschen Juden
    192
Rembrandt, Dutch ship 152–3
Reuss, Heinrich (Prince of Köstritz)
    58, 95–6
Ribbentrop, Joachim von 185–6, 191
Ringberg family 151
Ripken, Georg 177–8
Robat Karim 140
Röhr, Walter 50, 53, 60, 67, 97, 100,
    119, 146, 149–52
Romania 44
Rome 1, 166, 174, 186–7
Roos-Keppel, Sir George 33, 35, 63,
    66, 74, 85, 105

Rosenberg, Alfred 187
Royal Air Force 2
Royal and Imperial East Indian
    Detachment 165
Royal Navy 13–14, 87, 89
Ruhland, Karl 92
Russia 3–4, 8, 10–11, 13–15, 17, 19, 25,
    28, 30–1, 34, 36, 40–1, 44, 48–9,
    56, 58–9, 61–6, 68, 75, 80, 89–92,
    94–6, 105–6, 111, 116, 118–22, 131,
    133, 135–7, 139, 141–2, 145–9, 159,
    163–5, 167–70, 172–3
    First Army Corps 36
    German invasion of 1941 187, 190
    Russian Empire 7, 24
    Russian Revolution (1917) 99, 123,
        168
    see also Soviet Union
Russo-German Alliance 170
Russo-Turkish War 6
Rwanda 5

Safi-Abad 137
Saleh Mohammed 161
Samarkand 4, 11, 68, 97
San Francisco 23, 51–2, 156–7, 183
Sar-i-Pul 134, 138
Sarwar Sultana Begum 160
Sayed Ahmed 51, 120, 151
Sayyid Kemal 176
Schoch, General Gustav von 38
Schreiner, Captain Jakob 86
Schulenburg, Fritz-Dietlof von der
    193
Second World War 42, 169, 180
Seeckt, General Hans von 170
Seiler, Fritz 56, 106, 141–3
Serbia 30, 89
Shah Ali Reza Khan 161
Shah Shuja 117
Shanghai 152–7
Sheberghan 134–6
Shiraz 31, 91, 126–7, 131, 141–3
Shuja-ud-Daula 132
Shushtar 50
Siemens 179
Silk Letters Conspiracy 125

Silk Road 147, 150
Simla 63, 67, 83, 93, 109
Skobolev, General Leonid 11
Society of the Servants of the
    Powerless 52
Sommer, Rudolf 139
Soraya, Queen 1, 173, 187
Soviet–Afghan War (1979–89) ix, 3,
    132
Soviet–German Non-Aggression Pact
    (1939) 182, 185
Soviet Union 163, 167, 170, 178, 191
    see also Russia
Spiller, Helmut 127–8
SS Ecuador (USA) 153–4
SS Maverick 32–3
Stark, Freya 46–7
Stratil-Sauer affair 172
Stratil-Sauer, Gustav 171
Subhan Khan 51
Subhas Chandra Bose 181
Sultan Ali 128
Sykes, Brigadier General Sir Percy
    141, 197
Syr Darya see Jaxartes River
Syria 5, 10, 31, 46, 166, 172, 183–5

Tabas 62–3
Tagdumbash Valley 147
Tajik forces 132, 146, 176
Tajikistan 132–3, 147, 175
Taklamakan Desert 150
Taliban ix, 23, 35, 132, 193
Tamerlane 25, 133, 149
Tangistan 127, 143
    tribesmen of 50, 126
Tanzania 5
tarantulas x, 62, 69, 135
Tarzi, Mahmud 22, 29, 92–3, 100, 116
Tashkent 4
Taurus copper mines 10
Taurus Mountains 12, 46, 57
Tehran 13, 36–7, 49–50, 56–8, 64,
    90–1, 95–6, 106, 125, 128, 137–40,
    143, 197–8
Thesiger, Frederic John Napier see
    Chelmsford, Lord

Thomas Cook & Son 7–8
Tibet 14, 179
Togo 5
Treloar, Sir William 8
Triple Entente 28, 94, 105, 111, 155
Trotsky, Leon 123
Turkestan 21, 84, 86, 99
  Afghan 25, 119
  Chinese 149
  Russian 11, 19, 120, 205
Turkey 6–7, 8, 10, 19, 27, 30–1, 34,
    40–5, 47–9, 54, 56, 68, 73, 79, 85,
    89, 94, 96, 103–5, 111, 113, 116,
    126–7, 143, 163–4, 172, 184–5, 191,
    195
Turkish Army 6–7, 11, 65, 67, 77, 80,
    84, 87–8, 94–6, 100–1, 139, 141–2
Turkish Navy 6
Turkmenistan 106, 133–4

U-Bahn trains 2
Ukraine 190
United States of America xi, 3, 31,
    51–2, 91, 139, 151, 153, 157, 163,
    166, 177, 194
  entry into Second World War 155,
    157, 184
  terrorist attacks of 2001 193
Urumqi 150
US Geological Survey 164
Uzbekistan 4

Verdun 157
Versailles, peace negotiations 107,
    160, 163
  Treaty of 164–5, 168, 170, 174, 179

Victor Emmanuel III, King of Italy 2,
    174
Victoria, Queen 5–6, 16, 18, 75
Voigt, Günter 46, 118, 120, 169–70
Volunteer Units East 192

Wagner, Kurt 46, 119–20, 134, 143, 165
Wakhan Corridor 15, 123, 146–7
Wangenheim, Baron Hans Freiherr
    von 49
Wassmuss, Wilhelm xi, 39–40, 43–5,
    47–50, 56, 77, 90, 95, 126–8, 139,
    141, 143, 196
Wassmuss–Niedermayer mission 48
Waziri frontier tribe 85, 188
Waziristan 83, 188–9
Weimar Republic 164, 170
Weizsäcker, Ernst von 192
Wilhelm II, Kaiser of Germany x,
    5–11, 25, 38, 49, 52–3, 79, 163
Wilhelmstrasse 158, 182–3
Witzel-Kim, Dietrich 189–90
Wuhan 151
Wylie, Sir Francis Verner 190
Wyllie, William Hutt Curzon 30

Yarkand 147–50
Yazdan 63, 65
Young Afghan Movement 29
Young Turks 29, 39

Zahir Shah, King of Afghanistan 121,
    163, 167, 177–8, 180, 182–3, 185–7,
    190
Ziemke, Kurt 175